BOISE

BOISE
An Illustrated History

For Fred and Carol
with best wishes

Arthur A. Hart.

By Merle Wells and Arthur A. Hart
Picture Research by Arthur A. Hart

Sponsored by the
Idaho State Historical Society
and Idaho Statesman

American Historical Press
Sun Valley, California

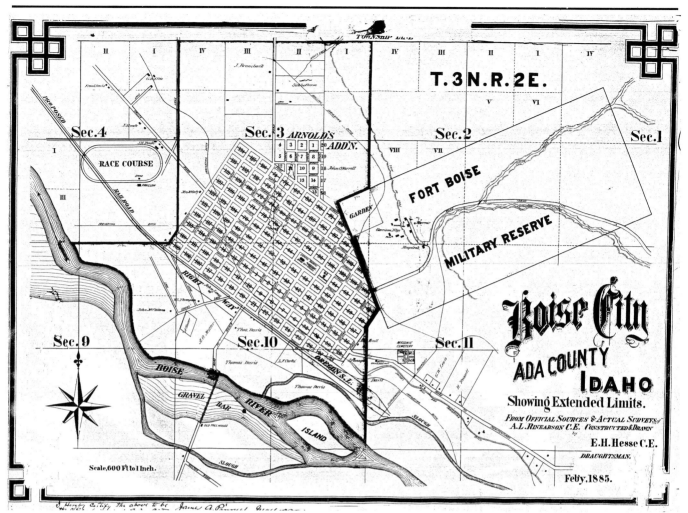

The 1885 Map of Boise City.

Frontispiece
Idaho's Capitol is reflected in its close neighbor, the state office building popularly known as "The Hall of Mirrors." The architects' intention was to create a structure that would nearly disappear by reflecting its surroundings rather than dominating them. Courtesy, Arthur A. Hart

© American Historical Press
All Rights Reserved
Published 2000
Printed in the United States of America

Library of Congress Catalogue Card Number: 00-108797
ISBN: 1-892724-13-8

Bibliography: p. 254
Includes Index

CONTENTS

Introduction   9

Chapter I
Indians, Trappers, and Emigrants: To 1862   9

Chapter II
A City Along a Trail: 1863-1868   17

Chapter III
In Search of a Railroad: 1868-1889   33

Chapter IV
Progress of a State Capital: 1890-1899   55

Chapter V
A New City Emerges: 1900-1912   69

Chapter VI
Consolidation and Stability: 1912-1929   81

Chapter VII
Depression and War: 1930-1945   97

Chapter VIII
Postwar Industrial Expansion: 1946-1962   109

Chapter IX
An Era of Adjustment and Change: 1962-1982   119

Chapter X
Dramatic Growth in an Electronic Age   151

Chapter XI
Chronicles of Leadership   171

A Timeline of Boise's History   252

Bibliography   254

Acknowledgments   255

Index   256

INTRODUCTION

Many cities have grown up in a pattern typical of urban development in large Eastern or Midwestern regions. Others have distinctive population elements or locations that made them different from most communities. Boise's history is special rather than conventional. A remote mountain and desert location, rather than an odd demographic composition, accounts for Boise's unusual development. No other American community of 100,000 or more is located nearly so far away from ocean ports and from any other city of comparable or larger size. That kind of isolation has done much to shape Boise's past. No other major-city state capital that needed rail service had such a hard time obtaining convenient modern surface transportation. And no other city had an easier time gaining a large modern airport. As a result, Boise emerged from a difficult past into a more pleasant modern era of community expansion, which justified so great an investment of pioneer effort to build a city of distinction in a wilderness far beyond Eastern and Western frontiers of settlement.

Even though they had to overcome exceptional obstacles in establishing a remote community, Boise's founders preferred to build a town that differed as little as possible from their earlier homes. To accomplish their goal, they had to adapt familiar national or regional styles and traits to meet some unusual local conditions. Desert lands had to be irrigated, but tree-lined streets and green farm lands with orchards replaced sagebrush rangeland. Boise's architecture and cultural traditions replicated traditional forms and customs that kept up with national trends rather than developing along innovative lines.

Visitors to Boise often expressed surprise at how quickly a small modern city arose in a remote desert wilderness. Two examples, one from 1879 when Boise had been settled for 16 years and a second when Boise had developed for 50 years, illustrate this point. T.F. Miner published an interesting description of Boise in his *La Grande Gazette* late in October 1879: *Boise City has been well called "Queen City of the Mountains." It is making rapid strides in improvements, and its streets give one an idea of its importance among the Idahoans. In the stores, at the hotels, among the corrals, and yes, among the distributors of wet goods, all seem busy, and the appearance of the military among the citizens gives a jaunty effect that can be indulged in only by cities favored with a military garrison. The private residences have a clean, inviting, home-like appearance—most of them being embowered in groves of shade and fruit trees, while small fruits and shrubbery seem to grow spontaneously, undoubtedly, however, aided materially by the irrigating ditches, which are met in all directions. The fences and surroundings are kept clean and tidy, and one can almost imagine himself transported to some old New England town, where cleanliness and order are strictly maintained in the city government.*

John Lamond of Edinburgh noted a great deal more progress after a half-century of settlement. Boise, he indicated, was:

a lovely city, one of the most beautiful cities of the West. It has a magnificent square in which the Capitol stands, the streets are broad and spacious, the buildings are stately, and at night are literally ablaze with electric lights, so that alike by day or night the visitor is bewildered by the fact that this city, so fair and attractive, is the creation of yesterday.

By this time, Boise was changing culturally also. A generation or two of effort went into remolding Boise's original frontier society into a typical national pattern, but after a reasonable amount of friction and political conflict, Boise developed an acceptable set of institutions and values not easily distinguished from those of most other Western communities.

Boise's distinction arises from overcoming difficulties in establishing a traditional culture in an unusual environment. That achievement is typical of Idaho's history. As a state which had to be assembled—because of conditions entirely beyond local control—from geographically isolated, divergent sections brought together by political boundaries at variance with natural areas of communication, Idaho represents a triumph of politics over geography. Boise had to lead a number of distant communities, each with good reasons to prefer different political arrangements, in forming a workable state government in defiance of conventional wisdom. That experience also shaped Boise's past. Yet a traditional state government emerged in spite of natural barriers. Regardless of limiting economic and political local conditions, Boise's founders and developers persisted in building a city and a state of which they could be proud. Before they were done, they could be thankful that they hadn't been able to succeed in attracting an enormous population that would have destroyed a number of environmental assets which provide a major share of Boise's attraction.

Not everyone who came to early-day Boise managed to adjust to pioneer life in a strange environment. Some gave up and searched for less demanding surroundings. But a few thousand held out and built a strong community regardless of obstacles they encountered. Because they were a highly select group with memorable achievements to their credit, Boise's pioneers have commanded more respect than frontiersmen gained in less demanding settings. They were innovative in such matters as the development of a pioneer, natural hot water heating system, but generally sought out standard frontier opportunities to improve their lot. Retaining national economic and cultural values, they sometimes

Wooden waterwheels lifted irrigation water from the Grove Street ditch for trees and gardens to the north. Amateur artist T. Slight painted the lush Grove Street, looking east, in 1897.

were pioneers in important reforms and sometimes proceeded rather conservatively. A number of intermountain localities share a similar pioneer tradition and experience. Yet diversity of geographical setting and cultural institutions sets them apart. Their distinctive local histories account for their reaching an eventual national uniformity in community development and appearance. Boise's transition from a gold rush supply center to a candidate for urban redevelopment is instructive both for understanding local institutions and for appreciating a significant aspect of national history.

A variety of episodes in Boise's development, some more dramatic than others, can be identified in a sequence of pioneer and urban experiences. After a gold rush era gave way to two decades of waiting for a railroad, Boise survived a period of

Populist and labor unrest prior to 1900. Then a burst of city building and rapid growth preceded two more decades of consolidation and near stagnation. Moderate growth resumed during an era of economic depression and war, followed by a generation of industrialization, community planning, and urban expansion. Modern Boise emerged from a complex series of developments that collectively account for building a city of trees in a desert wilderness, where more than 54,000 emigrants passed by before anyone figured out how to establish a permanent settlement there. Unlike those more cautious pioneers who were satisfied only with conventional farming settlements further west in Oregon's Willamette valley, Boise's founders had to accept considerable risk in developing a different kind of country in which they had little or no experience. But when they got done, they felt they had accomplished a lot more than their less daring associates who preferred a more ordinary kind of existence.

Chapter 1

INDIANS, TRAPPERS, AND EMIGRANTS
PREHISTORY TO 1862

For two decades prior to 1862, thousands of emigrants on their way to western Oregon came right through Boise's future site with little or no thought of settling there. Aside from Mormon colonizers in Utah, Western settlers of that time were not interested in desert homes. Even though they could have saved more than 400 miles of difficult travel, none of them seized the opportunity to stay until gold discoveries in 1862 suddenly provided an economic foundation for a new community. This prompted a considerable number of Oregon Trail emigrants to return and take notice of the fact that the Boise area provided an attractive environment to establish new homes. Other Western adventurers joined them. Boise almost immediately grew into a community of regional importance in a land of opportunity.

Boise is favored with a magnificent location. Timbered mountains and sagebrush deserts provide the diverse terrain characteristic of many Pacific Northwest communities. The Boise area has a forested ridge only several miles away and a tree-lined river running through the desert valley. These natural surroundings developed over millions of years of geological and climatic transformation.

Southwestern Idaho has been shaped by global surface forces of great magnitude. Although some places have extremely old, exposed rock formations, dating back a billion years or more, Boise's surroundings do not. Boise's rock formations generally were part of a submerged marine shelf west of a central Idaho coastline that shifted as ancient oceans moved about. About a hundred million years ago, while North America gradually was moving westward away from Europe, important

Facing page
Idaho Indians gathered every summer near the mouth of Boise River to catch salmon, trade, and enjoy themselves. Fur trappers came to the river in search of beaver, and they named this and two other streams "Wooded River," or Boissée, but only this one retains its French name. Courtesy, Arthur A. Hart.

Lava beds, such as these at Craters of the Moon National Monument, were created by lava flows that poured over southern Idaho for millions of years. When broken down by weathering and erosion, the various kinds of volcanic debris became the rich desert soils that have made irrigated agriculture in the Boise area profitable for the past 100 years. Courtesy, Arthur A. Hart.

granitic mountain ranges were compressed and thrust up. When California's Sierra Nevada was rising farther west, Boise Ridge—a granite edge of a large Idaho mountain block that had gradually cooled and crystallized at great depth—began to emerge as well. South and west of Boise Ridge, a broad valley formed, as the land sank and was eventually occupied by a broad Snake River plain. Major Columbia lava flows blocked ancestral Snake River's course farther northwest, creating a large interior lake more than 100 miles wide. Boise Ridge and a few local rock formations from that old lake (known geologically as Payette Lake for Payette-area rock structures quite unrelated to modern Payette Lake) represent Ada County's oldest rocks. Really quite new by geological standards, and far more recent than many other Idaho deposits, they show what a recent land Boise occupies.

When Snake River finally cut through lava obstructions below present-day Weiser, geologic Payette Lake was drained and Boise's future site became dry land. Later flows of Columbia basalt (named for their age more than for their origin) left lava outcrops north of Boise and created an additional series of shallow lakes from which a more extensive Idaho rock formation emerged around Boise. During this time, major rock fractures allowed surface water to sink deep into hot rock and come back up as extensive warm springs. Over millions of years, this hot-water zone helped consolidate surface sands into sandstone—a conspicuous feature adjacent to Boise, where tablerock and lower sandstone ridges provided commercial building material. Natural hot water has provided an important Boise attraction ever since.

Erosion of sand and gravel from Boise Ridge and adjacent Idaho batholith highlands, coupled with recent Snake River lava flows, finally provided Ada County with its present land surface. Wind-blown soils, interspersed with lava and eroded gravel, helped fill southern Idaho's vast Snake Plains. The result was a several-hundred-mile valley, which interrupts a long series of north-south ridges originally extending from Utah and Wyoming to Oregon and Washington, and has had great cultural significance from prehistoric times on down. Boise's location owes much of its importance to a strategic setting in that natural route of transportation and trade.

Spectacular, geologically recent events have had a notable impact on life around the Snake and Columbia rivers. More than 12,000 years ago, a huge continental ice sheet projected into northern Idaho and extended across much of Montana. Great Utah and Nevada lakes resulted from a colder and wetter climate that produced glaciers and ice fields farther north. Boise occupied an intermediate valley, which had a wealth of grass and trees in a general ice-age climate. Large and sometimes ferocious animals—many of them now extinct—roamed through Boise's grazing lands. People had followed them from Asia across a broad Siberian-Alaskan plain, exposed when sea levels were depressed greatly because a large volume of ocean water had been deposited as ice sheets and pluvial lakes on more than one continent. Elephant hunters reached southern Idaho more than 14,000 years ago, when a warmer and drier climate began emerging. Catastrophic floods and colossal volcanoes occasionally interrupted normal life in those years. When Lake Bonneville, a large Utah ancestor of Salt Lake that projected into Idaho and Nevada, overflowed and surged down Snake River some 18,000 years ago, a torrent equal to several Amazon rivers roared by present Ada County for six months or so. Farther away, a series of still larger lower Snake and Columbia floods caused havoc. A 2,000-foot northern Idaho ice dam was washed out one hot afternoon about 12,000 years ago. A sudden deluge, equal to ten times the flow of all the world's current rivers combined, flashed across Idaho and eastern Washington, ripping out soil that has still not been replaced. North Idaho's topography created a series of such disasters, as ice flows expanded and receded, and early people who traveled through Boise were affected, sometimes only remotely, by such incidents. Volcanic disasters, both local and regional, also provided variety to life around Boise. When a mountainous volcanic explosion created Crater Lake about 6,900 years ago, ash deposits covered Boise Valley and lands far beyond. A colder climate change interrupted a general warming trend during periods of widespread volcanic ash, which temporarily helped restore cooler weather.

Early Boise-area hunters pursued a variety of prehistoric elephants, camels, giant bison, sloth, and other creatures (some still indigenous to Idaho). When a gradually warmer climate emerged some 8,000 to 12,000 years ago, their elephant and camel herds moved farther northwest in search of greener terrain, and many Boise hunters had to follow them. New cultural traditions replaced those of earlier inhabitants, and a more diversified economy developed.

Boise-area peoples felt no need to engage in sophisticated agriculture, although they were aware that some Southwestern tribes cultivated corn and other crops. Before 1600, they subsisted mostly upon local salmon (an abundant resource) and camas, bitterroot, and other vegetables they dug from natural fields. Shoshoni mountain sheephunters inhabited an adjacent wilderness area, and

Snake River's canyon was created in a relatively short time by the great Bonneville flood, which occurred about 14,000 years ago. The river has continued to wear its way down through successive layers of ancient basalt, which resulted from millions of years of vast lava flows. Courtesy, Arthur A. Hart

deer and elk were available around Boise. Although extensive travel, with only pack dogs to help haul supplies, was not very convenient, early Shoshoni travelers covered a considerable range of country.

After Spanish settlement of New Mexico in 1598, mountain and plains tribes gained new mobility when horses of Spanish origin became available for transport. Prehistoric horses had roamed around Boise for several million years, and earlier Boise peoples had access to them until their disappearance several thousand years ago. Through southern plains intermediaries—a Shoshoni band known in Texas and New Mexico as Comanche, but linguistically indistinguishable from 18th-century Boise Shoshoni—horses spread northward. Boise Shoshoni buffalo hunters could cover great distances in a seasonal migratory cycle that included the upper Snake Plains.

This 18th-century innovation allowed for the incursion of a variety of Plains Indians to Boise in search of salmon. An important summer trade festival, which came to be known as the Sheewoki fair, attracted Indians from a wide area. Like similar regional intertribal lower Columbia and Mandan village gatherings, this annual event gained major cultural significance. For a month or two during fishing season, Indians traded horses, arrows and arrowheads from diverse sources, buffalo hides and dried meat, ornamental seashells, and even wives. Gambling and ceremonial dancing were other features of this regional trade fair, which lasted until Boise was settled. Northern Paiute from Oregon and Nevada, Umatilla, Cayuse, and Nez Perce from farther north, Cheyenne and Arapaho from Col-

Wilson Price Hunt's party met disaster at Caldron Linn, a terrifying narrows where the entire flow of Snake River passes through a gap less than 30 feet wide. After that, the party broke into small groups and spent a miserable winter walking to the mouth of the Columbia River. Courtesy, Arthur A. Hart.

orado, and Crows from Wyoming joined Northern and Western Shoshoni in a grand intertribal gathering. Held in an area where a number of important rivers (Boise, Payette, Weiser, Malheur, Owyhee, and Snake) converge, this camas and salmon festival brought increased traffic over traditional routes from Salmon Falls and Camas Prairie that became important fur trade and Oregon Trail avenues of transportation to lower Columbia and Pacific Coast trade centers. Boise grew up at a point where this long-established pathway of westward communication descended from a long desert stretch to a welcome, tree-lined river favored with an abundance of salmon.

Snake Country exploration had been considered by famed explorers Lewis and Clark when they crossed into Idaho in 1805, but they could not afford to wait six months for the spring grass that they were told was essential for such a desert trip. They also feared that a Snake Plains route would take them to Mexico instead of to Oregon. A private concern, John Jacob Astor's Pacific Fur Company, finally brought overland explorers to the Boise area in 1811. An advance detachment of Astorians, led by Donald Mackenzie, came through Boise early in November, with Wilson Price Hunt's band following on November 21. Famed author Washington Irving—who wrote an account of the explorations of Mackenzie and Hunt—describes Hunt's arrival in Boise (then a Shoshoni encampment) as fortunate:

Dubbed "Perpetual Motion" by his contemporaries, Donald Mackenzie is one of the legendary figures of the fur-trade era. As a coleader of John Jacob Astor's ill-fated Overland expedition of 1811-1812, Mackenzie performed incredible feats of endurance and determination.

> The next day brought them to the banks of a beautiful little stream, running to the west, and fringed with groves of cottonwood and willow. On its borders was an Indian camp, with a great many horses grazing around it. The inhabitants, too, appeared to be better clad than usual. The scene was altogether a cheering one to the poor half-famished wanderers. They hastened to the lodges, but on arriving at them met with a check that at first dampened their cheerfulness. An Indian immediately laid claim to the horse of Mr. Hunt, saying that it had been stolen from him. There was no disproving a fact supported by numerous bystanders, and which the horse-stealing habits of the Indians rendered but too probable; so Mr. Hunt relinquished his steed to the claimant; not being able to retain him by a second purchase.
>
> At this place they encamped for the night, and made a sumptuous repast upon fish and a couple of dogs, procured from their Indian neighbors.

Boise's trees in a desert setting inspired fur hunters to name the river and valley after them. Depending upon whether they spoke English or French (*boise* in French is translated as "wooded" in English) they began to refer to it as the Wood River or the Boise River. French Canadian trappers eventually were able to make their form, *Boise*, prevail after 1836, although most early maps refer to Wood River. (Francois Payette, who managed Hudson's Bay Company's Fort Boise for many years, deserves a great deal of credit for this result.)

Boise River had superlative beaver resources, but early attempts at fur trapping ran into resistance from local Indians, who still congregated there for their Sheewoki fair. John Reid, who had come through Boise with Donald Mackenzie initially, returned two years later to establish a temporary trader's post where the Boise

In 1834 Hudson's Bay Company established Fort Boise, a fur-trading post at the mouth of Boise River. Travelers bought provisions at the adobe-walled fort until its abandonment in 1855. Changes in the rivers' courses have obliterated the original site.

and Snake rivers join. But an energetic band of Bannock Indians wiped out Reid's entire force early in January of 1814. Only Marie Dorion and her small children survived. They had to make a terrible winter trip west to meet Donald Mackenzie, who was returning to Montreal after Astor's Pacific Fur Company had failed. Mackenzie returned in 1816 as a North West Company partner. He was back through Boise Valley in 1818 and arranged for a trappers' rendezvous there in 1819 to supply his North West Company Snake Brigade. He decided to construct a permanent fort at Reid's unsuccessful Boise River site that summer. Renewal of Indian resistance to intrusion into their summer-festival site defeated Mackenzie's resolute attempt. He staged a large Indian peace convention on Little Lost River in 1820, but his proposed Fort Boise could not be constructed until 1834.

Mackenzie went on to other opportunities, and his fur hunters worked elsewhere for two years. In 1824 Alexander Ross brought back Mackenzie's Snake Brigade (by now a Hudson's Bay Company detachment) to resume trapping around Boise. Accompanying some of his old Cayuse friends, he attended another grand Indian peace convention in an Arapaho camp near present Caldwell on July 19, 1824. Peiem, a prominent Boise Shoshoni leader, presided. Ross regarded this assembly as an appropriate conclusion to Mackenzie's efforts and was enthusiastic to participate.

In 1824 Ross was disturbed to encounter mountainmen, based out of St. Louis, representing Jedediah Smith and William H. Ashley, who were expanding their Rocky Mountain fur trade into Great Britain's Snake Country beaver empire. Sharp competition resulted. Hudson's Bay Company fur hunters trapped vigorously in an effort to turn their highly productive Snake region into a land barren of beaver resources. Depleting resources in the Snake Country, they felt, would protect them from St. Louis competition in Columbia and Fraser river lands farther northwest. Mountain Men representing William H. Ashley's and Jedediah Smith's interests helped them accomplish their objective with great enthusiasm. By 1826, Boise fur hunting was largely taken over by St. Louis trappers, although Peter Skeen Ogden brought Hudson's Bay Company trappers back in 1827 and 1828 to make sure that Boise-area fur resources would remain depleted, and an annual Hudson's Bay Company expedition visited Boise until as late as 1832. Captain Benjamin L.E. Bonneville, a United States army officer out hunting furs, also found Boise's location more than ordinarily attractive:

> The country about the Boise (or Woody) River is extolled by Captain Bonneville as the most enchanting he had seen in the Far West, presenting the mingled grandeur and beauty of mountain and plain, of bright running streams and vast grassy meadows waving to the breeze.

Washington Irving, *Adventures of Captain Bonneville*
After a Boston merchant, Nathaniel J. Wyeth, established Fort Hall in 1834 to dispose of his large stock of surplus trade goods, Thomas McKay countered with a Hudson's Bay Company post soon known as Fort Boise. He chose the location favored by John Reid and Donald Mackenzie, which no longer excited fierce Indian resistance. From 1834 until 1855, McKay's British outpost operated successfully through a time of fur-trade decline. Within two years he succeeded in forcing Wyeth to negotiate for a sale of Fort Hall to Hudson's Bay Company officials, who finally took over in 1838. Emigrants headed for western Oregon began to account for most of Fort Boise's business after 1840, and provisions obtained there often proved essential to their survival in their long westward journey. Disruption of Indian life caused by heavy Oregon Trail traffic—particularly overgrazing of a broad zone along important traditional Indian routes—finally led to trouble. Alexander Ward's emigrant party was nearly wiped out in a clash near later Middleton on August 20, 1854, and army retaliation escalated Indian hostilities to such heights that Fort Boise had to be abandoned. United States acquisition of Idaho in 1846 had left Hudson's Bay Company authorities with no further interest in Fort Boise, aside from an eventual claims settlement, and fur-trade activities began to give way to emigrant trade. Oregon Trail travelers continued to appreciate their access to a tree-lined river, which they reached at the future site of Boise, more than 40 miles above Fort Boise. But little else remained of white activities in southern Idaho.

Prior to 1860, hardly anyone anticipated that a Boise settlement would outgrow all other Oregon Trail cities west of Topeka. A few trees in the desert provided a welcome change of scenery for settlers from Kansas and Nebraska towns traveling to Oregon City, but Idaho was expected to remain largely unsettled for another half-century. Gold discoveries, commencing with Elias Davidson Pierce's strike in Clearwater country on September 30, 1860, suddenly changed that prospect, however. From 1856 to 1860, Idaho had been given back to the Indians. Then, in only two years, Idaho gained large settlements that transformed Boise from an Indian to a white community.

Top
The Mountain Men were a colorful crew of adventurers who lived dangerously and worked hard in wilderness never seen before by white men. On weekends modern-day "mountain men" relive an era for which they were born too late. Their costumes are researched meticulously and made as authentic as possible. Courtesy, Arthur A. Hart.

Above
Beaver dams abounded along the Boise when the first trappers arrived. Cottonwood, aspen, and willow supplied both food for beaver and building materials for their houses and dams. Limbs intricately woven together enable a beaver dam to hold water.

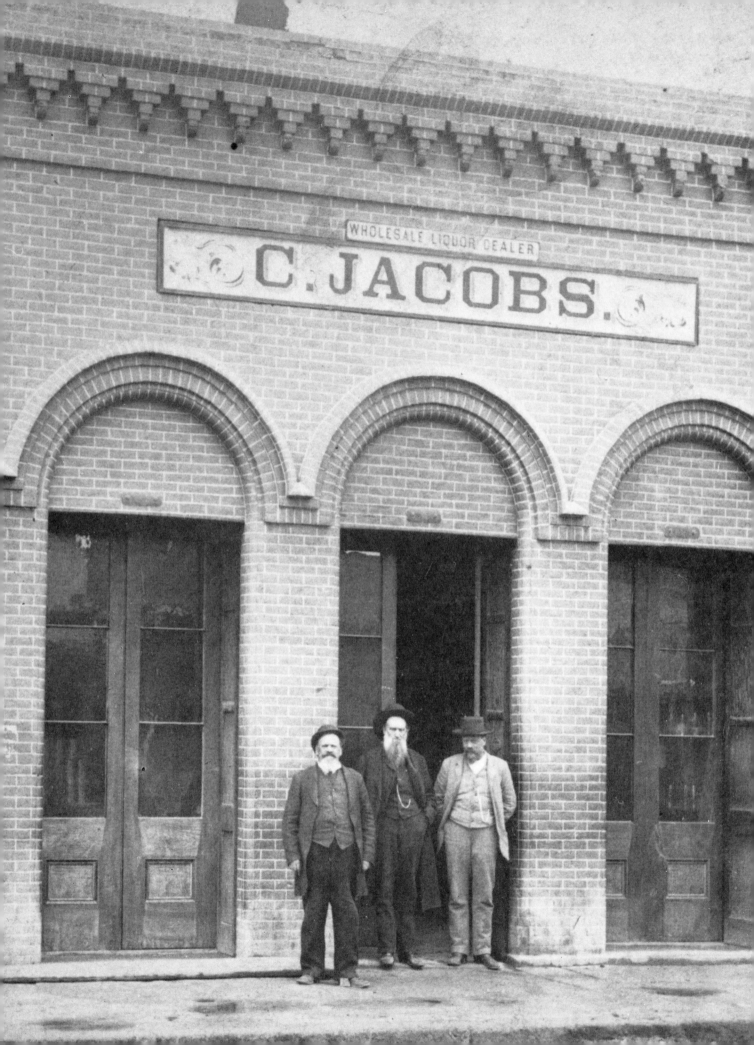

Chapter 2

A CITY ALONG A TRAIL
1863-1868

*M*ost people declined to be swept up in the wild enthusiasm of the 19th-century gold rushes. But those who did uproot themselves from family and home to pursue a fortune usually had a great adventure that they never forgot. More often than not, they found the adventure but not the gold, although enough prospectors emerged as wealthy men to sustain the hopes of those who failed. As a result, Western gold rushes persisted from the days of the California '49ers to the early part of the 20th century.

Gold had been known to exist in the Boise Basin for almost two decades before anyone took a serious interest in mining it, a delay that proved fortunate. A gold rush before the summer of 1862 would have resulted in extreme hardship. An exceptionally cold winter of 1862 was followed by spring floods that have not been matched since. When George Grimes and Moses Splawn brought their discovery party to the Boise Basin in June of 1862, it took them an entire month just to get through high water around Snake River. But they found gold on August 2 near what is now Centerville, which a week's prospecting proved could accommodate thousands of placer miners.

Thousands of miners did show up in the fall, rushing to get ready for the mining season that they knew would follow a spring runoff. Pioneerville, Idaho City, Placerville, and Centerville all sprang up as instant cities late in 1862. Congress established Idaho as a large new territory on March 4, 1863, and because of mining activity, Idaho City (then known as West Bannock) briefly surpassed Portland in population, becoming the Pacific Northwest's largest town for awhile. Additional mining districts sprang up around Rocky Bar and Silver City.

Facing page
Cy Jacobs, one of Boise's earliest merchants, owned a general store at the corner of Seventh and Main (where Idaho First Plaza stands today), headquarters for a remarkably diversified business that included a gristmill, distillery, packing plant, soup and candle factory, and feed lot. Jacobs had large mining enterprises in many Idaho camps, and "Jacob's Best" rye whiskey was locally famous.

Major Pinckney Lugenbeel of the Ninth United States Infantry led an army detachment into Boise Valley to establish Fort Boise in 1863. After building the fort's first buildings, he moved on to other assignments.

All of these mining camps needed supply bases and a governmental center. Enterprising community developers soon founded Boise to meet that need in southwestern Idaho. Boise's founders, principal among them H.C. Riggs, took great pride in establishing a strategically placed community with an unusually bright future. Attracted by the business and professional opportunities available in a new mining region, they set out to build a major city in a desert wilderness. Nearby mines provided the wealth needed to finance the expensive buildings that would soon be erected hundreds of miles from any large Western community of that era.

Besides the wealthy mining camps, Boise Valley farms also offered an important economic base for a commercial center. Commercial agriculture—as contrasted with the frontier subsistence farming that was common initially in Western expansion—got off to a fast start in easily irrigated river bottom lands. By 1864 all convenient crop lands were taken up and put into production during a less sensational, but equally hasty, farmers' rush that was inspired by the needs of the miners. A great many farmers had hastened to Boise Basin late in 1862, and some of them saw that they had a better chance for success with farming—which they understood—than with mining, which they did not. By February of 1863, farmers were already beginning to settle around Boise and, by June, three cabins were completed in that vicinity. Others appeared farther away along the river.

A crucial factor in developing Boise, and particularly in determining an exact townsite location, was the army's need for a regional military post. After the Hudson's Bay Company's Fort Boise (a nonmilitary installation) closed, an army escort system had been employed to protect Oregon Trail emigrant parties west of Fort Hall. This system scarcely worked at all. General George Wright learned of an Indian attack on emigrants not far from Castle Creek, and recommended the construction of a military Fort Boise on October 10, 1860. The outbreak of the Civil War made this an unfortunate time to obtain approval. More concerned with Civil War battles than with fighting a few Boise Indians, army authorities postponed taking on Wright's project. Renewed Shoshoni and Bannock hostilities in 1862, followed by the pressures created by a major gold rush, brought a much stronger demand for a fort from General Benjamin Alvord, on October 14, 1862. Even though Civil War campaigns were going badly, General Wright finally obtained army authorization, January 14, 1863, for construction to begin the following summer. Major Pinckney Lugenbeel set out with some Washington Volunteers on June 1 to find an upper Boise Valley site and to build a new post there. By that time, Jefferson Standifer's Placerville Volunteers had entered the area to retaliate against local Indian bands. His company annihilated one Malheur band and threatened so many others that Indians soon were hard to find. When constructed, Fort Boise was needed more to protect Indians from angry miners than to defend frontier roads and settlements, but in 1864 trouble around mining camps in central Oregon eventually spread to Idaho, and Fort Boise finally became necessary as a base for Indian campaigns.

Reaching Government Island near what is now Fairview Bridge on June 28, 1863, Lugenbeel's army construction company scouted for a good location for a military post. They needed an Oregon Trail

location that was close to a future intersection with freight roads
leading to a large group of Boise Basin and Owyhee mines. Lugenbeel celebrated July 4—when victories at Gettysburg and Vicksburg
marked encouraging turning points for the Union—by selecting a
Cottonwood Gulch-Idaho City road site for Fort Boise. Construction
began on July 6 on an initial set of log buildings, and the platting of
the new town followed a day later.

Boise was organized in a town meeting held on July 7, 1863, 17
years before Idaho would become a state. Henry Chiles Riggs—
whose uncle, Joseph R. Chiles, had shown great industry in developing a practical California Trail route—arrived at Fort Boise the day
before to assemble a meeting, in a cabin belonging to Tom Davis and
William R. Ritchie, to work out the city plat. Their meeting site was
placed in what is now a block between Main and Grove near Eighth
Street. Boise's townsite occupied a small area between Fort Boise
and a riverside farm (eventually Julia Davis Park) that Davis and
Ritchie had started on February 6. Lots were reserved for 20 sub-
scribers, including Lugenbeel and some of his army comrades.
Sherlock Bristol, a Methodist minister associated with Davis and
Ritchie, presided, and a variety of interests was represented. One of
Thomas McKay's sons, still regarded as having a Hudson's Bay Com-
pany affiliation, was on hand. He had gotten Bristol, Davis, and
Ritchie interested in Boise Valley farming. William Purvine and
John Creighton, express operators, and John M. McClellan and
Richard "Beaver Dick" Leigh, both local ferrymen, had transportation
enterprises. James D. Agnew joined H.C. Riggs in a business en-
terprise that combined a saloon with a livery stable, providing
refreshment for man and beast. Cyrus Jacobs, whose father-in-law
Joel Palmer had engaged in important Oregon Trail promotion, was
persuaded to develop his mercantile establishment—at first housed
in a tent—in Boise, instead of taking his stock of goods on to Idaho
City. Another pioneer Boise store, Crawford, Slocum and Company,
went unrepresented but quickly found permanent quarters, as did
B.M. DuRell and C.W. Moore, whose store offered banking services

Right
The Cyrus Jacobs house, built in 1864 near the corner of Sixth and Grove streets, is the city's oldest surviving brick building and is listed in the National Register of Historic Places. Jacobs' store was only a block and a half away.

Above
Cyrus Jacobs was elected mayor of Boise in 1880. Mrs. Jacobs, nee Mary Ellen Palmer, was the daughter of noted Oregon pioneer General Joel Palmer. The prominent couple was married in Oregon in 1856 and had six children.

and ran a freight line as well. A.G. Redway, sutler for Fort Boise, arrived July 10 to open a store. All this construction, including work at Fort Boise, ensured that Riggs' townsite development would succeed.

With four stores, a meat market, Samuel Adams' blacksmith shop, and two early hotels, Boise got off to a promising start. Tents and log buildings were gradually replaced by substantial brick structures. Charles May, who came from Walla Walla, Washington, to provide monumental sandstone officers' quarters and a sutler's store at Fort Boise, took on city building projects as well. By September only three other Boise Basin and two Montana mining camps exceeded Boise in population. More importantly, Boise's 725 inhabitants included 135 women and 74 children. Only Lewiston, another mine-distributing center a little more than half as large as Boise, had a comparable family representation. But with only 18 percent women and 10 percent children, Boise still seemed more like a mining camp than a traditional farming center. Even at that, about 12 percent of all Idaho's women and children lived in Boise, a town that accounted for only two percent of Idaho's 32,342 people. A sufficient number of children were on hand, though, to justify a private school that winter.

Ambitious to advance beyond its assured status as a regional supply center, Boise put in a strong bid to become Idaho's permanent capital. In an earlier move that had antagonized southwestern Idaho (which contained half of Idaho's population), Governor William H. Wallace had decided to organize Idaho's territorial government in Lewiston on July 10—just when Boise was being founded. The decision to organize the government in Lewiston, which slighted Idaho City's superior claim, gave Boise an opportunity that would not otherwise have been available.

If Wallace had chosen Idaho City, Boise would have had little chance, and even less justification, to displace a much larger and older rival. In Lewiston, however, which also wanted to become permanent capital, Boise had a rival located in a North Idaho mining region that had gone into abrupt decline. No North Idaho town—including Florence, which only two years before had attracted more than 10,000 miners—was as large as Boise. And substantial mountain barriers isolated Lewiston from a significant percentage of Idaho's people.

Inaccessible from southwestern Idaho, Lewiston was an unacceptable choice as capital to miners from East Bannock and Virginia City, who had rushed to the new camps on the upper Missouri when they had been transferred from Dakota to Idaho by Congress. Boise agents finally struck a deal with Virginia City, under the terms of which Boise would·become capital of Idaho while Virginia City, which represented a smaller mining area than the Boise Basin, could have a new territory of Montana to preside over. Only a last minute defection by two Idaho City legislators, who still wanted their town to become the capital, defeated enactment of this arrangement on February 4, 1864. But after part of Idaho was detached to become a new territory of Montana, on May 26, 1864, Boise no longer faced any serious obstacle to becoming capital of what remained.

In preparation for its anticipated prominence in government, Boise took on an improved appearance and offered important additional amenities later in 1864. After a year of development, Boise had "about sixty buildings of various shapes, sizes and construction." Most were "lumber, interspersed with adobe, and peat or turf." Aside from residences, Boise had "nine stores for general merchandise, two livery stables, two breweries, one butcher shop, two blacksmith shops, a lumber yard, a tin store, one bootmaker, one tailor and five saloons." An attorney, three or four doctors, and a surveyor rendered professional services. Early stores—even large ones—were simple in construction. James Crawford and Jerry Slocum had erected an adobe store with six-inch boards used only as part of a shingle roof that was supported by "tall cottonwood poles set in the ground endways. The building was never honored with a floor, other than the ground." Yet this pioneer structure stood "as firm as ever" for more than a decade.

Boise also got a triweekly newspaper. James S. Reynolds' *Idaho Statesman* provided essential press coverage after its founding, July 26. A Radical Republican, Reynolds differed politically from town founder H.C. Riggs and most of his readers; rejoicing at Confederate victories, they were running short of occasions to celebrate. Regardless of divergent political views, however, Riggs and Reynolds worked together to promote the community. Transcontinental stage service to a rail connection in Atcheson, Kansas, was gained August 1. Ben Holladay's Overland Stage Company, which connected in Boise with Columbia River lines, carried overland mail as well as passengers. Boise now had a two-week eastern postal connection. A handsome new Overland Hotel was opened a month later, greatly improving upon the facilities offered by three earlier hotels. More schools were opened, and a decision by Boise's numerous merchants, on August 4, 1864, to close their stores on Sundays gave a more staid appearance to what was still a frontier town.

Speeded by the availability of finished lumber—including doors, molding, and similar building materials—provided by Albert H. Robie's large new sawmill in August, Boise's commercial struc-

Henry Chiles Riggs, Boise's leading founder, created a county named for his daughter Ada. He was instrumental in having Boise made capital of Idaho Territory in 1864.

The Idaho Tri-weekly Statesman *began publication in Boise City on July 26, 1864. James S. Reynolds edited and published this Radical Republican newspaper in a territory with a majority of Southern Democrats. He carried on a running feud with the* Idaho World *of Idaho City from this small building at Seventh and Idaho.*

Hosea B. Eastman, a native of New Hampshire, ran the Idaho Hotel in Silver City with his brother, Manson. In the 1870s, the brothers moved to Boise, where they operated the Overland House (shown here), located at Eighth and Main. In 1905 the new Overland (later Eastman) building was erected on the same site. Lithograph by Charles Ostner, 1878.

tures and residences took on quite a different appearance from the rough log cabins and hastily erected stores of its beginnings. Important community needs still remained to be met. Idaho City, for example, had more than one theater but Boise had none. When John S. Potter's dramatic company, on August 12, 1864, offered "the first night of a theatre of any sort in Boise City," it had to adapt a local barroom for the performances. Other presentations included Dan Rice's traveling circus and a minstrel troupe. On August 29, Julia Deane Hayne, rated as "the most popular and talented actress on the Pacific Coast," commenced a series of Boise dramatic productions. Boise's proximity to Idaho City's substantial mining audiences, which attracted performances from as far away as California, enabled an otherwise remote and isolated community to offer cultural attractions. Local talent added to the efforts of traveling performers to produce a variety of superior programs.

A major increase in Missouri refugees reinforced Boise's Confederate population in 1864. Running low on resources as they headed west, many of the refugees, when they reached Boise, could go no further. Although the Missouri influx represented something of a strain upon community charitable facilities, they nearly doubled Boise's population to 1,658. Only Idaho City (which had grown slightly to 7,000) and Placerville were larger. Although the town now had a higher number of families (including 318 children), its percentage of male population exceeded two-thirds and Boise continued to resemble a mining camp more than an established community. But Boise was beginning to show signs of permanence.

Progress along quite a different line—making provision for Boise's local Shoshoni population, which was gradually being displaced by mining and farming activities—also came late in 1864. In the Treaty of Fort Boise, signed October 10, 1864, Governor Caleb Lyon arranged for cession of Indian claims to Boise Valley in return for an unspecified consideration. Since Lyon did not know exactly what should go into the treaty, he left blanks to be filled in by Washington authorities prior to Senate consideration. After well over a century, the document has still not been completed or ratified by the Senate. But an initial, if ineffective, effort to acquire title to Boise Valley was commenced. Governor Lyon was impressed by the excellent farming and mining prospects of the Boise area, so recently transformed by the two-year gold rush. The governor, when he returned to Lewiston, was accompanied by H.C. Riggs.

Riggs, elected to Idaho's second legislative session in 1864, handled Boise's interests with superlative skill and energy. Idaho, at the time of his election, was still a large mining territory with a substantial population, 90 percent of which lived in the southwestern mineral region near Boise. Riggs soon managed to have Boise designated the territorial capital, effective December 24, 1864, and also prevailed upon his colleagues to set aside a new county, named for his daugher Ada, for which Boise would serve as the seat of government. Through Riggs' efforts, Boise's future as a political and economic center was seemingly assured.

Lewiston's leading citizens, however, refused to give up their drive to have their community—the population of which had now dwindled to 359—designated the permanent capital. Lewiston attorneys went to court, questioning the legitimacy of the territorial leg-

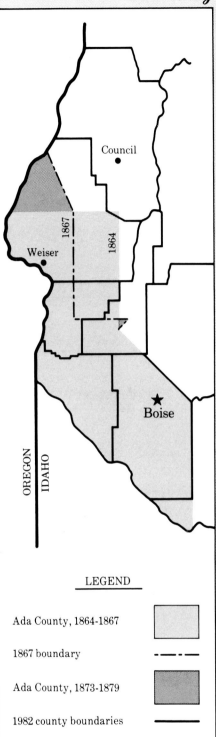

Ada County's courthouse was erected in an almost rural setting in 1881 and stood where the present courthouse stands. County commissioners and other officials pose in the foreground.

Henry Chiles Riggs, a founder of Boise, created a new county and named it for his daughter Ada, shown here circa 1885. Henry Riggs named a son "Boise."

LEGEND

Ada County, 1864-1867

1867 boundary

Ada County, 1873-1879

1982 county boundaries

Oregon Territory, a United States possession acquired by an agreement with Great Britain in 1846, included Ada County from 1848 until 1859. Incorporated into Washington Territory (1859-1863) and Idaho Territory (1863-1890) prior to Idaho State's admission into the Union, Ada County was included in Wasco County, Oregon (1848-1859), Spokane County (1859-1861), Shoshone County (January 9-December 10, 1861), and Boise County, Washington, before becoming part of Idaho on March 4, 1863, and gaining independent status on December 22, 1864. Several major boundary adjustments subsequently affected Ada County when Canyon County was approved in a local referendum in November 1892. A Confederate Democratic stronghold until 1882, when anti-Mormon Republicans took over for a decade, Ada County voted Populist in 1892 and for a fusion of Populist, Democratic, and Silver Republican slates in 1896. Ada County has remained Republican since then, except for the Democratic interludes of 1916 and 1932-1936 and the occasional election of popular candidates of other parties in unusual circumstances.

Caleb Lyon, governor of Idaho Territory from March 1864 until June 1866, was one of the most colorful and eccentric characters in Idaho's history. A contemporary Idaho official described him as "egotistical and ambitious, a scholar, a poet, and an art lover, but ... a conspicuous and dangerous failure as an executive."

islature. Since no one could determine when Idaho's representatives should actually have convened, Lewiston's probate judge ruled that Idaho no longer had a legitimate governing body and that all actions taken late in 1864—including Boise's designation as capital—had no validity. Annoyed by such a turn of events, Idaho's eccentric governor, Caleb Lyon, fled from Lewiston on December 29, 1864, saying that he was going duck-hunting. His departure left Idaho without a chief executive. Territorial Secretary C. DeWitt Smith, who would have functioned as acting governor, had not been able to reach Lewiston for six months because of an Indian war involving Nebraska and Wyoming tribes.

In desperation, Lewiston's law enforcement authorities then locked up Idaho's territorial seal and archives—all they had left of Idaho's government after Governor Lyon's clever escape—in their county jail. For three months, an around-the-clock armed guard thwarted all Boise efforts to spirit off the files. Governor Lyon took off for Portland, San Francisco, and Washington, D.C. Idaho's Supreme Court had not succeeded in organizing as yet, so Boise's attorneys had no way to appeal.

Secretary Smith decided to try to reach Idaho by way of Panama and San Francisco, providing him an opportunity to consult with Governor Lyon in Portland. Ascertaining the problems awaiting him in Lewiston, Smith quietly arranged at Fort Vancouver for military support to enable him to carry out his official duties. After his arrival in Lewiston on March 2, 1864, Smith spent more than a month devising a strategy for gaining control of his official files, which still remained under hostile guard. Accompanied by Boise conspirators, he pretended to go on daily horseback rides for his health. Eventually, he was able to escape to Fort Lapwai long enough to obtain an army detachment that overcame Lewiston's guards (without a violent clash) and allowed him to depart with his official files. After six weeks of well-planned effort, he reached Boise on April 14. Idaho finally had a functioning government again, and Boise remained capital from then on.

Aside from getting Boise selected as permanent capital of Idaho, Riggs had arranged, by a legislative act of December 12, 1864, for Boise to establish a city government. Boise's 1864 charter, however, required ratification in a special election before incorporation would become effective. Discouraged by an exceptionally severe winter and reluctant to assume any additional tax burdens, Boise's voters rejected their charter, by a 24-vote margin, on March 25. Like Lewiston, Boise had gone into a temporary decline, brought on in part by terrible winter weather and spring floods. Even after a mild 1864 winter and a continued 1864 gold rush, however, mining, stockraising, and farming all entered an abrupt recession. Living conditions still were quite primitive, even for citizens fortunate enough to have a house. A house with two rooms was regarded as luxurious, and Acting Governor Smith, while happy to find Boise "a pleasant place" in which to function, noticed the great contrast to communities a decade or so older, such as Portland.

Boise still lacked churches, but Episcopalian and Baptist services were held when clergymen were available in 1864 and 1865. Sunday schools were run by volunteers. Early in 1865, at a time when Boise's taxpayers declined to assume any responsibility for city government, a public school was started. With several private schools in operation, at least the educational needs of Boise's children were not neglected. Such advances, though, did little to relieve Boise's "Wild West" atmosphere. Governor Smith, a devout Methodist, complained that he had "found this country the home of refugees from justice; of men that delighted in crime, and boasted of their evil deeds—even seemed proud of them."

Serious efforts to develop a local desert oasis also were under way. Local canals were expanded in 1864, and a substantial community ditch company was incorporated, by legislative action, on December 21. Tom Davis had started Boise's tradition as a city of trees by planting 7,000 fruit trees early in 1864, and although he could not commence harvesting his orchard until 1869, his efforts led to increased activity that year. Phillip Ritz, who specialized in introducing trees to communities in the Pacific Northwest interior, had brought a large stock to Boise in November of 1864; but even fast-growing poplars, cottonwoods, and willows took some time to mature. When C. DeWitt Smith arrived with Idaho's territorial archives, he found Capitol Square's "virgin soil . . . innocent of a single tree, except a few scattering sage-brush." Governor Smith noticed in July that the land Boise farmers had to deal with was, "indeed a desert ground, and hard to cultivate. And the food here is rough and unpalatable. No fruit—no vegetables—but Onions and *Pop corn* and potatoes."

Many early Boise residents lacked some of the qualities needed for adapting to pioneer desert life. Substantial numbers of people, who could not adjust to a community without cultural activities and "modern conveniences," simply left for places similar to their old homes. Some, like Governor Smith, did not even manage that. Embarking upon a regional tour of Idaho's mining camps, he got as far as Rocky Bar. There, on August 19, after too strenuous a chess game, he suddenly expired from the unfortunate effects of a "dismal and melancholy disease." Boise remained capital of Idaho, but once again was without a territorial government.

With no executive, and with litigation clouding the legality of almost all of Idaho's statutes (including provision for Ada County and for Boise's status as territorial capital), Boise's energetic promoters arranged to have Horace C. Gilson appointed as secretary and acting governor on September 29. Gilson, "a small gambling bar tender" whom Smith had found in San Francisco, had dubious "moral antecedents." But at least he would retain Idaho's capital in Boise. Governor Lyon finally returned to Boise on November 7, reassuming his duties in the face of a generally hostile Confederate Democratic legislature. Every councilman and all but one representative opposed Idaho's prodigal governor.

A political conservative with ambition to make Boise a state capital within a year or two, Governor Lyon pursued an erratic course that got him into serious difficulties. He suggested some astounding projects to promote Boise and all of Idaho. These included truly ambitious plans to mine Owyhee diamonds he had heard about somewhere. He also wanted to alleviate national problems of Reconstruction by bringing an enormous colony of freed Southern slaves to Idaho to mine enough gold to retire a large national Civil War debt. Such a migration would solve Southern racial problems

Top
In January 1866 Boise's Baptist congregation erected the second church building in the city. First Baptist Church stood on the northwest corner of Ninth and Idaho streets. Lithograph from Elliott, History of Idaho Territory, *1884.*

Above
Episcopal Bishop Daniel S. Tuttle, a blacksmith's son, won the hearts of Boiseans soon after he arrived in 1867. He traveled to remote Idaho villages and mining camps for almost 20 years, preaching greatly effective sermons. Bishop Tuttle House, adjoining St. Michael's Cathedral, was named in his honor.

and provide Idaho sufficient population to become a state, which Lyon would gladly serve as United States Senator. To accomplish such an ambitious and elaborate plan, he needed an Idaho railroad. Anticipating a profound postwar opportunity for economic development, he advised Idaho's Confederate Democratic legislature that they faced a new era:

> The temple of war is closed. No more shall its iron-mouthed and brazen-throated cannon peal forth dread "misereres" over half a thousand battlefields, where sleep their last sleep—the victor and the vanquished. No more shall the ear of night be pierced with the echoes of fierce assault and stubborn defense from encompassed and beleagured cities. The conflict is over, and with it expired the cause.

With wartime distraction set aside, Lyon proposed roads, steamboat lines, and railroads as appropriate peacetime enterprises. He wanted to connect Salt Lake steamboat service by rail to an Old's Ferry-Salmon Falls steamboat line then projected to provide inexpensive communication with another Blue Mountain rail line to Umatilla's Columbia steamboat connection. This proposal, he speculated, would leave Boise with:

> less than four hundred miles of railroad to build to render a branch Pacific railroad a success, whose entrepot will be Portland, and its terminus Great Salt Lake City. This route is some five hundred miles nearer China and Japan than the trunk road through Nevada and California, and by your endorsement of the state of facts in a proper way by memorial, it cannot fail to attract favorably the attention of Congress, that we may have the same chartered rights and government bounty to induce its construction that has been given to other measures of a similar character. Thus the Columbia River, the natural avenue of commerce, would attract the trade of the Orient and Occident, as well as form the last grand link in this truly national highway. Oregon, as well as the territories of Montana and Washington, will be the gainers by its progress and completion.

Somewhat dazzled by Lyon's rhetoric as well as bemused by his half-antagonistic, half-conciliatory political approach, Idaho's legislature decided not to wait for Congressional action, but to incorporate an Idaho, Salt Lake, & Columbia River Branch Pacific Railroad Company, which was done on January 11, 1866. Dubious of Lyon's Salmon Falls steamboat enterprise, the company was authorized to construct a rail line from Salt Lake west to Old's Ferry. A bipartisan syndicate of Lyon and some prominent local leaders, Idaho's new railroad corporation also included Oregon Steam Navigation Company investors from Portland, along with Ben Holladay (whose Overland Stage Company operated west to Boise) and some New York investors. Tammany boss William Marcy Tweed (later to become notorious for his Tweed Ring operations), who had some dubious Rocky Bar mining investments, also was represented as an incorporator. All these diverse talents managed to accomplish nothing as Idaho railway builders, but their efforts indicated that there was strong interest in such a project prior to 1868, when Boise embarked upon serious efforts to obtain rail service.

Lyon's sequence of failures extended far beyond his railway proposal. His diamond mine lacked diamonds; his gold mines for freed slaves went into abrupt decline; his constitutional convention never was assembled; and his Indian policy offended enough influential politicians to ensure his dismissal from office. After sounding ferociously anti-Indian (a popular position at the time), he resisted efforts to wipe out local Shoshoni bands in an early stage of Idaho's Snake War of 1866-1868. Idaho was deprived of a territorial government when Lyon once again departed inconspicuously from Boise on April 21, 1866. Gilson already had quietly absconded on February 10, taking along Idaho's entire territorial treasury of $41,062. He was next reported seen in Hong Kong and finally was pursued across Europe by one of his Boise bondholders. Lyon, not to be outdone, made off with all of Idaho's Indian funds, amounting to $46,418.40. Idaho now lacked not only territorial officials but a treasury as well. Boise continued as capital, but without much evidence of territorial government to support any pretensions to political importance.

Adding to the potential loss in civic pride inherent in administrative collapse of Idaho's territorial government, Boise's electorate contributed to municipal chaos early in 1866. Legislative action approved on January 11 had given Boise another opportunity to experiment with city government. A new city charter, which eventually served Boise for almost a century, allowed no option of voter approval. In order that all "inhabitants of said city may enjoy the immediate benefit" of city government, Boise was required to elect a mayor and council on May 6. Yet resistance to organization of municipal government failed to disappear simply because the issue was not submitted for approval. An anti-charter party, with candidates pledged to refuse to take office, prevailed on election day. Legislative direction thus was thwarted by city officials who adhered to their campaign promises. Boise's tradition of independence from legislative control was reinforced.

A new governor, D.W. Ballard, helped restore Boise's importance as territorial capital very quickly after his arrival, June 14, 1866. A physician from Lebanon, Oregon, Ballard had to rely upon his Boise medical practice to retain financial solvency during most of his term as governor. Governor Ballard was a Radical Republican, representing a Yamhill group of Oregon politicians in their feud with Idaho's Confederate Democratic legislature, and he faced determined opposition from a majority of Boise's citizens. Yet some important problems were cleared up. Idaho's Supreme Court finally managed to organize and to review some appeals, including Boise's argument that Idaho's recent legislatures were legal and that Lewiston's claim to being territorial capital was spurious. Boise's two-to-one Supreme Court majority rejected Lewiston's arguments on June 16. North Idaho, which had gone almost unrepresented in Idaho's previous legislature, began to participate again. But Lewiston, mostly by means of nearly unanimous northern support, spent more than two decades in an almost successful effort to separate from Idaho. Boise politicians occasionally would endorse Lewiston's aspirations, but whenever a project to release North Idaho stood a chance of success, Boise leaders would undermine it. Sectional hostility erupted from these conflicts, and Boise's history (as well as Lewiston's) has been affected considerably by the feuds resulting from Idaho's odd territorial boundaries, which are inconsistent with the Pacific Northwest's political geography.

During a time of great national tumult over Radical

Boiseans James S. Reynolds, founder and owner of the Idaho Tri-weekly Statesman *(seated at right), David W. Ballard, governor of Idaho Territory from 1866 to 1870 (standing at center), and Lafayette Cartee, pioneer nurseryman and surveyor general of Idaho (seated at left), pose in about 1867.*

Central Hotel, which opened in 1866 as Hart's Exchange, stood at the corner of Seventh and Idaho streets now occupied by Boise City Hall. Its rooms were rented for sessions of the Idaho legislature before the Territorial Capitol was completed in 1886. Lithograph from Elliott, History of Idaho Territory, *1884.*

Reconstruction, Governor Ballard simply could not avoid a clash with Idaho's overwhelmingly Confederate fourth legislative session. With a good share of Missouri refugees still living in the area, Boise joined most of Idaho's mining towns in upholding President Andrew Johnson in his clash with Radical Republican Congressional leaders, who gained strength in 1866. Considering that Idaho, as a territory, had no Congressional vote, national issues received exaggerated attention in Boise. Meetings in Hart's Exchange—a new hotel that suffered damage during Ballard's legislative war—Idaho's legislative leaders investigated such issues as who had stolen the entire federal territorial treasury (Gilson had kept his depredation secret until then) and why they were about to be denied their pay. Idaho had been operating largely without the federal funds that were supposed to be made available to maintain territorial government. After Gilson's defalcation, territorial credit was so bad (nonexistent, in fact) that his successor had to advance governmental operating expenses from his own personal funds.

Solomon R. Howlett, who had taken over as secretary when Gilson absconded, then arranged to cut off all legislative salary payments, for which he had no funds anyway, because most members had been Confederates. Their response was explosive enough to cause Governor Ballard and Secretary Howlett to doubt if they would escape alive. They arranged for protection from Fort Boise, and the arrival of a file of soldiers, on January 12, 1867, really set off an explosion. Legislative resentment against military intimidation came close to getting totally out of control. Threats to burn down Boise were made, along with other suggestions for retaliation. Serious disorder eventually was averted, however, and a truce (described by Owen Wister as "The Second Missouri Compromise" in a short story he later published in *Century*) was effected. From then on, Boise was threatened less by legislative exuberance.

After legislative attention was no longer diverted by perplexing national issues, Boise's continuing problems of city government were addressed. Under an act of January 11, Boise's voters were given a third opportunity to organize their city. This time, only 10 days were allowed for an election campaign. Two slates of candidates for mayor and council—both in favor of organizing a city government—were presented in response to this new opportunity. But another anti-charter party was organized unexpectedly on January 19 and swept into power two days later by a margin of 277 votes to only 133 for both original sets of candidates. As a consequence of such determined resistance, Boise's new mayor refused to take office and his city council declined to organize.

Reluctance to organize as a city did not keep Boise from attaining greater regional importance. B.M. DuRell, a pioneer merchant who had begun to offer limited banking services, decided to expand his financial empire, which already included Idaho City and Silver City branches. Along with other merchants, he had been willing to accept gold dust, which would at least be protected in his safe. Merchants also dealt in territorial warrants, which were accepted at heavy discount, particularly at times when Idaho's treasury was empty and when redemption might be delayed for years. United States notes—regular paper currency called "greenbacks" in those days—also circulated at a discount. Idaho, though, had so much imitation gold dust—known as "bogus"— that regular paper money had better acceptance than in many other places where adulterated or fake gold created less of a problem.

Boise's economy needed efficient banking services, which DuRell finally arranged to provide. On a trip to Washington and Boston, he managed to procure a charter for his First National Bank of Idaho. National banks had been provided as an emergency Civil War financial device in 1863 when overinflated United States currency was declining excessively in value. But four years later, DuRell found that all $300 million in authorized national bank capital had been subscribed, so that no new charters were available. To overcome this obstacle, he had to locate and purchase subscription rights that had already been issued in Boston.

Returning to Boise, DuRell opened his new bank on June 6, 1867, with C.W. Moore as his business partner. Regular banking services gave Boise essential financial services, including interest-bearing deposit, issue of notes that circulated as greatly needed additional currency, discount of commercial paper and loans, and bank correspondence with institutions in other cities for transfer of funds. Through control of projects and enterprises for which they could ex-

Judge Milton Kelly, who succeeded James Reynolds as editor and publisher of the Idaho Tri-weekly Statesman, *was noted for strong political views and scathing verbal attacks on his opponents. In keeping with the tradition established by Reynolds, Kelley's running feuds with the editors of the* Idaho World *of Idaho City and the* Owyhee Avalanche *of Silver City delighted readers and helped to sell newspapers.*

tend or deny credit, bankers exercised decisive influence over community development. By gaining a strong national bank at an early date, Boise gained an important advantage at a critical stage in Idaho's economic development. Only a few Pacific Coast cities had nationally chartered banks by that time.

While DuRell was obtaining his bank charter, another kind of enterprise distinctive in Boise's development got under way. Like Idaho City, Boise had a hot springs nearby. Idaho's City's warm springs had been developed into an early resort and, on May 1, 1867, James Pollard opened a Boise warm springs resort at a favored site behind Table Rock. Eventually taken over by Milton Kelly and known as Kelly's Hot Springs, this resort served as a community attraction for many years. Warm Springs Avenue was developed as an elegant residential street leading to Kelly's Hot Springs.

Later in 1867, a compelling need to have a mayor directing its affairs overcame Boise's persistent reluctance to become a city. After a four-year delay, public land surveys began, so that Boise could have a townsite. (Until that time, aside from William Craig's Oregon donation claim near Lewiston, Idaho's residents all lacked title to their lands.) In order for anyone to gain title to a city lot, a townsite had to be patented. Only a mayor could provide that essential service. Boise's 1867 mayor still insisted upon respecting his campaign pledge never to assume office, but he agreed to resign in order to allow someone else to become mayor. One councilman out of four also declined to accept office, but three were enough to organize city government and to appoint a new mayor under Boise's 1866 city charter.

H.E. Prickett, who later became an Idaho Supreme Court Justice, finally was prevailed upon to act as mayor, November 18. A substitute councilman, Supreme Court Justice John Cummins, was obtained as well. Cummins arranged to set up a $600 loan fund at 24 percent interest in order to raise funds to patent the townsite. These loans were then used as credits to people who purchased townsite lots. Boise's original city officials also arranged for a volunteer hook-and-ladder company to provide fire protection. A regular election, on January 6, 1868, voted in officials for full terms, and no more anti-charter candidates were chosen. A *Statesman* account noted, however, that "little interest was taken in the election, except by the gamblers and their confederates who rolled out to a man and worked from morning to night." For a number of years, many prominent citizens engaged in strenuous efforts to abolish the city charter and government, but their campaigns failed and Boise's city government continued to operate.

Boise still remained a frontier community when city government began. Indian tensions, relieved temporarily by Caleb Lyon's Bruneau Treaty of April 12, 1866, soon grew into a series of frustrating encounters that became known as the Snake War of 1866-1868. Fort Boise served as an army operating base for Owyhee and Oregon engagements that continued with little or no success until General George Crook took over late in 1867. Rather than wait until spring to retaliate against Indian bands, which had made stage operations hazardous over a wide area, he set out on a winter campaign. This energetic innovation in Indian warfare, which other army commanders soon adopted, was used to advantage in subse-

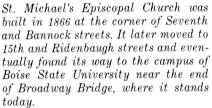

St. Michael's Episcopal Church was built in 1866 at the corner of Seventh and Bannock streets. It later moved to 15th and Ridenbaugh streets and eventually found its way to the campus of Boise State University near the end of Broadway Bridge, where it stands today.

quent seasons as well. Fort Boise offered an important additional contribution to local development. Expenditures for military supplies did much to maintain Boise's economy during years when mining was in decline. Boise's social life also centered around Fort Boise, as did a considerable share of community cultural activities. Even after Crook's extended Snake campaign came to a conclusion in California's Surprise Valley near Fort Bidwell in 1868, Fort Boise continued to sustain important community functions.

Evidence of Boise's permanence had continued to accumulate in 1866 and 1867, despite the decline in mining activity. Important lode-mining enterprises, with major stamp mills installed at Rocky Bar, Silver City, and the Boise Basin, had offered great hope in 1864 and 1865. Such operations would support Idaho's economy for years, since lode properties required more miners, large capital investment, and could not be exhausted in a few short seasons. But early stamp-milling experiments largely failed in 1866 and 1867. Because they were in remote country with very difficult access, and involved technology not adequately developed for most major mines, they proved more expensive than available investment resources could support. Yet lode operations had a bright future regardless of serious obstacles, which actually prolonged their period of activity. Boise clearly could rely upon a long-term mining economy that would support local farms as well as city businesses and services. New, more substantial buildings were constructed and an Episcopalian church was completed in time for services to commence on September 2, 1866. As trees grew and better houses replaced the early cabins, Boise gradually began to look more like the established town that permanent residents hoped to develop.

Chapter 3

IN SEARCH OF A RAILROAD
1868-1889

*E*arly 19th-century community developers had taken advantage of power sites, of strategic canal and river locations, and of railway enterprises in building cities that gained major regional or national importance. Good rail service was regarded as an essential condition for serious community promotion. Like promising towns everywhere, Boise had unlimited confidence in rapid growth. Transcontinental rail service was a condition essential for that purpose. Chicago's rise to ascendancy over St. Louis, which had previously dominated western economic expansion, showed exactly what might happen to a city that was surpassed as a rail center.

Far Western cities, however, eventually had a different experience from that of St. Louis and Chicago. Cheyenne, despite a transcontinental railroad advantage, failed to eclipse Denver, which soon got rail service, too; Ogden did not displace Salt Lake; Tacoma did not catch up with Seattle; and other early rail centers did not necessarily supplant older, established communities. In a much more modest way, Boise also demonstrated that a Far Western town could survive as an economic center despite long delays in gaining convenient rail service. But in all these cases, railroad connections seemed essential, and Boise's promoters went to great lengths to realize that ambition. When Boise's community leaders organized an ambitious campaign in 1868 to gain rail service, they had to incorporate their planning into a complex national transportation development. A national rail network was being extended to California as rapidly as possible. What Boise needed, however, was a line to Oregon.

Many years before, in 1840, Asa Whitney had suggested a

Facing page
In 1895 James Lawrence (in the doorway) owned the Spider Web Saloon in partnership with Madison Smith (center, in shirtsleeves).

Lafayette Cartee was Idaho Territory's surveyor general in the 1860s and 1870s and the leading nurseryman of early Boise City. General Cartee's ranch began near the corner of Fourth and Grove, where his elegant house and stable were located. Cartee took an active interest in the improvement of Idaho livestock as well as horticultural varieties.

Snake River route to Oregon. His original transcontinental railway proposal fitted Boise's needs very well. But such a project was conceived prior to United States' acquisition of Oregon, Idaho, and California, and so could not materialize for almost 30 years. First a wagon road had to be opened (Boise's Oregon Trail location on that route was favorable). Next Eastern and Western terminals had to gain Congressional support, and several cities vied to become a terminal. A series of Pacific Railroad surveys (1853-1855) provided route information for almost every reasonable prospect except Asa Whitney's Snake River route to Portland. Intense rivalry among prospective Northern and Southern terminal cities prevented Congressional action until 1862, when Civil War politics blocked Southern aspirations for a line. By that time, California's gold rush enabled San Francisco and Sacramento to supplant Portland as prospective beneficiaries. Portland and Boise had a better natural route that avoided obstacles as serious as California's Sierra Nevada. California's population and mining advantages overwhelmed Oregon's claims, and after improved financial and land grant supports were offered in 1864, Union Pacific construction from Council Bluffs and Central Pacific road building from Sacramento got under way.

By 1868 both lines were approaching a junction somewhere in Utah. Loans and land grants depended upon how many miles each company succeeded in building, so they engaged in a wild race to gain as much support as possible. Boise's promoters watched this contest with great interest, because they needed to obtain a connection to a Utah or Nevada railhead. Since no one would be interested in building more than 240 miles to reach a town of less than a thousand inhabitants, they had to capitalize upon Idaho's mining needs and potential industrial traffic. They also had to take advantage of a location along a prospective route to Portland.

In Portland, Oregon Steam Navigation Company officials, who already had important Idaho investments at Silver City, had an understandable interest in gaining transcontinental railway access. Union Pacific managers also saw an advantage in gaining a Snake and Columbia connection to Portland. Their chief engineer, Grenville M. Dodge, found this alternative to California's High Sierra Nevada crossing offered an important economic advantage. Dodge had checked out a Snake River transcontinental possibility while employed as a Pacific Railroad surveyor in 1853, and continued to support that route to Portland. His 1867 investigation disclosed a practical Snake River opportunity, which confirmed his opinion that "'ere long it will become the great through route from the northwest, and control the trade and traffic of the Indies." Such a prospect provoked determined opposition from California's Central Pacific builders, who gradually were constructing their part of an overland railroad from Sacramento toward an eventual Union Pacific junction at Ogden. They consistently refused to allow a Boise-Portland connection west of Ogden, because they wanted to monopolize transcontinental traffic on their line. Idaho promoters, aware of Central Pacific hostility, went ahead to support a plan for a Union Pacific branch line in 1868. But they could not anticipate a convenient Central Pacific connection at Kelton.

An elaborate territorial railroad convention assembled in Boise,

January 6-8, 1868, to call attention to Idaho's transportation needs. Setting aside bitter partisan differences, Democrats and Republicans worked in surprising harmony after many years of bitter strife. Delegates from all sections got together to adopt resolutions in favor of a Snake River line that would serve Boise. Silver City's delegation preferred a Central Pacific branch from nearby Nevada, and did not want to mention Boise's route specifically. But Central Pacific opposition to a Boise-Portland outlet defeated their proposal. Idaho's population had declined since 1864, but major lode mines at Rocky Bar and Silver City were waiting for rail transportation so that they could be developed. Once these two camps developed large-scale production, they would support an increased farm population and a more substantial trading center in Boise. Idaho Supreme Court justices and substantial business leaders joined legislative members and attorneys in asserting a broad Idaho interest in rail service. Idaho's Congressional delegate and governor added their influence in an assembly designed to impress Union Pacific and Oregon Steam Navigation Company management. For two decades, Boise had to continue this railroad campaign.

By 1868 Boise had grown into a permanent settlement with about 400 buildings, including some 250 private dwellings. Business and professional establishments continued to show a diversity appropriate for a remote, self-sufficient community. Two churches and 20 saloons suggested Boise's western orientation remained unchanged after Idaho's gold rush had receded. A variety of other enterprises indicated Boise's self-sufficiency as a community lacking rail communication:

Wholesale and Retail Stores, 18	Breweries, 5
	Drugstores, 2
Butcher Shops, 3	Hotels, 3
Cabinet Makers, 3	Bakeries, 4
Blacksmith Shops, 5	Paint Shops, 2
Photograph Galleries, 1	Wagonmakers, 4
Fruit and Vegetable Stores, 5	Restaurants, 3
	Shoemakers, 1
Barber Shops, 3	Tailors, 2
Livery Stables, 3	Gunsmiths, 1
Stage Offices, 2	Physicians, 4
Jewelry Stores, 1	Dentists, 1
Banking Houses, 2	Carpenters, 4
Lumber Yards, 1	Milliners, 1
Boarding Houses, 2	Corrals, 6
Printing Offices, 2	Mills, 2
Distilleries, 2	Flour Mills, 3
Law and Government Offices, 32	

Unlike some of Idaho's gold camps, which were made up mainly of single miners, Boise was a city of families who had come to settle permanently. Four elementary schools enrolled more than 200 children, but in 1868 "higher education" was limited to a dancing school or two and to music courses. A large number of law offices was appropriate for an isolated center of government.

Aside from wagonmakers, harnessmakers, cabinetmakers, and

Above
Joe Misseldt was one of Boise's popular German citizens. He operated the City Brewery two doors west of Sixth and Main until he drowned in his cistern in 1879.

Right
James Lawrence advertised his Naked Truth Saloon in the Boise City Republican *on March 1, 1886.*

THE
NAKED TRUTH
SALOON.

JAMES N. LAWRENCE, PROPRIETOR.

ADVERTISEMENT OF AN HONEST RUM-SELLER AS IT SHOULD BE.

FRIENDS AND NEIGHBORS:—Having just opened a commodious shop for the sale of liquid fire. I embrace this opportunity of informing you that I have commenced the business of making

Drunkards, paupers and beggars for the sober, industrious and respectable portion of the community to support. I shall deal in family spirits, which will incite men to deeds of riot, robbery and blood, and, by so doing diminish the comfort, augment the expenses and endanger the welfare of the community.

I will undertake at short notice, for a small sum, and with great expectations, to prepare victims for the asylum, poorfarm, prisons and gallows.

I will furnish an article which will increase fatal accidents, multiply the number of distressing diseases and render those which are harmless incurable.

I will deal in drugs which will deprive some of life, many of reason, most of property and all of peace; which will cause fathers to become fiends, and wives, widows, children orphans and all mendicants.

I will cause many of the rising generation to grow up in ignorance, and prove a burden and a nuisance to the nation.

☞ I will cause mothers to forget their offspring and cruelty take the place of love.

I will sometimes even corrupt the ministers of religion; obstruct the progress of the gospel; defile the purity of the church, and cause temporal, spiritual and eternal death; and if any should be so impertinent as to ask why I have the audacity to bring such accumulated misery on the people, my honest reply is "Money." The spirit trade is lucrative and some professing christians give it their cheerful countenance.

I have purchased the right to demolish the character, destroy the health, shorten the lives and ruin the souls of those who choose to honor me with their custom. I pledge myself to do all I have herein promised. Those who wish any of the evils above specified brought upon themselves or their dearest friends, are requested to meet me at my bar, where I will for a few cents furnish them the certain means of doing so.

February 24, 1886.

other local manufacturing establishments that might lose business to nationally distributed industrial products, practically all of Boise's business enterprises would benefit greatly from rail service; so, too, would Fort Boise. An 1868 Oregon railroad meeting called upon Congress to subsidize a Snake River line in order to reduce transportation costs to military posts. Such savings would pay for building a railway to Boise and Portland.

Even without accounting for military advantages, a Union Pacific extension to Boise and Portland would become profitable. In 1868 and 1869, J.O. Hudnut surveyed that route and confirmed Dodge's confidence in adding Idaho's mines to a growing Union Pacific transportation empire. Boise alone accounted for 8,000 to 12,000 tons of freight each year. Rates from Portland by steamboat to Umatilla of $30 a ton, followed by still higher freight wagon costs over an Oregon Trail Blue Mountain route, offered considerable inducement to Midwestern suppliers interested in southwestern Idaho markets. Hauling in the stamp mills and mining equipment involved still greater effort and expense. Forty freight wagons had been required to bring a single Rocky Bar stamp mill from Umatilla past Boise to a remote mountain basin, and other heavy freighting projects proved very attractive to enterprising suppliers and shippers.

North Idaho had no serious alternative to an Oregon Steam Navigation Company Columbia River route, which profited from high monopoly rates, but Boise's gold-rush trade had been able to go east to Salt Lake or southwest to Sacramento and Red Bluff. California Steam Navigation Company rate competition had forced Portland's charges, high as they were, down to a point of unprofitability. Central Pacific service to Winnemucca had then displaced Sacramento's river route to Red Bluff as a contender for Boise traffic. A Union Pacific challenge in 1868 or 1869 had great merit. But Congress ignored a proposal to subsidize an Idaho, Oregon, and Puget Sound railway venture, combining Union Pacific and Brigham Young's Mormon interests. Even though Dodge reported that Idaho traffic alone would increase to $25 million in annual mining and farming wealth, Union Pacific managers could not take on such a project just then. An effort to build as far west as possible, in order to reach a good Idaho terminal point northwest of Salt Lake, almost succeeded. But Central Pacific insistence upon Ogden as its permanent connection blocked a direct Union Pacific extension to Boise and Portland. Even after completion of its transcontinental railway to a Central Pacific junction, on May 10, 1869, other obligations and insufficient resources prevented Union Pacific expansion into Idaho.

Boise had to be content, for more than a decade longer, with cumbersome stage and freight service to a Central Pacific connection 240 miles away at Kelton, Utah. Freighters to Toano, Elko, and Winnemucca, Nevada, also competed for Boise traffic. These connections, realized in 1869-1870, provided a vast improvement over earlier transportation facilities. But rapid population and commercial growth, long contemplated as a result of rail service, was deferred. Boise had only about 1,000 people in 1870, and many prominent leaders who had come during an exciting gold rush era moved to other mining areas where rail service provided for earlier development. An isolated community remained to work for a railroad that still was essential for rapid growth.

Federally funded improvements, aside from an improved transportation system, continued to support Boise's economy from 1869 to 1872. Governor D.W. Ballard selected a territorial penitentiary site next to Table Rock on January 28, 1869. After a considerable construction hassle, the promising institution opened for business on March 22, 1872. More importantly, a concerted drive to obtain a branch mint had led to a more elegant building project—a United

Above
By 1884 Boise's U.S. Assay Office had begun to acquire a parklike setting, and its full block of century-old trees are still a city amenity. From Elliott, History of Idaho Territory, 1884.

States Assay Office—starting on June 28, 1869, and continuing until gold and silver bullion was accepted for purchase, March 2, 1872. Territorial Secretary Edward Jay Curtis also invested in an office building, known as the Stone Jug, to house territorial executive offices in 1869. All of these improvements emphasized a need for better transportation

One railroad scheme followed another after Boise's stage and freight traffic was reoriented to Winnemucca and Kelton transcontinental connections in 1869 and 1870. Some suggestions came from farther northwest. A La Grande convention created Boise interest, June 26, 1869, with a Puget Sound-La Grande-Boise-Green River Union Pacific extension. A Portland, Dalles, and Salt Lake company gained another Boise convention's endorsement on November 22, 1871. A later Boise meeting took up an 1869 suggestion, April 3, 1872, to construct to Winnemucca as a Central Pacific alternative. But when W.W. Chapman addressed a Boise assembly, December 27, 1873, he was able to obtain an energetic local committee to devote a lot of effort on behalf of his Portland, Dalles, and Salt Lake company in 1874. His timing, however, proved distinctly poor. Jay Cooke's Northern Pacific failure had set off an 1873 international financial panic that delayed other railway enterprises as well. Union Pacific construction scandals received unwanted publicity, and Congress, as a result, lost enthusiasm for additional railway grants. Boise, along with many other Western communities aspiring for modern transportation, simply had to wait.

Less expensive communication systems could be handled more easily. A telegraph line reached Silver City from Winnemucca, August 31, 1874, and service was extended to Boise a year later. But even that enterprise scarcely could be financed during a severe national economic depression. California escaped financial hardship for two years after Jay Cooke's 1873 disaster, and some of Idaho's miners and developers benefited by San Francisco's apparent economic strength. But California's reprieve proved temporary. W.C. Ralston's Bank of California failure, in August of 1875, ruined Idaho enterprises as well. Silver City's productive mines, which had con-

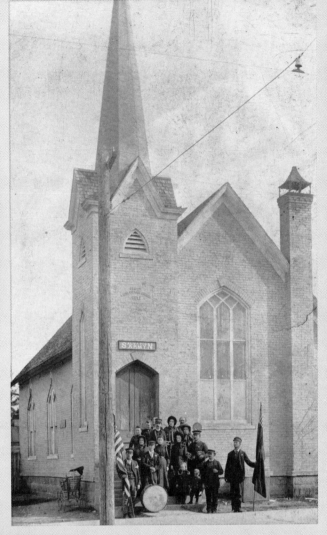

Clockwise from top left:
First Baptist Church, a handsome brick building built in 1892, stood on the northeast corner of 10th and Jefferson.

First Presbyterian Church at 10th and Main was built in 1878. The Salvation Army used the building in 1897, before the structure was torn down to make way for the Idanha Hotel in 1900.

Boise Presbyterians constructed a new church in 1894 at the corner of Ninth and State. Like most 19th-century churches, it was built in Gothic style with prominent stained-glass windows.

St. John's Roman Catholic Church was built on the northwest corner of Ninth and Bannock in 1876. The building was used until 1906 when the congregation moved into the basement of the cathedral on Eighth Street. Bishop Glorieux's residence, the brick building at right, was completed in 1886.

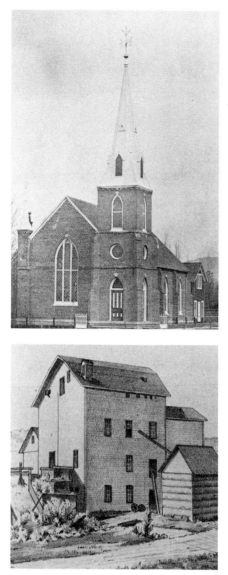

Top
Boise's Methodists built the largest church in the city in 1874-1875. The First Methodist Church stood at the corner of Eighth and Bannock, where the Hotel Boise (now the Hoff Building) was erected in 1930.

Above
The Ridenbaugh Mill was located at the foot of the Bench across the river from town. A south branch of the river once ran past the spot, making the area between the mill and the main stream an island. William Morris, Ridenbaugh's father-in-law, developed this flour mill, and the land above it became known as Morris Hill. Lithograph from Elliott, History of Idaho Territory, *1884.*

tributed greatly to Boise's economy, shut down permanently. New mines there could not be developed for another decade. Idaho farms and mines were set back for several years, although some Boise-area irrigation canals began to expand onto bench lands that could not be brought into cultivation when gold rush markets had stimulated Boise's original agricultural development.

An enlargement of Boise's farming area beyond river bottom lands required substantial capital investment. Road and bridge improvements, made necessary when a great 1876 flood shifted Boise River's main channel to a course nearer town, also proved costly. Finally, in 1878, when an improved national economy encouraged more ambitious irrigation projects, William B. Morris undertook a major canal expansion in an area affected by the 1876 river channel. In 1877 he invested $60,000 in getting a seven-mile canal—soon operated by his nephew, W.H. Ridenbaugh—onto bench land above Boise. Opened in 1878, the canal eventually was extended to 53 miles. Morris also acquired an 1865 canal, which had floated logs to and provided power for H.P. and J.C. Isaac's sawmill, flour mill, and distillery. But these investments absorbed all his resources, so that his canal project had to wait for government development almost 30 years later. This situation was typical of Western canal enterprises of the time, when most large irrigation projects exceeded a private company's ability to finance the canal and storage construction required for successful development. More than transportation improvements—essential as they were—was needed for agricultural expansion around Boise.

Boise's community leaders faced a variety of other problems during their long campaign to build an attractive city of trees in a desert wilderness, but they continued to display a unity of purpose and action that had been recognized ever since an initial bipartisan group of civic leaders ignored their Civil War political differences in order to advance an energetic program of community development. As a result of many years of concerted effort to advance their community's interests and their personal careers, they gained a reputation for success that had some negative connotations as well. Sectional leaders from other parts of Idaho complained (as was traditional in most Western territories) that they exercised excessive political power. After national exposure of a staggering series of post-Civil War corrupt government practices at all levels—national, state, territorial, and local—malfeasance frequently was assumed as conventional official practice. A dramatic exposure of New York City's "Tammany Ring" popularized an all-too-prevalent impression that many cities were managed by corrupt, sometimes bipartisan rings. Sectional jealousies in most Western territories combined with this impression to produce a series of controversies in which territorial capitals were assumed to be dominated by corrupt rings. New Mexico had its "Santa Fe Ring," Montana had a "Helena Ring"; and Washington had an "Olympia Ring." Idaho was likewise represented by its "Boise Ring."

Often the product of the fertile imagination of opposition leaders, who may have had grievances that were genuine enough, these rings evoked an excessive wave of controversy. The Boise Ring was no exception. Bitter factional battles among Idaho's territorial officials had plagued Idaho for a decade before 1878, when Governor

Mason Brayman got into a war against the Boise Ring. He had been warned in 1876 against Boise Ring machinations by Idaho's Democratic Congressional delegate, Stephen S. Fenn. North Idaho had elected Fenn to Congress in 1874, but his opponent, Governor T.W. Bennett, had deprived Fenn of his certificate of election, and had served most of Fenn's term by refusing to count numerous Democratic votes, which had been reported on forms that did not conform to legal requirements. This kind of irregularity had occurred frequently, but had never before been used as an excuse for reversing an election victory. After Fenn was finally able to rectify this injustice he warned Brayman (a Civil War general and prominent Republican) to watch out for similar Boise Ring evils.

Governor Brayman tried to govern like a Civil War general, which did nothing to improve his already poor relationship with many Idaho officials. Not surprisingly, he had a terrible time when he tried to capitalize upon a fight with a syndicate that Fenn had convinced him constituted a corrupt political ring. Brayman wanted to get rid of some Boise Ring federal appointees to create job opportunities for his family and friends. When they refused to retire quietly, he got into a bitter conflict that led to displacement of a number of Boise's leading citizens from territorial office. But Brayman wound up a casualty of his own war. Even Idaho's Indian wars, fought during Brayman's term as governor, did not always match his Boise Ring confrontations. Idaho's territorial militia organized into Brayman and anti-Brayman factions that sometimes showed more enthusiasm for assailing each other than for chasing Indians. Even before Brayman got into these difficulties, he had had great problems in trying to induce Idaho's militia to follow a distant Nez Perce warpath. For a time, a victorious Nez Perce force appeared to be headed toward Boise after routing a larger United States Army detachment at Whitebird in 1877. Military preparations to meet such a contingency ensued without delay. Eventually, when that threat proved to be unfounded, Boise militia showed insufficient interest in defending distant Mount Idaho and Lewiston, so Brayman was forced to enlist 20 Bannock Indian scouts to accept territorial armament. Led by Buffalo Horn, they headed north to represent Idaho's militia during General O.O. Howard's long Nez Perce campaign.

After months of close observation of Howard's severe difficulties in pursuing Indians through rough country, Buffalo Horn concluded his Bannock forces could win a war of their own. Late in May of 1878, more than a decade of tension on Camas Prairie erupted into a southern Idaho Indian conflict. Buffalo Horn's faction at last had a chance to demonstrate its military talents. Boise again escaped attack, but Brayman had a hard time explaining his alliance with Buffalo Horn. His Boise Ring detractors, now engaged in a relentless war against Governor Brayman, denounced him for every kind of offense they could think of and Idaho's Indian campaigns provided them one of a host of opportunities.

Dismissing Brayman's responses as ''garrulous vaporings of senile vanity,'' a number of Boise's prominent leaders reacted bitterly when their governor prevailed upon President Hayes to replace Idaho's old territorial officials with a batch of newcomers, along with an old Rocky Bar resident. Diverted in part from community

Mason Brayman served as governor of Idaho Territory from 1876 until 1880. His term of office was marked by clashes with the Nez Perces in 1877, the Bannocks in 1878, and the Sheepeaters in 1879. Brayman's "war" with the Boise Ring occupied an even greater part of his attention during his tumultuous stay in Idaho.

Thomas W. Bennett was Idaho's territorial governor from December 26, 1871, until March 3, 1875. President Grant had appointed five others to the post before Bennett accepted it, and to everyone's surprise he served for more than three years. Governor Hawley, who knew him well, called Bennett "the most jovially reckless gentleman who ever sat in a gubernatorial chair."

Andrew McQuaid. George Banks. F.J. Parker. Jack Cambbell

Right
When the Nez Perce War broke out in 1877, there was widespread fear that the Indians might head south. Boise volunteers, led by famed Frontier Marshal Orlando "Rube" Robbins (center with shotgun), headed north to protect Weiser Valley settlers. The Nez Perce went east instead, but a year later Robbins fought in the Bannock War.

Below
Civil War General Oliver Otis Howard led the U.S. Army in the attempt to round up the Nez Perces in 1877. Howard University is named for this religious zealot who lost his right arm in the war.

development by these efforts, they managed to get Brayman removed. But when his successor learned of a totally unsatisfactory situation that had developed in Idaho's territorial government, he refused to accept office and got another territorial appointment. Brayman finally served out his term after all, but his Boise Ring escapade contributed little to peace and good will during an already trying time in municipal history.

Before Mason Brayman's Boise hostilities had ended, Fort Boise's Indian campaigns also were concluded. In 1879 Idaho's Bannock disturbance was followed by a series of army expeditions to relocate a remote Shoshoni group known mainly for their skill in hunting mountain sheep. The expeditions succeeded in leaving 51 aboriginal Salmon River mountain inhabitants and Bannock war refugees without winter supplies. They finally agreed to evacuate their remote wilderness homeland to settle at Fort Hall. Another small "Sheepeater" band escaped unnoticed for several years, so Fort Boise no longer appeared to have much of a military function. Redesignated as Boise Barracks in 1879, the army outpost continued to help support Boise's economy until 1912. New buildings there matched some of Boise's growth, as an era of Indian wars gave way to a time of urban expansion and recovery from mining failures that had restrained local development for a decade.

Boise's prospects for rail service began to revive at this time. National economic prosperity returned sufficiently in 1879 for Jay Gould to start some important Union Pacific expansion projects. Gould had gained national notoriety as a railroad and market investment manipulator. Wanting eventually to reach Puget Sound, he started with a plan for Utah & Northern Railway extension northward across southeastern Idaho in order to reach Butte and Helena. This narrow-gauge line—shorter and less costly than a Boise and Portland investment—put little strain on his resources. He also had firm promises, never actually realized, of substantial Montana subsidies to assist in construction. Idaho consistently refused to offer subsidies, and Boise's more expensive project had to wait. Just after Utah & Northern contractors crossed from Idaho into Montana, other rail construction (also made possible by a more attractive investment market during a period of national economic recovery) created a situation that promised to be resolved in Boise's favor. After 1880 Union Pacific management no longer could delay their program to add a Portland outlet to their growing transportation system.

Construction of new Pacific Coast rail lines provided both a threat and an opportunity favorable to Union Pacific expansion through Boise. After taking over some of Ben Holladay's Willamette Valley rail enterprises, Henry Villard added Portland's Oregon Steam Navigation Company to his transportation empire in 1879. Consolidating his holdings into a reorganized Oregon Railway & Navigation Company, he sought a Union Pacific partnership in his enlarged venture. While waiting for a favorable response, he began construction of his Columbia River rail segment. Another Pacific Coast development also frightened Union Pacific officials, who were aware of their vulnerability in Ogden. But as long as Union Pacific and Central Pacific managers had no option but to use each other's line for transcontinental rail traffic, both were protected from outside competition.

In 1880, however, C.P. Huntington's Southern Pacific—a Central Pacific expansion and California affiliate—was about to achieve independent outlets through New Orleans and through a Santa Fe rail connection to Chicago. Union Pacific officials, realizing their predicament once Central Pacific traffic could be diverted from Ogden by way of an alternate Southern Pacific route, could not hesitate. Sidney Dillon decided that a Portland outlet could no longer be delayed. Combining forces with Henry Villard, he prepared to build an Oregon Short Line route to connect with an Oregon Railway & Navigation Company terminal where Idaho and Oregon meet along Snake River. Boise's hopes for rail service became realistic when Dillon had to respond to a Central Pacific competitive threat by taking advantage of a new Portland opportunity.

By 1880, when railway competition provided assurance that Union Pacific's Snake River line would finally be built, Boise had grown into a town of about 1,900 people—almost 1,000 more than were counted a decade earlier. Main Street had gained a more permanent appearance, with substantial brick buildings replacing many earlier wooden structures. Large new mansions, some of them reflecting contemporary architectural style, enhanced Grove Street's aristocratic residential area. Capitol Square still was vacant. But within a year, Boise received a legislative charter for an independent school district that was prepared to build a large new graded school. The consolidation of school districts, which was gaining acceptance nationally, led to the replacement of one-room schools, where pupils of different ages were schooled together, allow-

Colonel John Green was affectionately known as General Green during his long stay in Boise as commander of the barracks. The military post, which was vital to the frontier town at first for the protection it offered, always had economic and social significance for Boise City.

Facing page:
Top
John Lemp's Grove Street house exemplifies the Gothic Revival taste of the 1870s. Members of the prosperous German brewer's large family pose on the two-story veranda surrounding the house in about 1890.

Bottom
Boise druggist William Nye owned one of Grove Street's most attractive residences of the 1870s. Elliott's 1884 History of Idaho Territory included lithographs, such as this one, intended to show what a genteel and sophisticated place the capital city was after only 20 years of existence.

Left
Surveyor General Lafayette Cartee was Boise's leading nurseryman. His Gothic Revival cottage and lush grounds at Fourth and Grove are shown here in 1958, shortly before the Cartee mansion was demolished.

Below left
Christopher W. Moore, a founder of the First National Bank of Idaho, built the finest house in the territory on Grove, increasing that street's reputation as the city's best neighborhood. After Moore moved to Warm Springs Avenue in 1892, the building came to be known as "The Delamar," a famous Basque boardinghouse. Lithograph from Elliott, History of Idaho Territory, 1884.

Right
Cynthia Mann, one of Boise's most beloved schoolteachers, is shown surrounded by a group of her proteges in 1890. She taught at Cole and other public schools, and for many years she instructed local children in literature and the arts in her own home.

Above
Central School was completed in 1882. Ostner's statue of George Washington and the Territorial Capitol are in the distance. From Thayer, Marvels of the New West.

ing older ones to help the younger ones but providing limited opportunity for advanced instruction. Boise's consolidated school district was able to commence a high school, but anyone interested in higher education still had to leave Idaho to find college or university opportunities.

Months before June 16, 1882, when Oregon Short Line construction crews crossed from Wyoming into Idaho on their way toward Boise and Huntington, Boise's railroad negotiators had good reason to expect they were going to encounter serious problems. Boise had a fine Oregon Trail location with superior access to major mines, but emigrant road and railroad grades demanded very different location requirements. Rather than descend steep, difficult grades to reach Boise, Oregon Short Line surveyors preferred a route directly down Indian Creek. Company officials remained unimpressed when Boise's businessmen reminded them of the major investments that had already been made in an established community, but the company proposed instead the formation of a townsite development corporation. This thinly concealed Union Pacific front organization, the Idaho and Oregon Land Improvement Company, would cheerfully provide a new Boise River city at Indian Creek from which rail service could be offered to Boise, about 29 miles upstream. Boise countered with a proposal for only a 15-mile branch line to an existing Boise-Silver City stage station on Indian Creek. The offer was rejected, again because of the hills that would have to be crossed. Boise railway promoters then undertook to defeat the U.P. by taking up whatever decent land was available at their Boise River-Indian Creek location, so that no competing city could be built at Boise's branch railroad junction. (At least, this is the way U.P. townsite promoters viewed the Boise action.)

After moving westward past American Falls to Shoshone, Oregon Short Line construction was halted for a time. Boise's incipient battle over a rival townsite was deferred for a season because Henry Villard's Oregon Railway & Navigation Company construction toward Huntington and an Oregon Short Line connection was running far behind schedule. Rather than end up with a line that terminated nowhere (since Huntington remained unbuilt), Sidney Dillon's Oregon Short Line took time out to build a branch to Hailey, where Idaho's new Wood River lead-silver mines needed immediate rail service. Meanwhile, Boise promoters built up hopes of obtaining an Oregon Pacific-Chicago Northwestern connection with a coastal outlet at Newport, Oregon. In case this connection should fail to materialize, John Lemp arranged for an extremely difficult route survey up Boise River's south fork canyon to provide Oregon Pacific Camas Prairie access to Ogden. Another unlikely enterprise would have given Boise a narrow-gauge line through difficult canyons to Atlanta and Vienna, where important mines were developing.

Proceeding west again, railroad builders completed their line down Indian Creek on September 6, 1883. At this point, Idaho and Oregon Land Improvement Company managers outmaneuvered Boise's opposition by establishing a new townsite in Alkali Flat. Located on a lower Indian Creek expanse of uninhabitable land that Boise's railway interests had regarded as not worth acquiring, the

Charles Ostner's 1878 view of Boise City was lithographed in San Francisco. When the lithographer redrew the original sketches on stone, Boise's Lombardy poplar trees were changed into evergreens by an artist who had never seen the city. The view is from the hill behind Fort Boise, looking south to the Owyhee mountains.

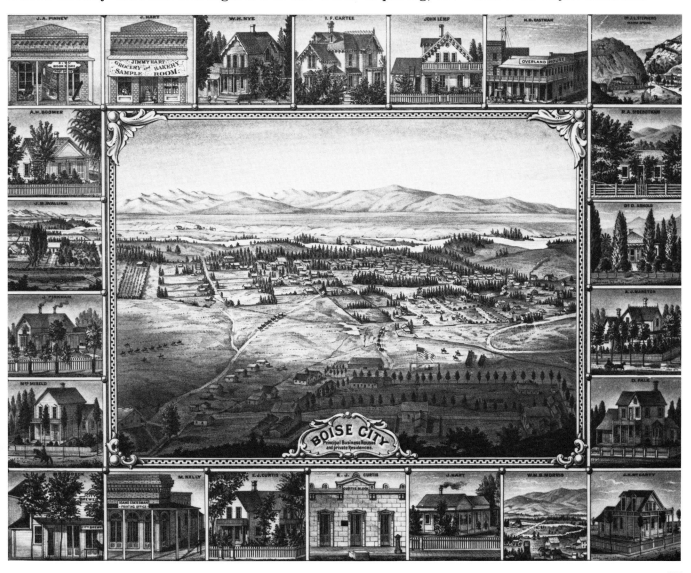

German immigrant John Lemp was a pioneer Boise brewer, civic leader, and mining and real-estate investor. After his election as president of the Turn Verein Society in 1870, Lemp went on to become mayor in 1875. John Lemp's popularity derived partly from his pleasant custom of donating kegs of free beer to help celebrate holidays and other special occasions.

townsite was decked out with an array of August Christmas trees to impress a special trainload of Iowa investors. The Boise Board of Trade responded to the ruse of the promoters with a long denunciation of their "villainous and unprincipled conduct." Deploring efforts "to gratify the greed of a few impecunious adventurers," John Lemp and his Boise business associates assailed their new townsite rivals as "a gang of unprincipled, impecunious and insatiable cormorants ... who invade our country as do the leprous hordes of China, solely to 'pillage and depart'. ..." The Alkali Flat syndicate, however, did not lack resources. One member had been wealthy enough to purchase a United States Senate seat a decade earlier—an investment ruined by exposure of his finagling that forced him to retire. Another went on to become one of Pittsburgh's most illustrious multimillionaires with a long record of distinguished service as Treasury Department secretary. Boise's problem, though, was how to avoid displacement by a nearby rail center, in a situation similar to Reno's success in competing with Carson in Nevada.

Responding to an urgent appeal for help, Union Pacific President Charles Francis Adams came to Boise on October 17, promising that with local support in obtaining a right of way, a river branch would be constructed without delay. Boise met his terms and grading finally got under way. But another national financial panic in 1884 interfered, and a year later construction had to be suspended. Also ruined by that national economic collapse, a monumental Boise Valley canal project funded with New York capital was set back for two decades. Boise had to remain satisfied with stage and wagon freight service to Kuna, 15 miles distant on Indian Creek, for four years. That was a great deal closer than Kelton, but still unsatisfactory. During that time, a grand effort was made to develop a central valley rail center in Caldwell, which would have become Boise's rail terminal if Adams' initial Oregon Short Line branch had been completed. Caldwell, though, could not profit very much from a central location in a valley where widespread irrigation could not be developed for another two decades. Boise merchants and distributors already had been successful in obtaining Central Pacific freight-rate rebates from San Francisco to Kelton so that California suppliers could retain their trade prior to Oregon Short Line construction. They managed to preserve their business, even though they had to operate at a considerable disadvantage from a wagon road location in an area where their competitors enjoyed rail transportation.

In spite of their disappointment at having their railway station in Kuna, Boise investors took advantage of other technological advances that were transforming everyday life at that time. A Boise phone exchange began operation as part of a New Year's Day celebration in 1884, with service extended to Caldwell on January 19. Utilizing a Ridenbaugh Canal power source, an electric company was incorporated on October 4, 1886. Failure of the company's contractor to get the plant installed delayed the opening of an electric lighting system for nearly a year, but Boise was making an effort to keep up with modern inventions that were available in most progressive communities. (In Idaho, Ketchum's Philadelphia smelter had a small electric light plant in 1882; and Hailey, with major lead-silver mines to speed up community development, had installed a city system in 1887.) In 1885 and 1886, an elegant territorial capitol

Left
Dr. George P. Haley, a longtime Boise physician, placed great faith in electricity as a healing agent and owned exotic equipment.

Below
John Hailey, known as "stagecoach king," "sheep king," and territorial congressman, was the first head of the Idaho Historical Society when it became a state agency in 1907. The town of Hailey was named for him and in 1910, Hailey's History of Idaho *was published with an appropriation from the state legislature.*

was under construction, and new downtown business buildings continued to add to Main Street's increasingly substantial appearance.

Civic improvement, however, was not attained without a considerable amount of dissension. In order to obtain capitol construction funding, Territorial Secretary D.P.B. Pride (whose Boise Ring legislative management operations astonished some of Idaho's more experienced politicians) had to gain Mormon votes for his project even though he and his associates professed to be sincere and diligent anti-Mormons. (In those days, a national and southeastern Idaho antipolygamy tumult forced most successful Idaho politicians to turn anti-Mormon after 1882.) In return for a promise that Governor William Malcolm Bunn would veto Idaho legislation forbidding any Mormon to vote, hold office, or serve on a jury, Pride got enough support to overcome Hailey Ring opposition to capitol appropriations. Some Boise businessmen had to put up a $5,000 bond to guarantee Bunn's veto—a precaution that proved wise when Bunn was forced, by threats of physical violence, to rescind his promised veto. A number of prominent Boise leaders were left disenchanted with Pride's Boise Ring operations. Serious charges also were published against Bunn, who was represented by some prominent Philadelphia antagonists as ''a professional gambler, libertine, and a notorious scoundrel,'' who had, as a ''youth, bore the unenviable reputation of a pickpocket.'' Boise's citizens were advised: ''For the sake of your sons and daughters and the reputation of your infant State give this man a wide berth—or your boot at the end of his spinal cord.'' Knowing that he had no future as governor during

President Grover Cleveland's incoming Democratic administration, Bunn retired from Boise after a bitter fight. A disagreeable factional battle split Pride's Boise Ring into hostile elements that struggled for city and territorial control until after Idaho became a state in 1890.

By 1886, when a second construction project was designed to bring rail service to Idaho's capital city, Boise had a good share of reasonably wealthy people. But none of them had fortunes sufficient enough to build 20 miles of railroad. All community resources available for that purpose had been devoted to a Union Pacific failure to complete a Boise Central rail line to Caldwell. A new syndicate of townsite developers, free from a Union Pacific association, emerged in 1886 to promote a compromise route based on Indian Creek halfway between Kuna and Caldwell. James A. McGee, who had been instrumental in starting a new community of Nampa, finally managed to interest J.F. Curtis of Boston in his Idaho Central rail connection project, which was incorporated June 26, 1886. Curtis arranged to finance a relatively inexpensive grade from Nampa to Boise. Mormon contractors from Montpelier, experienced in Oregon Short Line construction across Idaho, completed Curtis' project in three months, attracting surprisingly little notice. Surprised to find that a rail line had reached their community, about 1,000 people went out, on Sep-

H. Seller's Valley Store at 805 Main Street was located next door to the First National Bank of Idaho's second home. The four arch-topped sign boards list the many items carried by a Boise general store in the mid-1880s. The Valley Store also housed Edward F. Fowler's watch, clock, and jewelry store.

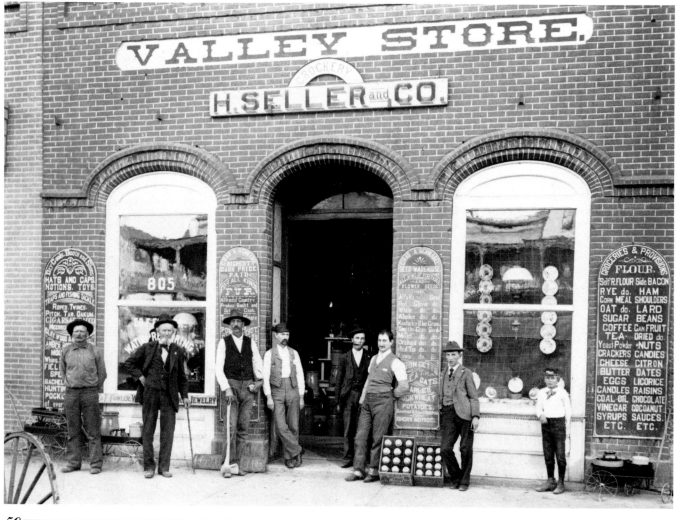

Among the most influential men of their generation in Idaho politics were (from left to right) D.P.B. Pride, E.J. Curtis, Joseph Perrault, and Silas Moody. Curtis, secretary of Idaho Territory for a generation, was acting governor so often during Idaho's turbulent Territorial days that his contemporaries called him "Governor Curtis."

tember 4, 1887, to greet a train that had arrived a day earlier:

> The road from town to the depot was lined with people nearly all day. The distance is about a mile, and the more fortunate rode in carriages, others in lumber wagons, and others on horseback, while hundreds of men, women and children walked over.

Nine days later, Boise got around to staging an enthusiastic welcoming ceremony. They had only a branch line, but that was enough just then. Rail service had a considerable impact upon Western community development. Important adjustments had to take place. A *Salt Lake Tribune* observer, in a perceptive analysis, noted that when rail service reached a new Western community:

> suddenly the occupation of a great many teamsters, blacksmiths, wagon makers and hotel keepers is taken away, and the farmer, who has always enjoyed heavy prices for his produce, finds that there are neither men nor animals to consume what he has, and that if there were he would be placed in direct competition with other farmers five hundred miles both east and west of him. ... And the merchant that for years has worked in the careless way of the West, charging heavy profits, because in the very nature of the business he has to lose a good many debts; suddenly sees some shrewd man from the East with only a little capital sit down beside him and reduce the profits to a minimum. ... Gradually, however, business adjusts itself.

In common with other instances of technological displacement, expanded rail service soon provided new opportunities to injured enterprises. Freighters and merchants shifted operations to new mining areas that could be developed with improved transportation, while increased population finally converted rail service from a calamity to a blessing. For Boise, heavy initial Idaho Central traffic included many carloads transporting a mill that had to be freighted

Above
Peter Sonna's building at Ninth and Main was constructed in 1888 to house his hardware business downstairs and an opera house upstairs. It featured the latest in store construction: cast iron columns, iron roof cresting, and large plate-glass windows. Sonna, noted for his generosity and public spirit, was elected mayor of Boise in 1893.

Boise did not have the large cultural elite that Mary was used to associating with in her Hudson Valley homeland, but that could hardly have been expected in a small frontier community. If she had taken a representative sample of 2,000 people in New York or Boston, she would have been exceptionally fortunate to have done so well. Yet her perceptive impression of Boise's pioneers and their attitudes reveals much about frontier society:

> *It took strong men to succeed and build up the town. We can make light of it—coming here after things are comfortable— but one has only to look from the pretty bowery streets in summer, the little lawns and fruit trees, out on the desert beyond, to see what these men have done in about thirty years. Like all self-made men, they are prone to worship the work of their own hands.*

One of the 19th-century's most popular authors and illustrators was Mary Hallock Foote, who lived in Boise from 1884 to 1895. She had come there with her husband, A.D. Foote, a talented mining engineer from a prominent Eastern family who numbered among his cousins Henry Ward Beecher and Harriet Beecher Stowe. A.D. Foote designed Boise Valley's irrigation system, but

Mary Hallock Foote, shown here in 1890, spent many difficult but creative years in Boise Canyon and on a farm where Hillcrest Country Club now stands.

This 1889 illustration, published in *Century Magazine* in the series "Pictures of the West," uses the house just south of present-day Lucky Peak Dam as its setting.

his canal enterprise was plagued with financial difficulties from the start. As a result, Mary Hallock Foote's Boise period was extremely productive; she wrote novels and published numerous articles and illustrations in such national magazines as *Century* and *Scribners* to support her family and help finance the irrigation project.

A revival of interest in the literary and artistic career of Mary Hallock Foote has come in recent years with the publication of two books—Wallace Stegner's novel *Angle of Repose* (1971), which was inspired by her experiences and won the Pulitzer Prize; and *A Victorian Gentlewoman in the Far West: The Reminiscences of Mary Hallock Foote* (1972), edited by Rodman W. Paul.

The Footes lived in this lava rock house with wraparound veranda in Boise River Canyon from 1885 until 1889.

on to Matt Graham's remote Silver Mountain development. Despite a million-dollar investment, Graham's mill never produced anything because of a total absence of ore. But other large mining properties at Rocky Bar and Silver City finally were able to provide mineral values that benefited Boise and all of southwestern Idaho.

Increased population, not only in Boise but in all parts of Idaho, and superior communication had significant effects on Boise's future. North Idaho's plan to return to Washington Territory, which had gained Congressional (but not Presidential) approval as part of a scheme to incorporate all of southern Idaho into Nevada, was thwarted, February 29, 1888, by a Congressional committee impressed by Idaho's renewed vitality. Boise finally had a chance to entertain Idaho's state constitutional convention on July 4, 1889. By August 6, a state constitution was approved for submission to Idaho's voters that fall. In only a decade, rail transportation had transformed Idaho from a sparsely populated, sectionally divided territory into an active region with good prospects for state admission. Geographical barriers still split Idaho into two distinct sections, but somehow they were going to have to work together to secure statehood, and Boise was assured of a position as state capital whenever admission might be achieved. Boise's railroad was only a branch line, but it formed part of a transportation system essential to community and state development.

William Thayer's Marvels of the New West, *published in 1889, included this engraving of Main Street, looking west from Seventh. High-wheeled bicycles were the newest transportation craze, but covered freight wagons pulled by six or more horses were a more common sight. The coffeepot sign advertised Coffin's tin shop.*

Chapter 4

PROGRESS OF A STATE CAPITAL
1890-1899

*O*nly a day after an impromptu demonstration of enthusiasm over Idaho's somewhat unexpected admission as a state, Boise held a superlative 1890 Fourth of July celebration. Cannons at Fort Boise boomed their traditional salute, and a large crowd participated in day-long festivities leading to an evening display of fireworks. Parade Marshal Orlando Robbins "appeared on Main Street mounted on the celebrated cavalry horse ridden at Chancellorsville by General Stonewall Jackson." (The highly unlikely identity of the cavalry horse responded to community needs, felt almost everywhere by 1890, to attach national importance to each local Independence Day celebration, no matter how improbable a claim was advanced.) Then troops from Fort Boise escorted Idaho's Governor's Guards—a brass band decked out in artillery uniforms. Six horses then drew Boise's traditional July Fourth "Liberty Car" down the parade route, carrying local beauties representing all states and territories. In a special ceremony, Governor George L. Shoup promoted Idaho's representative from a territorial to a state designation. An elaborate ship of state led a number of horse-drawn floats—depicting Idaho's mineral, lumbering, and business enterprises—down Main Street, followed by a long line of wagons. A long patriotic oration then was delivered. When July 4, 1890, came to an end in a fireworks display, a large number of Boise people were exhausted, but they knew they had celebrated Independence Day exactly as they should.

Idaho's state admission came at a time when Boise was experiencing sudden and rapid growth. On April 1, 1890, United States census takers found only 2,311 inhabitants. By July,

Facing page
The First Idaho Regiment boarded its train on Front Street on May 19, 1898, when war fever and patriotism were at a peak. The sinking of the battleship Maine *in Havana harbor stirred outrage against Spain, even though Spaniards had nothing to do with the explosion that caused it.*

however, a major New York Canal construction project employed hundreds of ditchdiggers, bringing renewed hope of large-scale settlement in nearby bench lands. By September 19, Boise's population had jumped to 4,026, a long-anticipated gain that might have occurred several years earlier if canal financing had been more dependable.

An ambitious plan to irrigate 300,000 to 500,000 acres below Boise had been proposed in 1882, when rail transportation promised to provide regional and national markets for commercial farming. A.D. Foote—a highly competent mining engineer who outlined most of southern Idaho's major canal systems—planned Boise's New York Canal as a combination mining and irrigation project. Snake River placers west of Boise, it was hoped, would amortize much of the initial cost, and Boise Valley farmers would utilize a large volume of residual water that would be made available for irrigation. The national financial panic of 1884 ruined Foote's funding arrangements, however, and for six years his enterprise had to depend upon the earnings of his talented wife, Mary, a novelist and an illustrator for *Scribner's Magazine*. Mary Hallock Foote brought literary distinction to frontier Boise, but she could not expect to support a major irrigation project from the sale of popular novels. (One of those novels, *The Chosen Valley*, dealt directly with Boise Valley irrigation.)

During the 1880s, the Liberty Car was the chief feature of Boise's Fourth of July parades, shown here in front of Good Templars Hall, two doors east of Sixth Street on the north side of Main.

Top left
Boise Rapid Transit Company's 1891 Car Number One, shown here humming along Warm Springs Avenue, was small but efficient. Thousands of Boiseans rode this line to the Natatorium, the success of which was closely linked to this inexpensive, modern form of transportation.

Top right
Streetcar barns, such as the ram-shackle structure attached to Cy Jacobs' gristmill at 14th and Idaho, were built in Boise soon after trolleys began running in 1891. The Edison gen-erator that powered the system ran on water from Jacobs' ditch, and on rare occasions when the ditch froze, the cars stopped running.

Middle
Passengers board streetcars at Seventh and Bannock streets in about 1915. Electric streetcars furnished Boise with cheap, efficient, and quiet trans-portation from 1891 until 1928. Booth Furniture Company (at right) operated only from 1909 until 1911.

Bottom
The motorman and conductor of the South Boise line pose on Broadway Avenue in about 1912. The banner advertises a performance of the San Francisco Opera Company at Riverside Park.

Right
Tea parties were one of the pleasures of a small Boise society in which everyone knew everyone else. Social interactions in the town can be traced from guest lists published regularly in the Idaho Statesman, *which also recorded what people did for entertainment, such as reading Dickens aloud, dancing, and playing whist.*

Above
Many elegant mansions were built along Warm Springs Avenue after the streetcars began running in 1891. Cattleman Robert Fraser built this towered beauty at 615 Warm Springs in 1894, and Governor John T. Morrison resided in it during his 1903-1904 term of office. The tower has since been removed and the porches enclosed.

Canal construction was suspended a year later, after New York and British bondholders got into a dispute. Only 14 miles of canal had been built out in a desert, with no connection to a river diversion point. An extremely expensive canyon ditch from Foote's diversion point had been started, but could not be completed for a decade. Foote had to switch his interest to another, more modest Boise Canal, and rapid development of valley farming land was put off until after 1909.

Not anticipating these delays in Boise Valley development, investors in other local enterprises had better luck. A Boise streetcar company had incorporated, in April 1890, to provide modern urban transportation, less than two years after a New York system had demonstrated that the replacement of horse-drawn streetcars with electric ones was practical. Rails were laid and equipment was acquired in time to begin service in August 1891. Cy Jacob's power plant for his flour mill (served by Ridenbaugh Canal water) was used to run a generator. Since extended transmission lines had not yet been developed, such a local power source was essential. Boise's electric streetcars ran for nearly four decades before city buses replaced them in 1927 and 1928.

Development of privately financed municipal water systems commenced in 1890, and an experimental, natural hot-water well was drilled late that year a mile or more from cold artesian wells then in service. Hot water was reached December 26; at greater depths, water of even higher temperature was tapped. Hot springs had been used for resort purposes since Roman times, and Kelly's Hot Springs, several miles from Boise, had been developed into a popular tourist attraction over previous years. But using natural hot water for residential and commercial power was a novelty. Warm Springs Avenue, which led to Kelly's Hot Springs, was about to replace Grove Street as Boise's most fashionable residential district, and a possible natural hot-water line through that development held great attraction. In 1890 hot-water drilling began, but no one could be sure whether such a system of power distribution would work. Enough of Boise's leading families were willing to attempt the enterprise to make it feasible, however, and in less than a year, a few mansions on Warm Springs Avenue adopted natural hot-water heating. More than 200 other homes soon followed suit. Extension of a hot-water line to serve about 40 business-district customers brought demand sufficient to reach a natural limit of available hot water. Except for the rare days of sub zero weather—which could be 10 years apart—natural hot-water provided more than adequate heat. Rates were extremely reasonable once installation costs and technological problems were met.

Geothermal power was developed commercially in Italy in 1904, and later in New Zealand and Iceland, as well as in a number of other places. Boise's pioneering system not only provided an important model for these international applications of hot-water heat, but also proved a popular local attraction. In 1892 a natatorium was built, offering a variety of social amenities in addition to a large hot-water swimming pool, all in an elegant architectural setting. Streetcar service along Warm Springs Avenue provided access to the Nat (as it was always known) at a site close to Boise's hot-water source. Kelly's Hot Springs went into decline after depletion of its source of hot water, which had nearly disappeared by 1918, but Boise's natatorium continued to thrive. After structural problems abruptly forced the abandonment of the Nat in 1934, Boise's natural hot-water heating service continued to operate. When a thorough rehabilitation became necessary in 1972, a user's cooperative took over and preserved this significant pioneer geothermal enterprise.

Boise's famous natatorium was not alone in providing features of architectural interest in a community remote from prominent national urban areas. Prior to 1890, a substantial business district consisting mostly of two- to three-story brick structures had emerged over the previous decade, although wooden landmarks still survived,

Below
Boise's Natatorium was a center of social life and recreation from the 1890s until its demolition in 1934 following a damaging windstorm.

Left
A 1908 Christmas postcard shows the Natatorium in the distance behind White City Park's "scenic railway" roller coaster. The amusement park next to "the Nat" featured a dance pavilion, boating, and other attractions.

Unlike its flimsy predecessor on the Bench, Oregon Short Line's 1894 depot on Front Street was a substantial structure of local sandstone decorated with bracketed eaves, swooping dormers, and a "Prussian helmet" tower. Some of the "stub line" locomotives were still of Civil War vintage.

including Overland House, Hart's Exchange, and Saint Michael's Church. Boise had been served by at least one architect as early as 1882, and in 1889 James King came from Huntington, West Virginia, to provide modern architectural design and give Idaho's capital city a more distinctive appearance. Business buildings, such as the Boise City National Bank (designed in 1890 and completed in 1892); government buildings for Idaho's state penitentiary and state Soldiers' Home; important private residences; and an Episcopal rectory were among King's contributions to Boise. Table rock sandstone and local brick were both called for in his designs.

Only a single structure still stands to attest to John C. Paulsen's brief architectural career in Boise (1891-1893). Boise's natatorium (similar to an earlier one Paulsen provided in Helena, where his main office was based), a distinctive Boise City Hall, and an elaborate Columbia Theatre have all been torn down. An apartment complex he designed for a former attorney general, Richard Z. Johnson, survives. Paulsen had considerable influence on Boise's late 19th-century appearance, and other skillful architects followed, despite a national panic that set back construction in Boise in 1893. A permanent Union Pacific passenger station was built downtown in 1894, when rail service was extended there. Frank Coffin managed to build his hardware store in 1894 at Eighth and Main in spite of financial obstacles, and Falk's Department Store followed in 1896 when national prosperity returned. Large new Baptist (1892), Presbyterian (1894), and Congregationalist (1896) church buildings, as well as a Jewish synagogue (1895), accommodated growing congregations as Boise's population increased, while Grand Army of the Republic and Masonic halls (both 1892) served civic and fraternal needs. Street paving and concrete sidewalks provided another modern aspect to Boise's appearance beginning in 1897.

With frontier life receding into history, Boise gained a complex of cultural institutions typical of older established communities. Church and privately sponsored schools, libraries, theaters, and hospitals flourished in Boise as they were doing elsewhere. A Catholic high school opened on September 9, 1889; after a year in temporary quarters, a permanent structure was completed to house the institution, Saint Teresa's Academy, at Fourth and Jefferson streets. When Saint Teresa's began classes in its new facility on September 20, 1890, it was the first of a number of Catholic high schools, which have been a prominent feature of Boise education ever since. Saint Margaret's Hall, an Episcopalian academy for girls, followed in 1892. After 40 years, Saint Margaret's became Boise Junior College, which eventually emerged as Boise State University. Boise Public Library also dates back to this era of cultural development. Boise's Columbian Club—a women's organization started in 1892 to help provide an Idaho exhibit for the Chicago World's Fair—went on to start a local library in 1894. Boise and Fort Boise each had circulating libraries as early as 1870, but permanent service was needed. In 1901, the Columbian Club's efforts induced Idaho's legislature to start a state library as well. Both libraries were housed in City Hall until Andrew Carnegie donated a building for the Boise Public Library in 1905.

Theaters and hospitals also gained importance. James A. Pinney's Columbia Theatre became a notable Boise landmark in 1892. With good facilities available at last, legitimate theater gained conspicuous local success. In 1894 plans were also under way for Boise to obtain a hospital. Catholic Bishop A.J. Glorieux persuaded an Indiana order to advance $25,000 for the construction of Saint Alphonsus' Hospital. Opened on December 27, 1894, on a site oc-

Below
Elvina Moulton, shown here in 1895, was a charter member of Boise's First Presbyterian Church. Boise has had a small black community since 1863.

Left
The Presbyterian Church, built in 1894, had a 350-seat sanctuary, a dramatic beamed roof, and colorful windows.

Frank R. Coffin resided in this magnificent Queen Anne mansion, one of the last great Grove Street houses. It was erected in 1892 at 1003 Grove just when the city's elite was beginning to build on Warm Springs Avenue and in Boise's north end.

Roman Catholic girls from Idaho mining camps were often sent to schools in Boise. These young musicians from Placerville attended St. Teresa's Academy in the 1890s.

cupied by Boise's earliest Catholic church, Saint Alphonsus expanded from a modest 25-bed facility with a staff of four to a reasonably large city hospital by 1902. A second hospital, Saint Luke's, was completed in 1900 with room for only six beds, but it soon developed into a major Episcopalian venture. Boise was now prepared to enter a new century of progress and achievement, well-equipped with community institutions and new leaders to achieve ambitious municipal goals for expansion and improvement.

Many new residents who settled in Boise after state admission began to show their influence in Idaho and city affairs quickly. Among them, William E. Borah, who arrived late in 1890, and Moses Alexander, who followed a year later, stood out as leaders of promise. Borah, a young attorney from Illinois and Kansas, was chosen as the main speaker at Boise's traditional Fourth of July celebration in 1891 and he rose to become Republican State Chairman in February 1892. By 1896 he was a candidate for Congress in Idaho's most exciting political campaign. Party organizations were shattered badly that year, and an unbelievably complicated political realignment ruined Borah's chances for victory, but he made a conspicuous start toward a distinguished career. Moses Alexander, a German Jew who arrived in Boise after running a clothing store in Chillicothe, Missouri, fared better initially: as a Democrat, he was in a position to replace veteran Mayor James A. Pinney in 1897. After two terms as mayor, Alexander gained enough recognition to enable him to go into state politics, and his long career brought Idaho considerable national distinction. Many other future community leaders settled in Boise at this time. Even though national economic chaos restricted their immediate opportunities for success, they went ahead to overcome financial obstacles to building a city of which they could be proud.

National economic troubles affected more than local business and building enterprises. Silver prices had been declining since 1888, and an abrupt drop in 1892 precipitated a violent North Idaho mine labor war in July of that year. In 1892 and 1893 a number of union of-

Idaho's Episcopal bishops lived in this house, built in the 1880s and enlarged in the 1890s. This turn-of-the-century photo shows the Bishops' House at its original location at the corner of Second and Idaho, before it was moved to the Old Penitentiary in 1975 and restored for public use. St. Margaret's, next door, was an Episcopal school for girls.

ficials were arrested on federal charges and placed in Boise's Ada County jail, where they decided (upon advice of James H. Hawley, their local attorney) that a large regional organization of miners' unions was needed. A powerful organization (Western Federation of Miners) was established in Butte in 1893, in part to cover Hawley's legal expenses in getting their union officials released. Hawley was finally able to demonstrate that they had been incarcerated by mistake.

Boise's unsympathetic federal court also provided a judicial blockade to another nationally important display of labor unrest in 1894. From across the nation, more than 20 of Jacob S. Coxey's "armies"—as they were called—headed toward Washington, D.C., to complain to Congress. A Northwestern army from Washington and Oregon, traveling by Union Pacific freight trains, crossed Idaho, frightening people along their route. Local communities soon realized, however, that Coxey's men were only ordinary, unemployed people who wanted to air their grievances. Oregon's detachment was allowed to reach Idaho without significant interference, but Boise's United States Judge James H. Beatty tried to halt their advance. A fairly large contingent managed to cross Idaho anyway, only to run into a similar blockade when they entered Wyoming. They had to "borrow" a Union Pacific train to make their trip—an action that did not appeal to Beatty or to some high railway officials either.

United States Marshall Joe Pinkham was dispatched to Wyoming with a force of 25 soldiers from Fort Boise and a dozen deputies, to round up as many Coxeyites as he could. Returning to Boise with 158 prisoners, he faced a major problem of housing that many people in boxcars and an empty roundhouse. U.S. Attorney General Richard Olney had decided to turn back Coxey's Northwestern army by winning a judicial proceeding in Boise, despite seriously inadequate facilities to detain and try them. A number of Coxey's leaders were sent to other jails in southern Idaho, but Boise's delegation of prisoners still increased to 184. They were finally sent to a camp at the Snake River bridge where they had entered Idaho originally, so that they gradually could be returned to their homes. Other federal judges followed Beatty's unusual precedent in dis-

James H. Hawley ran away from home at age 15 to follow the gold rush to Florence, Idaho, in April 1862. After working as a prospector and laborer in the mines, he prepared himself for law by reading in a law office until he could pass the bar examinations in 1871, a year after his first election to the legislature. Hawley, a Boise mayor and Idaho governor, was first and foremost an outstanding lawyer, specializing in mining, irrigation, and criminal law.

patching one of Coxey's entire armies to prison, and the Boise episode quickly assumed national importance during a time of economic disaster and unrest.

In 1896 efforts to complete A.D. Foote's major Boise Canal project inspired further conflict, although it remained localized. Foote's company water claim had lapsed, and two competing sets of farmers and developers tried to relocate New York Canal Company claims in January of 1896. In a clash on February 20, a syndicate of farmers drove out another group by forceful tactics that recalled Idaho's earlier mining-claim disputes. Litigation, which was appealed all the way to the Idaho Supreme Court, led to an award of different canal segments to each group of claimants. Prior to this settlement, on January 24, 1898, farmers went to work in slack seasons trying to dig the canal by themselves, although they did not get very far, at least relative to the magnitude of the project. In 1899 both canal interests were consolidated into another New York Canal Company owned by the farmers, who were thereby entitled to receive water in proportion to their shares of stock. Exempt by new legislation from taxation, this cooperative invested $100,000 necessary to complete a small canal connection that put a modest amount of water into their 25-mile main canal system. After 1899 water was at last available to begin irrigation.

Throughout these times of adversity, Boise offered a variety of recreational opportunities that compared favorably with those found in most other communities. Organized sports—in fact, physical games of any kind—did not gain currency in North America until a decade or two before Boise was founded, but by that time they were an established part of city life.

Baseball had started much earlier and had become a national pastime during the Civil War, when army units popularized it. Baseball had reached Boise by 1868 and local ballclubs were organized annually. The Fort Boise grounds provided sports arenas for townspeople and soldiers alike. By 1892 a Falk's Department Store team represented Boise in a semiprofessional regional league, and in 1894 Riverside Park provided them with a good playing field.

Roller-skating was another early pastime and Boise's Good Templars' Hall was used as a skating rink in 1870, shortly after roller-skating reached North America from Australia, where it had originated around 1863. Ice-skating and sleighing had been popular in Boise for an even longer time. Tom Davis operated a skating rink in 1869, and an ice boat was used in the winter of 1870, when lack of snow made sleighing impossible. During winters of heavy snow, especially 1865 and 1898, sleigh rides provided popular recreation. In accordance with a long-established local tradition, Boise's band used to go out to offer musical accompaniment for sleighing parties. After 1892 winter skating was popular at Boise's natatorium, where swimming in the hot-water pool could go on concurrently.

Modern football reached Boise in 1892, following an early soccer form that had been popular in Boise as early as 1869 and 1870. Annual Thanksgiving Day games, sometimes with neighboring towns, were featured.

Basketball came to Boise in 1897, shortly after being invented. Primarily a girl's game at first, basketball was soon incorporated into YMCA programs in Boise as well as nationally. Golf, which had ancient origins in Scotland but was slow to gain popularity in North America, also reached Boise at this time. Like most towns, Boise accepted new sports as soon as they were introduced and, particularly after 1890, organized sports assumed increasing importance in community life.

A much more serious "diversion" commanded national and local attention in 1898: the Spanish-American War. Boise had been caught up in the nationwide jingoistic fervor that led to our "misadventure" with Spain, and Idaho's National Guard eventually fought a spirited Philippine engagement—not against Spanish forces, but against Filipinos, who objected to being taken over by a new imperial power. This entire operation (particularly Boise's guards-

Facing page:
Top left
Moses Alexander came to Boise in 1891 and opened a small clothing store, which eventually developed into a chain. Alexander served two terms as mayor at the turn of the century and two terms as governor of Idaho during World War I. His public service was marked by social reforms, not all of which were popular.

Top right
Designed by architect James King, the Idaho Soldiers Home was built in 1894. When fire destroyed the onion dome in the center a few years later, the building was remodeled into a French chateau. The new roof also burned, but the building was patched up and used until 1973, when it was torn down to make way for Veterans Memorial State Park.

Bottom
William E. Borah made an immediate and favorable impression on Boise City when he arrived from the Midwest in 1890. His oratorical skills and keen mind were appreciated, and his law practice flourished while he began the political career that made him a national figure. In 1895 young Borah married Mamie McConnell, Governor William McConnell's daughter, in Boise.

This page:
Dentist and patient pose in a luxurious Boise dental parlor in the 1890s. It is hard to believe that this dentist, or any dentist of the time, ever performed extractions while wearing a tuxedo and white tie. Note the array of teeth around the elephant's feet in foreground.

Fire Department

Clockwise from top:
Boise volunteer firemen pose proudly with their new Silsby steam fire engine in front of Capital Market, the brick fire bell tower, and the former blacksmith shop that served as a fire hall. The firehouse later burned, and the engine was hauled out just in time.

Boise City had a professional fire department starting in 1903 when the new Central Station was built at Sixth and Idaho. The fire horses were trained to react quickly when the bell rang, and hanging harnesses dropped onto their backs could be buckled up in seconds.

Onlookers gather to watch the Metropolitan steam pumper extinguish a fire at Ribble and Brooks, 310 South Eighth Street, in 1905. Blacksmith shops had a high incidence of accidental fires.

Fire fighters parade at Sixth and Main streets in about 1911. Boise's fire department has paraded on the Fourth of July and other special occasions for more than a century. A first-class force of fire fighters has been a source of satisfaction and pride since 1876 when the first volunteer department was formed.

men's departure and return) brought considerable drama to Boise in 1899, providing an exciting, if somewhat inappropriate, close to a decade of change.

Even with only a limited irrigation project to spur development of valley farm communities, Boise and Ada County had grown substantially after 1890. With a population approaching 6,000 in its corporate limits, Boise continued to be Idaho's major urban center. Together with South Boise (then a separate, incorporated town), Idaho's capital city had doubled in size after 1890 to a population in excess of 8,000. More than an additional thousand lived around Meridian, a new farm community that had grown up about nine miles west of Boise. More than 200 each of Japanese, British, German, and Chinese natives were included among 1,500 aliens, whose proportion was declining as settlement grew. Canadians, Irish, and Swedes also were prominent population elements. With a total of more than 10,000 residents, Ada County was ready to expand rapidly, now that more farmland was becoming available for settlement. As a new century approached, there was confidence in Boise's future, which had a continually more dependable basis in agricultural and business achievement.

At 7:20 a.m., according to the Hesse and Sturges jewelry store's clock, a crowd gathered to view a fire in Frank Coffin's Pioneer Block. A ladder was extended up to W.E. Borah's second-story law office, which was emptied by helpful bystanders.

Chapter 5

A NEW CITY
EMERGES
1900-1912

*I*n 1900, Boise began to get a new skyline. The buildings of two or three stories that had been common for more than a decade were now overshadowed by John and Thomas McMillan's six-story Idanha Hotel. This elegant French chateau structure, designed by a prominent Boise architect, William S. Campbell, started a trend. In a dozen more years, four additional six-story buildings followed. These large structures and a group of other substantial office and business structures gave Boise an urban appearance that remained virtually unchanged for almost two decades.

As a symbol of community optimism and enthusiasm for 20th-century progress, Boise's new landmark proved fitting indeed. Just about everyone anticipated material achievement on an unheard-of scale, and such new inventions as automobiles, flying machines, and wireless telegraphy pointed the way. To bind 19th- and 20th-century excitement together, Idaho's Thunder Mountain gold rush—a classic 19th-century episode in an early 20th-century context—gave Boise and regional promoters an apparently unparalleled opportunity. In building fine hotels and in developing fabulous gold mines, Boise-area civic leaders looked with confidence toward a new day of community development and prosperity.

In their unrelenting drive for expansion, Boise developers continued to promote new rail and transportation projects that would enhance their position as a major distributing center. They had immediate as well as long-range goals. Construction projects were initiated for rail lines to Butte and to San Francisco, although neither project got more than a few miles. But that kind of distant connection, involving construction through

Facing page
On September 19, 1901, Boiseans turned out for a solemn memorial parade honoring President William McKinley, victim of an assassin's bullet at Buffalo, New York. Many old-timers in the crowd recalled mourning Lincoln in 1865 and Garfield in 1881.

Boise's 1901 Street Fair and Carnival was nearly called off when the news came that President McKinley had been shot. When the President's condition seemed to be stabilizing, the show went on. McKinley died just as the carnival ended, and Boise became the first city in the land with a ready-made memorial arch that only needed repainting.

Above
Rich gold and chromo designs decorate the cigar boxes that gleam in plate-glass and mahogany humidors and showcases in Samuel Parrott's elegant cigar store at 807 West Main Street in 1907.

extremely rough and difficult terrain, had to be achieved if Boise were to become a major rail center. A wagon road to Thunder Mountain, intended to channel great mineral riches and trade through Boise, also turned out to be overly ambitious. W.H. Dewey, a wealthy Silver City miner who was investing heavily in a monumental Thunder Mountain mining enterprise, got disgusted when Boise capitalists could not manage to build a Thunder Mountain road in time for his company to rush a large stamp mill to his nearly inaccessible property. Dewey decided to locate his fashionable Dewey Palace Hotel in Boise's railway outlet at Nampa, instead of in Idaho's capital city, and to help develop a rival commercial center. With Nampa and Caldwell both competing to replace Boise as a regional distributing center, a complex battle for supremacy ensued. Boise investors, however, wisely unloaded their Thunder Mountain interests at a profit at a time when a nationally publicized 1902 gold rush gained incredible notoriety. Millions of dollars—mainly from Pittsburgh investors—were used to produce about $350,000 worth of gold, and a series of Thunder Mountain road projects from a variety of Idaho communities accomplished almost nothing. Boise escaped a series of Thunder Mountain fiascos with notable capital gains and relatively modest losses.

Boise was denied many traditional opportunities for rapid growth after 1900. Lack of mineral and energy resources—coal, gas, oil, and iron—was discouraging. Enough possibilities remained, however, to enable business leaders aware of those limitations to succeed. Essential water supplies and recreational attractions compensated for other resource deficiencies. Boise's isolation from large commercial cities precluded any responsible effort to entice heavy industry into an uneconomic location. Thus, government, industrial management, and regional wholesale and retail distribution were Boise's main prospects for early 20th-century economic expansion.

Commercial farming and commercial forest products also helped to provide Boise a secure economic base. After a series of canal construction failures, increased irrigation finally came with reclamation project development. Important lumber companies overcame a complicated set of problems—timberland acquisition and local rail construction among them—to make substantial production possible. A favorable freight-rate structure, resulting in part from progressive regulatory reform, supported a wholesale distribution system that reinforced community development. State and national governmental services gained importance during Theodore Roosevelt's progressive era after 1900, and Boise also profited as an administrative center for both levels of agency activity.

As Boise approached economic maturity, social attitudes, too, began to change. New civic and church leaders wondered if Boise's red light district ought not to be suppressed. An informal licensing system regulated commercial institutions, known as ''parlor houses,'' by a system of police fines rather than by ordinance or statute. Some church leaders, appalled by the revival of anti-Mormon political antagonisms, began to direct municipal politics along new lines. Boise's frontier tradition of hurdy-gurdy houses and Levi's alley of easy virtue was losing some of its allure, and dens of prostitutes began to appear as less of a source for civic pride. Such a challenge to earlier values failed to gain immediate acceptance, but Boise's anti saloon league was making headway attacking both parlor houses and liquor outlets. In response to changing sentiment, Boise's old Overland Hotel saloon was known as the Overland Buffet after reopening in a replacement structure built in 1905.

New attitudes, more in line with later 20th-century thought, also were developing toward Boise's Chinese community. Long disparaged and persecuted, Boise's Chinese citizens began to command more respect. Idaho had received a large Chinese influx after Central Pacific railway completion had left great numbers of unemployed Asiatic railroad builders in Nevada and Utah in 1869. Within a year Idaho's typical miner had become Chinese, and Idaho

Above
Boise was one of only a few American cities that could boast laundries that used natural hot water at the turn of the century. The American Laundry Company began business in 1904 at the corner of 14th and Grove, and its successor still operates from the same location.

Below
In 1901 Ada County Sheriff Joe Daly poses with "Hogan the Stiff," Boise's town drunk. Poor Hogan is manacled to prevent injury to himself during fits of delirium tremens. Also included are the sheriff's wife and daughters (left), deputy Andy Robinson (right), and the sheriff's clerk (rear).

Right
Mayor Harry Fritchman (top center) poses with Boise's police department in front of City Hall in 1911. The bell-shaped hats and upraised nightsticks are reminiscent of London bobbies or Keystone Cops.

Above
Boise High School, designed by architect William F. Schrage of Kansas City, opened its new building to students in September 1904. Although the style of the building was praised, the workmanship was so poor that school board member Nathan Falk resigned on March 19, 1903, so that he would not be responsible for paying for work he felt was shoddy. The board rejected the work, and it was another year before the building was ready to use.

had more Asiatic miners than any other Western state or territory. Chinese immigrants had come from Canton in search of a mountain of gold, and had not really intended to pursue jobs in Boise laundries or similar lowly service occupations. But some Boise Chinese had accepted business or gardening jobs a generation or more before they began to gain local respectability.

A major Western effort to drive out all Chinese residents in 1886 was not received as well in Boise as in some other Idaho communities, but hardly anyone could really afford to defend them. Political charges were brought against an Ada County sheriff whose fees came partially from boarding county prisoners at a modest profit. The complaints he faced because of rounding up Chinese to fill his jail derived from objection to graft in government rather than from any concern for unfortunate sojourners from China.

In 1902 Boise's Chinese constructed an elegant temple, and a year later they welcomed Liang Ch'i-ch'ao to their community. Liang was an international celebrity who had helped to organize a China Reform Association to institute a constitutional monarchy in his native land. Boise's Chinese now gained favorable attention quite unlike their earlier reception. Liang estimated that about 400 were on hand to greet him, with Boise's Columbia Band heading the parade. Liang responded graciously that Boise was "one of the most attractive cities that he had ever visited." He was "banqueted and entertained in extravagant fashion by his countrymen, who hold him in high esteem." Boise provided some of Liang's most dedicated China Reform Association members, who, in turn, were gaining recognition as cultural leaders quite unlike traditional conceptions of Chinese laborers. Local Chinese still had to fear police raids, and a 1910 city ordinance required Chinese restaurants and apartments "to tear out all booths, trapdoors, basement apartments, sofas, and beds," because "sanitary and moral" reformers objected to small basement opium dens concealed in Chinatown.

Counterclockwise from top right:
Gwong Louie, a young Boise Chinese, poses amid delicate Oriental vases and woodwork in 1885. Thousands of Chinese came to Idaho beginning in the 1860s to work in Idaho's placer mines, and by 1875 hundreds had settled in Boise.

Boise's Chinese community celebrated the Fourth of July with firecrackers and a colorful cloth-and-paper dragon in about 1911. Central Lodging House was located upstairs in the old Perrault building at Seventh and Main from 1909 until 1923.

In 1924 Louie Lai ran the Mandarin Inn at the corner of Eighth and Grove. On Chinese New Years, or on special occasions such as christenings, Boise's Chinese residents often invited their non-Chinese friends to lavish banquets of special delicacies.

A Chinese farmer poses with his Model-T delivery truck in 1926. By that time Chinese farmers had been selling produce door-to-door in Boise for half a century. Photo by Walter Lubkin.

Slaughterhouse Gulch, shown here at the turn of the century, became The Highlands after it was developed into a fine residential suburb of the city.

By 1900, Boise's major minority element was Japanese. Recent arrivals, they had not yet had a chance to develop into a community as well-established as that of their less numerous Chinese neighbors. A small black community had also been present since gold rush days, and some representatives of most nationalities found their way into a mainly British and western European population, Boise's primary stock. Some of Idaho's mining camps attracted Slavic and Italian immigrants, but relatively few of a vast throng of Southern and Eastern European immigrants were settling in Boise.

Boise also was becoming more tolerant of another ethnic community that was gaining importance after 1900. Within a generation, Boise became the nation's Basque center. Basque enterprises in Boise go back to Jesus Uriquides' gold rush pack trains of 1863. His packers' Spanish village stood close to Boise's business district for more than a century, and his exploits in packing heavy mining machinery into extremely difficult, mountain wilderness camps had become legendary long before 1900. Basque sheepherders had gradually worked north from California and Nevada into Idaho. When they reached Boise, they generally got out of sheepherding as soon as possible, preferring other occupations. Boise also had acquired a substantial German community during several decades prior to 1900. A strong Turn Verein association built an important cultural center in 1906. Some Swedish, Norwegian, and Irish residents contributed to community diversity as well. All these groups brought distinctive cultural traditions to their new Boise community.

Boise's increasingly diversified economy encouraged a greater variety of peoples to settle in southwestern Idaho. Commercial logging contributed additional variety. Like mining and irrigation, a forest-products industry could be developed only by overcoming serious obstacles. Lack of an effective system for acquiring timberland impeded sawmill investment. In Idaho's early years, loggers simply cut timber from public lands—a procedure that became legal for limited mining purposes but fell into disrepute as commercial lumbering began to develop. Following the precedent set by farm homesteads, federal Timber and Stone legislation (1878) had contemplated small, family-size timber holdings. Individual families, however, could not operate commercial sawmills. To circumvent an unworkable legal arrangement, a system of indirect timberland acquisition through real-estate firms—which flourished in violation of federal statutes, but which might deliver title to lumber companies that could be sheltered from prosecution—was developed. In 1902 former Governor Frank Steunenberg managed to interest Wisconsin lumbermen in entering Boise-area timberlands already made available through earlier operators. By 1906 a Wisconsin-based Barber Lumber Company had completed a major sawmill just above Boise. At that stage, serious problems obstructed their enterprise. Company managers could not find enough experienced loggers to staff their operation. Silt from Boise Basin placer operations interfered with log drives through flat areas and quickly filled their mill pond. In 1906 a railway to Centerville appeared necessary, but a national financial panic of 1907 delayed construction. More timberland was necessary to justify the expenditures needed for a railroad, but state lands could not be obtained at a sufficiently low price. Additional Weyerhaeuser investors helped raise capital, but more was needed. At that inauspicious juncture, a complicated litigation attended Barber Company efforts to get started, delaying Boise expectations for a large timber industry until 1912.

Adjudication of Boise-area timberland titles brought national attention to an Idaho political clash between partisans of William E. Borah, who won a United States Senate seat, and an opposing faction that had preferred another candidate. Borah's opponents brought title litigation against his Barber Lumber Company clients and obtained a grand jury indictment against Borah for conspiracy in a timber fraud case. President Theodore Roosevelt and his attorney general had to intervene before Borah was vindicated in court. Boise received far greater publicity from another court case. Former Governor Steunenberg had been assassinated on December 30, 1905, in a matter totally unrelated to lumber development, resulting in trials of international notoriety. Borah and his attorney, James H. Hawley, participated in all of these contests. Hawley and Borah tried to convict a Western Federation of Miners' official—William D. Haywood, formerly of Silver City—for conspiracy with Steunenberg's assassin.

In 1886 Frank Steunenberg came to Idaho where he and his brother, A.K. Steunenberg, operated the Caldwell Tribune. *He was elected to the Idaho legislature in 1890, after having served at the Constitutional Convention the year before, and served as governor of Idaho from 1897 until 1901. He was assassinated in Caldwell on December 30, 1905.*

Right
Boiseans gathered to see and hear President Theodore Roosevelt in May 1903 on Jefferson Street in front of the old Capitol. It was only the second time a U.S. President visited Idaho. (Benjamin Harrison came to Boise in 1891 and planted an oak tree on the Capitol grounds.) Central School is in the background.

Below
Clarence Darrow attacked the testimony of Harry Orchard, confessed assassin of former Governor Steunenberg, in Boise's Ada County Courthouse in the 1906-1907 Haywood trial. Cameras allowed into the courtroom recorded the drama.

Haywood's case grew out of an earlier labor battle in North Idaho, where Steunenberg had proclaimed martial law following a dynamiting incident at a major mine concentrator in 1899. Harry Orchard, a disaffected miner who assassinated Steunenberg, made a sensational confession in which he credited Haywood and other federation leaders with employing him to blow up Idaho's former governor. Lack of evidence to corroborate Orchard's testimony forced a conscientious Boise judge and jury to discharge Haywood and another defendant. In a period when radical labor leaders had a hard time securing fair trials, this was an unusual outcome and Boise received a great deal of national publicity. President Roosevelt denounced Haywood and his associates as ''undesirable citizens,'' but massive labor parades (20,000 in New York and some 10,000 in Boston and Chicago) demonstrated against Western Federation prosecution in Boise. Hawley's and Borah's presentations against Haywood and Clarence Darrow's defense were given international press coverage, and Borah gained a national reputation just as he was about to commence a six-term Senate career.

The reporters and visitors who crowded into Boise as spectators for Haywood's trial found a rapidly growing community. Two large new cathedrals, Saint Michael's Episcopal (1902) and Saint John's

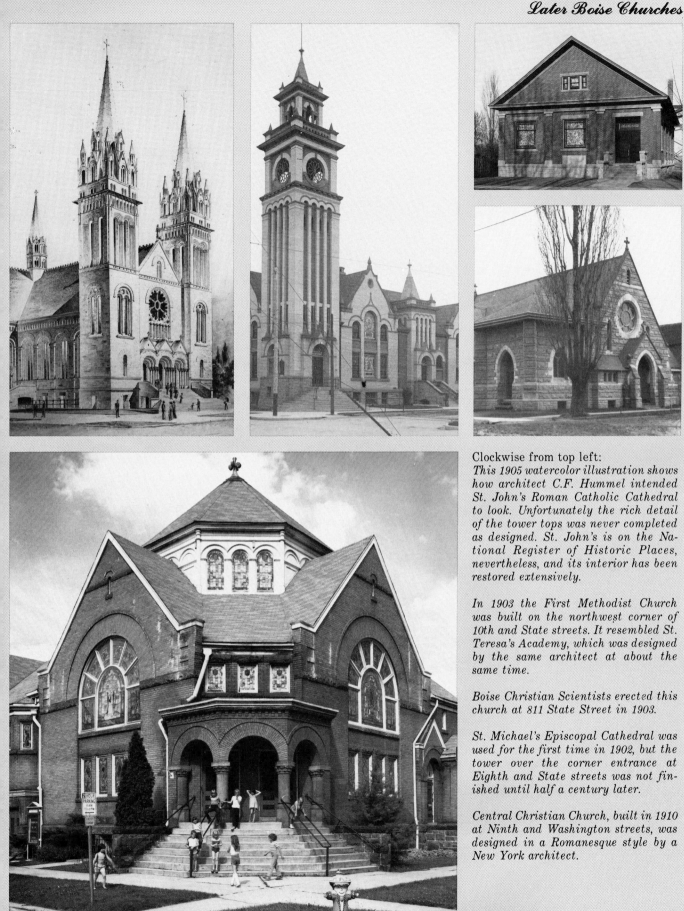

Clockwise from top left:
This 1905 watercolor illustration shows how architect C.F. Hummel intended St. John's Roman Catholic Cathedral to look. Unfortunately the rich detail of the tower tops was never completed as designed. St. John's is on the National Register of Historic Places, nevertheless, and its interior has been restored extensively.

In 1903 the First Methodist Church was built on the northwest corner of 10th and State streets. It resembled St. Teresa's Academy, which was designed by the same architect at about the same time.

Boise Christian Scientists erected this church at 811 State Street in 1903.

St. Michael's Episcopal Cathedral was used for the first time in 1902, but the tower over the corner entrance at Eighth and State streets was not finished until half a century later.

Central Christian Church, built in 1910 at Ninth and Washington streets, was designed in a Romanesque style by a New York architect.

In 1908, when nearly all vehicles were still horse-drawn, the veterinarian had an important calling. Dr. Clarence E. Thayer kept his rubbers near the telephone in his office at 708 Front Street, ready for his next "house call."

Roman Catholic (1906), helped serve its religious needs. A new federal building had been built in 1902, a new state capitol was under construction, and a large office building had replaced Boise's 1864 Overland House. Other ambitious projects were under way. A Boise Valley interurban streetcar system, powered by electricity transmitted from Swan Falls, began to provide service in 1906.

Boise's expanding population and economic enterprises were reflected in increased recreational and cultural opportunities. New sports joined established athletic contests. Tennis, with national beginnings around 1880, became popular in Boise in 1903 and 1904. Polo, which had been introduced nationally in 1876, gained regional currency later. But, in 1912, Boise quickly developed enthusiasm for polo, and other area teams started then as well. In baseball, no southwestern town could keep up with Weiser in 1906 and 1907. Weiser's pitcher, Walter Johnson, overwhelmed local batters. He set a record of 85 consecutive innings without allowing a hit until a Boise team finally stopped his winning streak with a 1-to-0 triumph. By that time Johnson was already signed to a major league team, where he went on to become a national legend.

Community support for a modest local symphony orchestra and for programs by nationally renowned artists continued a frontier tradition that dated back to Boise's origins 40 years earlier. A jocular Clarence Darrow, who appreciated his stay there, referred to Boise as "the Athens of the sagebrush." A surprising display of theatrical and cultural activity lent credence to Darrow's characterization. Boise had a long theatrical tradition, reinforced by James A. Pinney's Pavilion Family Theatre—a summer theater that opened August 4, 1902, next to his well-established Columbia Theatre. Four more theaters followed in only two years, although all of them had closed by 1906. Some reopened as motion-picture outlets, as did a 1905 theater that could not have otherwise survived. Two of Boise's more interesting enterprises of this era were a Main Street fire station, which was converted into a theater on May 9, 1904, and the Riverside Park Theatre, which opened May 30, 1904, with seats for about 2,500 spectators, and lasted until 1910. Another theater came in 1907, but Boise's only long surviving legitimate theater was provided by James A. Pinney in 1908. On September 17 of that year, he finally replaced his Columbia Theatre with considerable fanfare. Movie houses were gaining popularity at that time, but Pinney's Theatre was not converted to motion pictures until 1920.

Arrangements to enlarge Boise Valley's irrigation empire into a major United States Reclamation Service project had also been completed in 1906. By that time Boise River water claims for irrigation greatly exceeded available supplies, even in years favored by abundant runoff from a mountain snow pack. But after an extended legal proceeding, all water rights were adjudicated early in 1906, with rigid priorities established for claims based upon date of earliest diversion. A water users' association agreed, in 1906, to a value of $14 an acre for prior canals and improvements. This amount was credited to their accounts when a total Boise project cost was established for repayment of a completed system. A major diversion dam was located at a site that gave direct access to Boise Valley's New York Canal, which had been dug years before but had remained unconnected to a large water source. A smaller ditch had made only a

Idaho's senate poses in the old Capitol in 1909, as portraits of President Taft and Vice-President James S. Sherman overlook the proceedings.

modest amount of water available for a large project. Finished in 1909, Diversion Dam finally enabled farmers to enter a large tract of land planned for irrigation ever since 1882. This, in turn, required construction of a major storage dam that was begun two years later at Arrowrock.

By 1910 Boise had grown remarkably. Together with South Boise—still a separate village of 885 people—a population of 18,243 had been attained. Another 2,000 resided just outside those municipal limits, so Boise's overall total had risen from a little over 8,000 in 1900 to more than 20,000 by 1910.

More houses and business construction were needed to accommodate this growth. By 1910, a six-story Owyhee Hotel and another six-story office building had appeared. Completion of an impressive capitol dome and an additional six-story office building in 1912 gave Boise a skyline that lasted without much change until 1930. An interurban valley loop, also completed in 1912, gave frequent service between Boise, Nampa, and Caldwell. Although Boise's growth almost stopped for two decades, a respectable city had been built.

Chapter 6

CONSOLIDATION AND STABILITY
1912-1929

*A*fter a decade of preparation, large-scale expansion of Boise's regional farming and forest resources became practical in 1912. A substantial increase in Boise's project irrigation capability was arranged, and the long-anticipated clearance for major logging operations came on February 12, when timberland litigation ended. Weyerhaeuser Lumber Company interests could consider opening their Barber mill after a six-year delay, and two southwestern Idaho Weyerhaeuser companies finally could be consolidated. Boise-Payette Lumber Company operations commenced on March 9, 1914, as a result of this merger, and Intermountain Railway Company service to Centerville allowed the Barber mill to open a year later—nine years after construction had been completed. By that time, Panama Canal traffic gave Pacific Coast lumber producers a rate advantage in Eastern markets. Southern lumber companies also had closer access to Midwestern markets. But Boise-Payette developed a strong system of intermountain retail outlets that made Boise-area lumber production profitable for a time. Besides the costs of rail construction, Boise-Payette invested $660,000 in its Barber mill and box plant, and additional timber purchases boosted potential production to a still more promising level.

When Boise celebrated Washington's birthday in 1912, nearly all Boise citizens concurred that their rapidly growing community would expand to 100,000 or more in 10 to 15 years. But Boise suddenly stopped growing for more than 15 years, and a half-century would pass before a population of 100,000 was attained. A well-organized segment of Boise's citizenry, however, regarded standard progressive reforms—including

Facing page
In 1916 Boiseans flocked to the Intermountain Fair at Fairview and Orchard streets in Model-T Fords, runabouts, and touring cars of many makes.

initiative, referendum, and recall provisions—as appropriate for a new century and a community that they felt would soon undergo major expansion. An equally well-organized conservative leadership preferred to retain Boise's 1866 charter with its traditional mayor and city council unimpeded by safeguards against big city political bosses. Serious disagreements between the two factions ensued.

In a hotly contested referendum, Boise's progressives overcame business and financial interests to advance their reform campaign. Old political-machine practices were outlawed and the awarding of city franchises was regulated closely. Boise's mayor became a voting city council member and received a few additional responsibilities, primarily relating to conscientious law enforcement. A systematic reform campaign, with local as well as outside progressive leadership, was managed by a bipartisan organization of prominent civic leaders. The opposition to the reforms brought in outside help as well. Spokane had recently adopted similar reform measures, and both sides relied upon Spokane's experience. Boise's business district and its older established residential area opposed reform, but rapid population growth represented in new residential areas provided the majority necessary to effect municipal changes.

When a new mayor and city council were chosen from a large number of candidates (eight for mayor and 34 for council), a second election was necessary before any candidates could obtain a majority vote. Boise's progressives gained some council representation but did not elect a mayor in 1912. Aside from instituting government reform, many of the progressives were trying to get Boise to suppress prostitution and to outlaw saloons. (Boise's antisaloon league had gained control of Ada County's 1908 Republican convention, leading to 1909 local-option legislation allowing counties to exclude saloons.) In 1912 an Ada County local-option election against

Below
Construction began on Idaho's new statehouse in 1905 and was completed in two phases. The central block, shown here, was finished in 1912, and the senate and house wings were completed in 1920.

Right
Popcorn wagons, such as this one parked on Ninth Street between Main and Idaho, were a familiar sight on Boise's streets in the early 20th century. Fresh, buttered popcorn sold for five cents from richly decorated wagons.

Electric streetcars were the dominant mode of transportation in 1915. At that time more horse-drawn vehicles could still be seen on Main Street than automobiles.

saloons was defeated, but there was nearly enough strength among local progressives to emerge as a dominant force. In 1915 they were able to replace Boise's mayor (who regarded campaigning as unnecessary because his opposition was so quiet) with a progressive prohibitionist. Legislation to impose prohibition statewide went into effect in 1916 and, through control of Boise's government, progressives finally secured their long-awaited objective.

Boise's old city charter proponents managed to retaliate quickly after prohibition became effective. Mayor Jeremiah Robinson, who had already arranged for police raids upon houses of assignation, embarked upon vigorous enforcement of statutory prohibition of liquor in Boise. But with a local majority previously opposed to excluding saloons, he ran into a serious problem. Boise's progressive municipal reforms had included provision for recall elections of city officers. His opponents now used this device to force him and one of his progressive council members to compete in a special election, held June 1, 1916. Boise's Main Street vote—responsive to downtown business interests—had been unable to combat institution of a progressive system of city government in 1912 but supplied a modest majority (2,792 against 2,659) against Boise's prohibitionist mayor. That victory contrasted with their previous loss (2,625 votes for reform compared with 2,424 for retention of Boise's charter) in 1912. After only six months of prohibition experiment, recall of Mayor Robinson established that while saloons might not be allowed to operate openly, liquor-law enforcement would not be undertaken too seriously. A considerable element of discord entered into city election contests from 1912 to 1916, but another referendum on Boise's city charter could not be provided prior to 1918, so hostilities subsided for a time.

Boise's progressive leaders fared better in state administration than in municipal government. For five consecutive elections

Arrowrock Dam was the highest dam in the world when completed in 1916. Its reservoir filled the Boise River's valley and tributary creeks, providing flood control and vital storage for downstream irrigation. Lucky Peak and Anderson Ranch dams would later complete a system that made flooding in Boise Valley a thing of the past.

(1910-1918), retired Boise mayors were chosen as Idaho's governor. (No other Boise candidates ever have filled that office.) Through 1912 Boise's conservative leadership was favored, but in 1914 Moses Alexander proved that a Jewish candidate could be elected governor—an achievement that never had been accomplished in any state—and Alexander attracted considerable national attention. He was able to help his Boise progressive associates by approving a state prohibition act, and his administration emphasized professional efficiency in government, a standard progressive demand, in addition to achieving such reforms as industrial accident insurance and workmen's compensation legislation.

Nationally, Boise's progressive element compiled a still more impressive record. William E. Borah had gained a strong position early in his Senate career. Conservative Senator Nelson Aldrich of Rhode Island mistakenly assumed Borah was an antilabor corporation attorney and awarded him choice committee assignments. (Borah had been a successful corporation attorney, but believed labor should be organized into unions and that large business corporations should be controlled by antimonopoly legislation.) By 1912 he had served as Senate sponsor for two constitutional amendments (income tax and direct election of Senators) and for legislation establishing the United States Department of Labor as well as its children's bureau. New Senators rarely rose to prominence so quickly, and Borah was in a position to initiate a large dam-construction project, which accorded Boise better treatment than any other Western community, as well as an improved three-year reclamation homestead act. Federal water-conservation activities resulting from Borah's efforts had great importance for Ada County and Boise Valley farms, as well as for local business and general economic development.

In making a gradual transition in its economic base from mining to farming and logging, Boise became a great deal more dependent upon water storage for agricultural expansion and upon forest conservation for both timber and water resources. Natural resource conservation gained widespread national acceptance after 1900, and a federal timber-and-water-conservation program underwent important professional development. As significant aspects of progressive legislation and administration, United States Forest Service and United States Reclamation Service programs brought a new dimension to federal activity that had a substantial impact upon Boise's development.

Federal agency operations have always been prominent in Boise's economy. War department expenditures at Fort Boise had been important from 1863 to 1912, when Boise Barracks finally suspended operations. Boise National Forest had begun to compensate for that prospective loss in 1906, and a Reclamation Service Boise project had accounted for capital investment as well as for farm expansion from 1906 on. Early in 1912, reclamation engineers decided on a new design that increased Arrowrock Dam's height beyond any that had been attempted anywhere. Increased storage capacity would be obtained and Boise merchants and valley farmers both profited from the decision. When Arrowrock's spillway finally overflowed on June 28, 1916, and a full season of irrigation from Arrowrock became possible, Boise Valley at last had a surplus of water.

In 1916 Boise Valley had water for an additional 1,167 irrigated farms of 67,454 acres. At the time, it already had 2,635 farms on 151,212 acres out of a possible 223,866 irrigable acres. For further enlargement to occur, a long and complicated negotiation was required to work out arrangements for water purchase and cost repayment. A battle soon broke out between large owners and small farmers, who could qualify for Boise project water under an 80-acre reclamation limit. Another clash pitted established farmers with inexpensive early water rights against newcomers, who had to purchase higher-cost Arrowrock storage for their entire operation. Ada County farmers were more likely to get less expensive water, although a moderate number of them were developing new land that required a greater investment.

Expansion of Boise Valley farming capability with the construction of Arrowrock Dam came at an opportune time. Wartime dislocations in Europe after 1914 affected farm markets greatly, and rising agricultural prices helped retire irrigation development costs. Hostilities in Europe and military conditions in Mexico had other impacts upon Boise as well. Mexican border incidents in 1916 led to mobilization of Idaho's National Guard in Boise by July 6. Boise Barracks had been closed in 1912, although military camps sometimes occupied facilities at Fort Boise for a number of years afterward. A Mexican expedition camp was among them, but from July 1 to December 8, 1916, Idaho's soldiers were based in Nogales, Arizona, for Mexican border patrol. When war broke out with Germany, April 6, 1917, they were mobilized in Boise again. Expanded to 15 companies by August, they left early that fall for Charlotte, North Carolina, where they lost their separate identity by merging with an expeditionary force to France. Most Boise servicemen were drafted and commenced army life with recruits from other cities and states, and their contributions also cannot be separately identified. Boise engaged in bond drives and other support programs that assisted a

Crowds filled the corner of 10th and Front streets in 1917 when the Second Idaho Infantry left for training camp. Boise's depot was located on Front from 1894 until the mid-1920s, when the present depot at the end of Capitol Boulevard was built.

Members of Idaho's militia enjoy coffee and sandwiches in Boise's Front Street railway yard in 1917 before embarking for training camp. The elevated yard shack in the background became a crossing guard's shelter after the war and is now part of the Idaho Transportation Museum at the Old Penitentiary historic site.

successful military campaign in France in 1918, and Red Cross and other home-front activities figured prominently in Boise during that era. Boise, like many other American communities, was afflicted with a worldwide flu epidemic late in 1918.

As relations with Germany grew worse after 1916, and wartime fears of German spies and agents increased nationwide, Boise's intolerance of local German institutions and customs grew. Boise's long-established Turn Verein society had to be abandoned, and even German-language classes in public schools became suspect. With a German population larger than any other group's at the time, Boise suffered a substantial cultural loss. Fears that Russia's 1917 Communist revolution would spread to Idaho's logging camps (then an IWW stronghold influenced by William D. Haywood's radical union activities) and farms (where a socialist farmers' Non-partisan League was organizing a militant political movement) led to a "Red Scare" of national proportion. Efforts to prevent Non-partisan League speakers from appearing in Boise were thwarted by a resolute Ada County sheriff, who resisted claims that constitutional rights no longer applied in wartime. Senator Borah's strong position in favor of freedom of speech and against confusing Idaho farmers with Communist agents also helped. State and local councils of defense got into a complicated situation during that era of wartime hysteria, but Governor Moses Alexander, while unsympathetic to

IWW activities, preferred a relatively moderate course during a difficult confrontation. Boise finally avoided some of the worst Red Scare excesses, although Idaho's legislature in 1917 initiated a national movement to enact syndicalism legislation designed to suppress advocacy of violent, radical reform.

As capital of a predominantly agricultural state, Boise did not profit from national or regional trends after 1919. Postwar international economic dislocation made particular trouble for farmers, whose costs and prices had undergone a great wartime inflation. Then a dramatic postwar collapse brought ruin. Idaho's widely acclaimed potatoes, which commanded $1.51 a bushel in 1919, dropped to only 31 cents in 1922. Idaho corn fell as precipitously, from $1.65 to 50 cents a bushel by 1921. A relatively large number of Idaho banks failed, including some from Boise.

Wartime farm profits had gone into excessive costs for land investment. Debts were incurred that could not be serviced or retired for more than two decades when wartime prosperity once again restored farm income. During an era of national prosperity from 1924 to 1929, farmers continued to battle against financial depression. Boise did not grow during that era of economic adversity. With a population of little more than 20,000 after South Boise was consolidated with Boise City in 1918, Boise entered a period of stability that lasted a lot longer than anyone had planned.

National prosperity, while largely denied to local farmers, helped bring some important transportation benefits to Boise. Local capitalists and business leaders arranged a guarantee essential to encourage Union Pacific construction of a main passenger line to serve a large new depot not far from Boise's original station. More than half a century of effort went into this achievement, marked by a great celebration on April 16, 1925. The fact that Union Pacific passenger service would be discontinued less than half a century later scarcely could have been foreseen on that day of community rejoicing. Boise had, at last, obtained service that matched the favora-

Below
In 1924 the Church of Jesus Christ of Latter-day Saints built a tabernacle at 900 West Washington Street in a Colonial Revival style with a crisp Tuscan portico.

Left
Costumed girls turned out on April 16, 1925, to welcome the special passenger train that inaugurated service over a new rail loop that put Boise's recently completed depot on the Union Pacific mainline.

Sports in Boise

Right
By 1912 tennis had become a fashionable Boise sport, and backyard tennis courts had been built by a number of enthusiasts. Champions of the tournament held that year were Allen B. Eaton, in both singles and doubles with his partner, Pettingill, and Byron in women's singles.

Below right
Golf was originally played in sandy seaside courses called "links." Boise's foothills were just as rugged and primitive , and a good lie was hard to find, even on the "greens" made of raked sand. This Boise golfer of the early 1920s attempts a "baseball swing" bound to fail.

Facing page, clockwise from top:
Boise High School football players line up during the 1920s at Public School Field, now East Junior High.

The 1929 basketball team of Link's Business College poses in uniform. Boise women began playing basketball as early as 1896, shortly after the game was invented and a few years before men took it up.

Boise and Ontario polo teams compete in a 1912 game. Boiseans, with their long Western tradition of horsemanship and horse breeding, took to polo with enthusiasm.

Californian Walter Johnson came to Idaho to play semiprofessional baseball in the Idaho State League in 1906 and 1907. Playing for the Weiser Kids, in a league that included the Boise Senators and the Emmett Prunepickers, he literally "mowed 'em down" with his blazing fastball. In 1907 he was called up by the Washington Senators and became a sensation in the big leagues as well. Courtesy, Intermountain Cultural Center and Museum.

Above

Boiseans were enormously proud of the new auditorium and classical portico added to the high school in 1920-1921. Salt Lake sculptor Joseph Conradi, a native of Switzerland, carved the details and also donated the bust of Plato that decorates the pediment.

Below

Governor H.C. Baldridge (right) greeted Charles A. Lindbergh (left) in the fall of 1927, the year of Lindbergh's solo flight from New York to Paris. Thousands turned out to greet Lindbergh at the field that has become the Boise State University campus as he toured the United States in his Ryan monoplane, Spirit of St. Louis.

ble freight rate structure gained some two decades earlier, and that was what counted then.

New industrial advances, related primarily to automobile assembly-lines and to similar innovations in steel, rubber, oil, and coal production, affected Boise and Idaho primarily through consumer distribution and services rather than through local industrialization. Aside from lead, Idaho lacked resources related to this era of industrialization. Boise retained a variety of craftsmen organized into 16 unions. Some of the unions, which had joined to help organize Idaho's State Federation of Labor on May 20, 1916, had a dubious future. Boise's horseshoers union, which had organized early, went into eclipse not long after 1920 but eventually revived when Boise became a horse center again. Cigarmakers and streetcar men also had to adapt before long. But other crafts, such as tailors, carpenters, electricians, pressmen, typographers, musicians, and projectionists for movie theaters had a better, long-range future. Because Idaho's economy did not accommodate to national trends very well at this time, even those more promising crafts did not enjoy a major expansion after 1920.

Airline connections came almost as soon as main-line rail service. Planes had been coming to Boise for years, and Barney Oldfield had raced a plane with his car at Boise's Fairgrounds in 1915. When commercial airmail contracts supplanted army airmail deliveries in 1926, Boise was included in a national system inaugurated early that spring. With initial flights from Pasco and Elko, where connections were made to Salt Lake and San Francisco, April 6, Boise's service emerged through company consolidation into United Air Lines. United Air Lines now recognizes Boise's difficult flights (one of which went astray in a desert more than 80 miles away) as the company's inception. An airport was developed about halfway between Boise's business district and railroad station, and a great throng turned out to greet Charles Lindbergh there in 1927, when he made a national tour after his celebrated flight to Paris. Compared with a rail trip of nearly a week's duration, an air adventure from Boise to New York took only 30 hours. For people not accustomed to jet age speeds with six-hour transcontinental flights, that seemed remarkably fast.

Improved rail service and the modest beginnings of air transport affected Boise, but not as profoundly as the development of a flourishing national automobile industry. By 1916 a national road improvement program emerged with rapid expansion of car sales. Idaho took part in the construction of a highway network that gave Boise improved access to farm and mine communities over a large area. More venturesome drivers could undertake long trips to remote cities, particularly after 1920. With a sparse population, and difficult mountain terrain where construction costs were exceptionally high, Idaho had to overcome serious highway building difficulties. A federal aid program provided sufficient capital, though, to allow major road improvements to proceed. Stage lines, which after 1882 had become local connectors to railroads, now were motorized and extended. By 1929 Union Pacific Stages offered long-distance service through Boise as part of a national network of intercity bus lines. With that transition, Boise Valley's interurban electric trolleys suspended operations and Boise's streetcars were

Top
Charles F. Willard poses in front of his "pusher" model Curtiss—one of the first ever seen in Boise. Both the Wright brothers and Glenn Curtiss sent planes to Boise in 1911 for an exhibition at the fairgrounds.

Middle
Governor H.C. Baldridge posts an airmail letter in the slot of a Varney Airlines (later United Airlines) plane in 1926 as Senator William E. Borah and Mayor Walter F. Hansen look on. Regular airmail service between Pasco, Boise, and Elko began that spring.

Bottom
Speed sports attracted large crowds to the fairgrounds near Fairview and Orchard in the early years of the 20th century. This contest between Barney Oldfield in his Fiat Cyclone and DeLloyd Thompson in his airplane thrilled thousands on June 24, 1915.

Right
In about 1915 the Davidson children pose with their automobile, an obvious source of family pride, even though the young people are studiously nonchalant about it. Granite Hall, the Davidson home on Warm Springs Avenue, can be seen in the background.

Above
Wesley Andrews' 1920 postcard view shows the 1908 Pinney Theatre (left) and the 1912 Elks Lodge building. These two additions to downtown Boise were part of the architectural era when the city leaped into the 20th century with handsome new buildings in the latest styles.

replaced by buses in 1928.

The economic and social effects of widespread use of cars were felt in Boise and all of Idaho. Larger centers displaced small rural communities, now that farmers could drive farther to town, and Boise profited substantially from the increased mobility. Other expressions of the new freedom associated with cars affected Boise as they did every other community. John D. Hicks, in *Republican Ascendancy*, describes some of the more shocking social changes of the "Jazz Age":

> Long-established habits of churchgoing broke down as both saints and sinners took to the roads for Sunday drives and picnic lunches. The restraints that had once circumscribed courtship somehow lost their validity on and off the highways, and the chaperon disappeared. Women drivers found long skirts a dangerous anachronism, and shortened them. Criminals discovered in the automobile an easy means of escape from the scene of their crime, and often also a high degree of immunity from prosecution across state or national lines. As the highways grew more crowded the number of accidents increased; the automobile was soon to become a greater killer than any known disease, greater even than war itself. More significant still, the possession of a car did something to its owner; with all that power at his command, he was never quite the same man again. Indeed, this automobile psychology seemed almost to characterize the nation as a whole; the American people, like the drivers of many American cars, were relentlessly on their way, but not quite sure where they were going, or why.

Sales and service of automobiles, radios, and other modern conveniences assumed considerable importance in local economies. For a brief time, Boise had a small Ford assembly plant. Operated by Henry Ford's brother-in-law H.H. Bryant, who had a long-established Ford agency in Boise, it fitted a local manufacturing tradition that could not be retained in an automobile era. Centralized national fabricating and distributing facilities eliminated that kind of local enterprise and, while Boise once had been a stagecoach-manufacturing center, a similar possibility for cars simply was not feasible after 1920.

Large cities and local communities had their movie palaces, complete with theater organs designed to provide an atmosphere appropriate for silent films. A number of film theaters flourished along with Sonna's earlier opera house (1888) and James A. Pinney's large new 1908 theater, which shifted mainly to film performances. Finally, in 1927, Boise's Egyptian Theatre came just when sound films were about to replace a long series of old silent classics for which it was designed. Eventually rehabilitated into a modern movie outlet, this is Boise's only surviving silent-era theater.

Boise's long tradition of band and symphonic performances led to an important innovation in 1919. An annual community music week began that spring, with free performances provided each night by churches, schools, musical organizations, and talent selected for special productions. Ambitious pageants, dances, and dramatic pre-

Ben S. Eastman's two daughters pose in their Warm Springs Avenue home in the late 1920s, conveying the wealth and social position of the family.

Boise women brought Broadway to their hometown in El Korah Shriners' 1923 "Follies." The bobbed hair, as well as the costumes, symbolized a new postwar freedom—marked by fast cars, jazz, and bootleg booze.

sentations were included each May. Schoolchildren provided colorful annual lantern parades, and coordinated community participation resulted in distinctive programs offered on a special stage erected in front of Idaho's Capitol. Music week continued in a different format after 1940, and has spread to other communities. Programs have changed, adapting to contemporary taste, but substantial community involvement always has been a significant feature of this musical tradition.

State and national trends also affected Boise's municipal government. State rejection of Idaho's Non-partisan League proposals for major agricultural reform in 1928 led to the repeal of direct-primary legislation and to conservative minority administrations, which continued to hold office because of a progressive split into at least two parties. Eight years later, Boise followed by abandoning its progressive form of municipal administration. In 1927 Boise's 1866 city charter was reinstated and most progressive reforms were set aside. Boise did not return to partisan politics for city elections, though, so a major (and important) feature of progressive improvement in municipal government was retained. Lack of a practical method of expanding city boundaries after 1927 created later problems, but for a while Boise managed to get by without excessive difficulty.

National and international affairs continued to command more than ordinary interest in Boise. William E. Borah earned respect as one of a handful of outstanding Senators in United States history— a distinction that did not escape notice in his home town. Because of his thorough disapproval of Woodrow Wilson's peace settlement with Germany in 1919 and of international instruments (League of

Nations and World Court) to maintain it, he gained an international reputation that increased during his tenure as Senate Foreign Relations Committee chairman from 1924 to 1933. Not everyone in Boise adhered to all of Borah's liberal views—especially his long effort (with little national or local support) for United States' diplomatic recognition of Russia. But Borah had more support in his successful efforts to gain at least a modest naval-arms limitation and agreements for renunciation of war during an era in which the evils of modern war were particularly conspicuous. Borah's state campaigns to restore and continue progressive reform did not get anywhere until after 1929, largely because of partisan divisions that interfered with legislative action.

When the financial distress of farmers, compounded by wild securities speculation in 1928 and 1929, finally developed into a national economic disaster culminating in the stock market panic of October 24-29, 1929, Boise entered a new era of development. Calamity and banking failures eventually gave way to municipal expansion in spite of adversity, and economic depression turned into another period of modest growth, which had been denied during a time of national prosperity.

In 1929 the opening of a unique Boise restaurant was announced. The "Mechanafe," as it was later called, operated at 916 Main Street until 1933, when it moved to 211 North Eighth Street. The Mechanafe closed at the end of 1945.

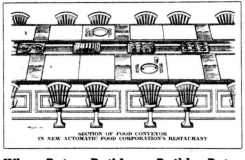

Chapter 7

DEPRESSION
AND WAR
1930-1945

Construction of a major new hotel symbolized a brief resumption of Boise's growth after 1929. Hotel Boise, completed in 1930, towered over all other city buildings except for Idaho's Capitol, located only a block away. Federal building expansion opposite Hotel Boise was also begun at this time. But further construction of large downtown buildings came to an abrupt halt when the stock market crashed, banks failed, and millions were thrown out of work. The Great Depression would test Boise, as it would the rest of the nation, but the city began to grow again.

Even prior to 1930, Boise's traditional logging and farming enterprises had become marginally profitable at best. After surviving a 1920 market collapse, Boise-Payette Lumber Company operations had returned as much as a 10-percent annual sales profit; from 1924 to 1929, however, net profits had slipped to only one percent. National prosperity after 1922 had not helped the intermountain farming areas upon which Boise lumbermen depended. But Boise-Payette's 1930-1932 losses of $1.8 million proved much more damaging to Boise's lumber-marketing fortunes. Bank failures and the closure of many retail outlets because of farm depression led to repeated shutdowns at Barber until 1934. With no logs readily available, Boise-Payette dismantled its Barber mill but continued to operate its larger Emmett plant. Severe retrenchment preserved a modest level of production until demand for local lumber returned after 1940.

Another agricultural price collapse compounded Boise's problems. Local banks, whether sound or not, faced a bleak future when their farm loans lost much of their value. Two of

Facing page
When 1,100 new members of the Civilian Conservation Corps from the Eastern United States arrived in Boise in 1934, local transfer companies helped haul them and their luggage up into Idaho's mountains, where most of the new camps were located.

Theater in Early Boise

Above
James Alonzo Pinney served three terms as mayor of Boise City, in 1882-1885, 1890-1893, and 1905-1907. Pinney, like many other early settlers, came west to California and then to Oregon and Idaho in search of gold, but made his fortune in business.

Right
Costumed dancers pose on the Pinney Theatre stage in about 1910. Mayor Pinney's new playhouse opened in 1908 on Jefferson Street across from his earlier Columbia Theatre.

Below right
Main Street in 1930 was enhanced by the exotic Egyptian Theatre which had (and still has) the only theater organ in town. An Egyptian theme was chosen for this "picture palace" after the discovery of King Tut's tomb in 1922 made Americans conscious of the glories of ancient Egyptian art.

Facing page:
Top
In 1910 the Boz, one of Boise's popular movie houses, was located on 1007 West Main. Owner W. Fred Bossner, who applied his own nickname to the theater, published this publicity photo.

Bottom left
Columbia Theatre, built by Mayor James A. Pinney in 1892, opened on December 12, with Julia Marlow in Shakespeare's As You Like It. For the next 15 years, nationally known musicians and dramatic companies performed regularly at the Columbia.

Bottom right
Mayor James A. Pinney's magnificent new theater, called the Pinney, had a huge interior space, with two balconies, box seats, and an orchestra pit, and provided facilities for elaborate stage shows as well as movies.

Right
During the bank crisis of August 1932, J. Lynn Driscoll put up a sign saying to his patrons, "If you want your money, come and get it." Enough confidence was restored by this bold action that his bank weathered a storm that closed all other Boise banks.

Above
James P. Pope served as mayor of Boise from 1929 until 1933. He joined William E. Borah as Idaho's other U.S. Senator in 1933, following the Democratic landslide victory.

Boise's three banks had to shut down for a time. One of the two shut down had to be liquidated, but the other—Boise's First National Bank, which had survived every financial panic since 1867—could be saved. In the perilous economic climate of the times, a series of regional bank failures could set off financial chaos. Federal authorities showed great concern when Boise's banks encountered serious trouble, but they failed to act quickly or decisively enough. J. Lynn Driscoll, whose First Security Bank was Boise's only surviving Federal Reserve outlet, arranged to have $500,000 in cash flown in (as inconspicuously as possible, to avoid creating any more panic) from Salt Lake City during a long run of withdrawals, on August 31, 1932. Driscoll showed enough courage to restore confidence and his bank was spared. Reconstruction Finance Corporation and Federal Reserve Board support finally were employed to avert total disaster. A successful First National reorganization restored Boise's original bank, and Federal Reserve officials finally could relax after that crisis passed. But soon they ran into still worse situations for which acceptable solutions could not be found. A complete shutdown of all national banks ultimately could not be averted in 1932.

Farm and urban economic distress provoked political disturbance as well as social problems for unemployed people. Boise voted in 1932 to reelect President Herbert Hoover, although with discernibly less enthusiasm than was shown four years earlier. Local farmers objected so firmly to Hoover's unsuccessful farm policies that Ada County went Democratic—a result not realized in a Presidential election since 1896, when Idaho's Republicans ran William Jennings Bryan. Senator Borah, who had done a great deal to gain farm support for Hoover in 1928, could not endorse him for another term, nor could he turn away an overwhelming Democratic sweep that also captured Idaho's state administration and legislature. Boise's Mayor James P. Pope became Borah's Democratic Senate colleague, continuing an Idaho tradition of having one Senator in favor of participation in the League of Nations and the World Court, and another Senator more responsible than anyone else for blocking such a development in foreign affairs.

Boise gained considerably from New Deal relief and recovery measures instituted after Franklin D. Roosevelt became President. Solvent banks were reopened after the "bank holiday" of March 6-12, and a new farm program eventually improved agricultural income. Roosevelt's Civilian Conservation Corps—in which young men, mainly from out-of-state, built forest roads and engaged in other public construction and conservation projects—undertook more work in Idaho than in almost any other state. Boise's Harry Shellworth, with a forest-industry orientation, was instrumental in arranging for many of the projects, which, along with other regional improvements, had substantial community benefits.

Until 1932, relief programs for unfortunate and indigent citizens had traditionally been a local responsibility, but neither Boise nor Ada County had sufficient resources to handle widespread unemployment and other problems caused by a severe depression. State government also lacked capability to respond to so drastic a situation. An early New Deal program of direct federal relief for those who suffered from industrial unemployment had to be instituted as an emergency measure. An entirely new era in city-federal relationships eventually grew out of national concern for urban crises such as this one. Substitutes for federal emergency relief, administered by cities and counties through a grants program, were employed when possible; but direct payments to unemployed workers were less expensive than elaborate construction or employment programs, and could be instituted more quickly. Except for unusually self-sufficient groups—particularly Boise's growing Mormon population—an elaborate federal relief system had become essential.

A variety of other New Deal projects also affected Boise. Public works construction included a modest office building, which eventually served as Boise's City Hall, a large Ada County courthouse, an art gallery, and the initiation of a state historical museum. An important Federal Writers' Project, managed by Idaho's distinguished novelist, Vardis Fisher, published useful volumes: an Idaho guide, an Idaho encyclopedia, and a literary work entitled *Idaho Lore*. During his Boise era, Fisher also published *Children of God* (1939), a nationally popular account of Mormon history, which resulted in more converts to Mormonism than he had anticipated. Fisher's project also included a Historical Records Survey of state and county governments, which preserved important information. Art projects also were undertaken, along with educational programs. Many Emergency Relief Administration and Works Projects Administration activities offered temporary employment to people who otherwise would have had to go on direct relief, a prospect most unemployed wanted to avoid. A National Youth Administration funded high school and college employment programs that benefited a substantial number of Boise's young people in search of education.

Repeal of federal and state prohibition of liquor sales, which had not been very effective in Boise since Mayor Robinson's 1916 recall election anyway, also came as one of President Roosevelt's

Above
Walter E. Pierce's firm led the development of Boise's residential neighborhoods and promoted much downtown construction for 40 years. Pierce built Hotel Boise, and Idaho's governors now live in a house Pierce built for himself.

Top
In 1930 Hotel Boise, the first tall building erected downtown in nearly 20 years, marked a new era in local architecture with its Art Deco styles. Large neon signs were placed atop the city's tallest building a couple of years later, but they were removed during a 1970s renovation when a restaurant was added to the tower.

campaign measures. Mormon areas in Idaho fought repeal, as di⟨ Governor C. Ben Ross, who would not act on the issue until con siderable national pressure was brought to bear. Idaho still had a⟩ antisaloon league tradition that was strong enough to prevent pri vate retail outlets from selling anything except beer. For wine an⟨ other spirits, Idaho went into a state liquor sales business, thus rais ing new problems that continued to be a source of political agitatior and legislative and administrative pressures.

Boise's response to New Deal programs varied considerably Senator Pope continued his firm support of Roosevelt's program an⟨ finally emerged as Senate sponsor for important revisions o⟨ Roosevelt's farm program. Senator Borah went along with some New Deal measures, but became a leading critic of others, includin⟨ Roosevelt's National Recovery Administration, which he denounce⟨ as encouraging business monopoly practices. Borah emerged as ⟨ leading contender for the Republican Party's Presidential nomina tion to oppose Roosevelt's 1936 reelection. Too independent to be ac ceptable to Old Guard Republicans, however, he ended up as a candi date for reelection to a sixth Senate term. With a record of servic⟨ longer than any other Senator's, he retained national prestige and ir a showdown with Governor Ross—who offered his first serious op position for reelection—Borah won by a wide margin. His Idah⟨ vote, in fact, exceeded Roosevelt's, and Boise continued to have tw⟨ United States Senators representing very diverse viewpoints in na tional and international affairs.

Federal recovery measures, added to Boise's natural position a⟨ a haven for refugees from dust-bowl communities, caused Boise (and in fact, the entire state) to gain residents even though farming com munities generally remained depressed. Boise also continued t⟨ develop cultural institutions important for future community growth. Foremost among these was a new college. Boise long had supported a superior elementary and secondary school system, and Roman Catholic elementary and secondary schools, including Saint Teresa's Academy, were part of the Boise community after 1889. In addition, an Episcopal secondary school—Saint Margaret's Hall—

Below
Vardis Fisher was Idaho's best-known author for a generation. During the Great Depression he edited two significant contributions to Idahoans' knowledge of themselves: The Idaho Encyclopedia *and* The Idaho Guide, *both funded by the Federal Writers Project of the WPA.*

Right
Anxious crews sandbag the area between Ninth and 11th streets during the April 1936 flood. Boise River flooded its valley for many thousands of years before Arrowrock, Anderson Ranch, and Lucky Peak dams were built in the 20th century. Boise Gas Company's tank is in the background.

operated from 1892 until 1932, when hard times interfered. Depression conditions, including youth unemployment and scarcity of funds for students who could not afford to leave home to attend a distant university, created the demand for a junior college. So Saint Margaret's became an Episcopal junior college until 1934, when financial problems forced Boise's Chamber of Commerce to reorganize it as an independent private institution. Two years later, Eugene B. Chaffee became president and gradually developed a strong, high-quality institution during his long tenure (1936-1966). In 1939 legislation was enacted to provide for district support, subject to voter approval, which was obtained that spring. From a truly modest $15,000 annual budget in 1936, Boise Junior College went on, with district support, to build a permanent campus at Boise's centrally located airport.

Boise had experienced all kinds of trouble in securing rail service, but air transportation was an entirely different matter. An excellent desert airport site, with enough space to allow for major expansion, was available close to town, and by 1940 military necessity encouraged federal funding that solved the financial problems of development. For a nominal acquisition investment that year, Boise was able to obtain a new airport with mile-and-a-half runways—a facility for larger aircraft than big Eastern cities had at that time. Developed as a large army air base for B-24 bombers, Gowen Field assumed wartime importance as a final training center for units headed for Europe. During a time of wartime dislocation, in which large numbers of Boise's young people served in remote Pacific and European theaters of operation, Gowen Field brought stability to Boise. Many airmen stationed there returned to settle after hostilities ended, and Boise wound up with a permanent airport capable of accommodating larger planes than commercial needs would require.

Aside from local opportunities for military service, Boise had a special involvement in distant areas as well. An international construction firm, Morrison-Knudsen (MK), which had started in 1912 when Arrowrock Dam was being built, had expanded greatly by 1930. Harry Morrison then organized a combine of six major construction companies to undertake large Western projects—including Boulder Dam and San Francisco's bay bridge—and MK became active in South America as well as in other remote places. A force of MK workers, many of whom were from Boise, was engaged in constructing a South Pacific military base at Wake Island when Japan attacked Pearl Harbor and followed with an expedition that captured Wake. MK continued, though, with large Pearl Harbor contracts and emerged from wartime service prepared to continue global operations on a large scale.

From the outbreak of World War II until 1945, Boise went through a sequence of wartime dislocation and instability. National industrial conversion to military production built instant boom towns in some areas—particularly around shipyards, aircraft factories, steel mills, and similar heavy industrial concerns. Boise businessmen contemplated applying for military contracts, only to discover that previously industrialized areas would be considered for expansion. A location remote from major population centers could not qualify. Many industries, such as shipbuilding, clearly were im-

Eugene B. Chaffee was hired to teach history when Boise Junior College opened in 1932, and in 1934 he was asked to become the new school's president, but refused. Asked again in 1936, he accepted the job and led the college for the next 32 years. His outstanding dedication and talent for inspiring community support made Boise College a four-year institution and laid the groundwork for a great university.

Music in Early Boise

Top
A children's orchestra performs during the 1934 Boise Music Week, a tradition started in 1919 and copied by other cities across the country. People of all ages and many talents participate in this annual community event.

Middle
The Columbia Band entertained Boiseans at public occasions such as parades, ball games, and political rallies at the turn of the century.

Bottom
Boise's long musical tradition owes much to its German-born citizens. Clarinetist Louis Steidel (back row), a shoemaker by trade, conducted Boise's 1887 symphony orchestra, and Adolf Ballot (front row, center), a watchmaker, played first violin. Two saddlemakers and a dentist also played with the 1887 group, which rehearsed and performed in Capital Hall on the south side of Main.

Facing page:
Top
Herman Kaiser and his "musical family" performed in their series of movie theaters in Boise, beginning with the Lyric on Main Street. Every member of the large Kaiser family played an instrument by 1910 (except the baby in the tuba, who hadn't learned yet). Herman Kaiser changed the name of his Kaiser Theater to Liberty Theater during World War I.

Bottom
Members of Boise's symphony orchestra pose at the Columbia Theatre in 1908, the last year of the auditorium's existence, before owner James A. Pinney built his new theater across the street.

Early dramatic and minstrel companies came through Boise, and a traveling circus performed in 1867. But local talent accounted for almost all Boise musical events before 1890. Some Boise and Idaho City artists and musicians also traveled widely. Sue Robinson Getzler, wife of a Boise expressman, appeared regularly with a dramatic and musical troupe. John Kelley, a talented violinist who adopted a local Indian child, had highly successful European and American tours with Willie, his "Snake Boy," who became a fiddler and was "supposed to be the greatest contortionist of his age living."

Pianos and organs reached Boise from Portland and San Francisco by 1864, and within a few years, a substantial majority of all Boise homes were equipped with them. Piano teachers were available as early as 1806. Boise's band began offering concerts as early as 1866, and from 1869 on, band programs were offered regularly except during 1878 and 1886-1887, when all instrumental players "left town seeking other employment."

Private and public schools offered music education as early as 1865, and music conventions—usually four- or five-day sessions - grew out of Boise's early singing schools. Frankie Miller, an Idaho City native who studied opera in Italy, returned to Boise as Madame F. Roena Medini in 1887 to offer a six-week series of music conventions that summer. When Peter Sonna's opera house opened on January 3, 1889, Boise's music and theatrical opportunities were increased greatly.

possible anyway. High pay in distant war plants attracted many industrial workers from Boise to other locations, while others volunteered for military service or were drafted. Compensating, in part, for these losses was a large force of Gowen Field Air Force officers and maintenance crews. Coming and going every six weeks, bomber units maintained an overall population level that was transient to a remarkable degree—somewhat reminiscent of an old gold rush camp, but more orderly. Some city schools had to be staffed by officers' wives who came and went as part of the pattern. Residents who did not have to follow such a schedule had to welcome those who did, helping them to adjust to the dislocation that characterized army life.

Right

The USS Boise had a distinguished battle record in World War II. The ship's silver service and parts of its equipment were returned to the city after it was decommissioned. Veteran members of the Boise's *crew still hold annual reunions.*

Below

U.S. Army Air Corps bombers stationed at Gowen Field in 1940 were early versions of production models made by tens of thousands after World War II started. The "pursuit planes" at upper right were biplanes that had advanced little since World War I. By 1945 wartime competition had produced the first jets.

In contrast to 1918, when local German Americans were given a particularly hard time, wartime animosity was more restrained. Boise residents of German or Italian extraction were not subjected to the kinds of attacks that had characterized the outbreak of hostilities a generation earlier. But Japanese Americans did not fare so well after 1941. Idaho was designated to receive coastal citizens (and aliens) of Japanese ancestry from Oregon and Washington in 1942. Largely because of the less than warm reception they received, the national government decided to intern them in a camp near Jerome and Twin Falls. Almost 10,000 Japanese were held there. Some were released to make homes in Boise, where they were accepted without excessive difficulty, aided in part by the efforts of church groups. But in many communities, American citizens of Japanese origin were excluded entirely. Boise's Japanese population was so small as to attract little notice, though outlying farming communities had a larger number of Japanese. Wartime hysteria gradually receded, in large part because of Japanese restraint in responding to a very difficult situation, and many Japanese Americans stayed on after the war.

Industrial production on an unprecedented scale was essential to a successful military campaign. In order to meet quotas on the output of ships, planes, tanks, and munitions, civilian goods were restricted and shortages arose. Some activities around Boise, such as gold mining, were dispensed with completely after 1942; but the extraction of strategic minerals continued in Boise's trading area throughout the war. Mining regulation shifted, therefore, rather than curtailed local industrial operations. Food production to maintain essential harvests had to continue with less local labor. Increased use of migrant labor from Mexico, as well as from Idaho's Japanese internment camp, helped solve the problem. Automobile production was shut down in 1942; gas and tire rationing was introduced; and a national 35-mile-an-hour speed limit was imposed to reduce tire wear. Government regulations to accomplish these changes were tolerated only because of the extraordinary military emergency.

Even though Boise had immediate access to an outstanding area of intensive farming, national shortages required food rationing of local products, including sugar and meat, and such imports as coffee. A national system of rent controls also applied to Boise, where inflationary pressures were less evident than in some places but still significant. Because national support for war objectives was essentially unanimous—in contrast to all previous wars in American history—rationing and price controls were accepted. War-bond drives and volunteer efforts to support soldiers, sailors, and airmen followed the tradition established in the World War I years.

Wartime residents of Idaho's capital city followed military operations in all combat areas with great concern, but took special interest in a South Pacific naval encounter that occurred October 11-12, 1942. Like many other cities, Boise had had a naval cruiser built under a 1929 authorization. Commissioned October 12, 1938, Boise's cruiser had served as Rear Admiral Husband Kimmel's flagship at Pearl Harbor in 1940 but was convoying troops to Manila in December 1941. When several cruisers intercepted a Solomon Island Japanese naval convoy, the *Boise* led off in battle, taking credit for sinking six Japanese ships but getting badly damaged. Unwilling to give up, the *Boise*'s crew, according to one account, "flooded her exploded magazine, put out her fires, shored up her wavering bulkheads, and plugged up her shell holes with bedding." A local bond drive raised funds for repairs, and Admiral Ernest J. King greeted her at Philadelphia, November 19, where the ship was rehabilitated and fitted with improved equipment. After action in Sicily and Italy, the *Boise* returned to South Pacific campaigns, serving as General Douglas MacArthur's flagship for part of his Philippine return.

More than four years of difficult army, navy, and air force campaigns of all important world powers of that era were required before German and Japanese military collapses finally brought an end to hostilities in 1945. With victory celebrations and a sense of intense relief that peace at last had been restored, citizens of Boise joined in a national effort to promote world reconstruction, and to develop a new nation in an awesome era of nuclear power that could be used for peaceful purposes as well as for military destruction. Wartime exigencies had brought important changes to Boise and a more diversified local economy, with significant industrial development, emerged during a period of national reconversion from wartime to peacetime pursuits.

Bathing suit fashions were modeled at the Natatorium in 1930.

Chapter 8

POSTWAR
INDUSTRIAL
EXPANSION
1946-1962

*A*fter World War II ended, food and housing shortages created problems that persisted for a year or two. Rent controls were continued and, in September of 1946, price controls on meat were revived. Meat products all but disappeared for a time, when valley farmers and processors could not afford to handle them. But eventually wartime dislocations, accompanied by spectacular inflation, receded with industrial expansion. Increased industrialization and housing demands brought expanded construction, and 1946 saw 219 new Boise dwellings (up from only 66 a year before) and 34 new commercial buildings, representing an increase over the previous year's 26. A large hardware supplier accounted for much of Boise's construction gains.

For a generation or more, Boise's ''aristocracy'' was amused to hear reports that, in order to keep a factory environment and industrial workers out of town, it was discouraging large manufacturing plants from locating nearby. Boise's developers denied such intentions. Large agricultural processing plants were built in other valley communities to be closer to their sources of supply. Nampa's major Pacific Fruit Express repair shop was placed at a rail center. Years before, Boise had profited from a regionally important sandstone export industry, which had supplied building material to Spokane, Los Angeles, Portland, New Haven, Omaha, and other Western communities. Mining equipment continued to be fabricated in Boise and, after sandstone became uneconomical as a building material, a steel products plant replaced Boise's Tablerock quarry. After wartime controls were finally lifted, Boise entered a new era of industrialization.

Facing page
By 1960 parking lots had replaced a few older buildings in downtown Boise, but the major clearing of the area south of Main during urban renewal was still 10 years in the future.

On June 8, 1950, Harry W. Morrison poses in front of Grand Coulee Dam, built by the company he started with Morris Hans Knudsen in 1912. Morrison-Knudsen became one of the world's largest international construction companies, with diversified interests on several continents, but its corporate headquarters, still expanding, have remained in Boise.

In addition to the construction gains, Boise benefited from the expansion of the school system. School additions and a new junior high kept pace with Boise's industrial growth in 1946. A year later, 120 new businesses, including 14 industrial firms, started in Boise. Steel-fabrication and machinery companies, as well as a paving company, were among the additions. Department stores were growing and bonds for a badly needed sewage disposal plant were mandated. Air service was increasing, reflecting community optimism for future growth. New subdivisions were developed and urban dwellers began to move into farm lands farther from town. This kind of growth, along with the expansion it brought in construction activities, assisted Boise's lumber industry during its crucial transition from a wartime to peacetime economy.

In addition to modest-sized local contracting and logging operations, postwar expansion especially benefited two major Boise concerns—Morrison-Knudsen and Boise-Payette. Morrison-Knudsen, with a highly developed international operation, had local construction contracts as well. Chief among these at the time was Anderson Ranch Dam, a 450-foot structure that was then the highest in the world. The half-mile-thick, earth-fill dam had long been needed to supply supplemental water to Boise Valley farms, but had been delayed by wartime priorities. Anderson Ranch Reservoir stabilized Boise-area farming in times of drought. Also of local importance, Morrison-Knudsen had developed a Boise plant to produce custom equipment for digging ditches, paving airports, drilling tunnels, and hauling concrete.

Boise's large lumber producing and marketing firm, Boise-Payette, also continued to operate at a high level of production. Following heavy wartime logging, the construction boom that followed the war was creating such demand that Boise-Payette's commercially available forests were virtually barren, leaving only timber that would take years to mature. Until 1948 Boise-Payette was prepared to suspend production and to retain only its well-organized system of retail lumber yards, which had accounted for most company profits anyway. For years logging operations had not paid much more than company freight bills, and if Boise-Payette had wanted only to support a railroad or two, company officials decided they might as well have gone into that business instead. Finally John Aram brought a new logging expansion program to Boise-Payette after 1948. Based upon retention of company lands and the establishment of permanent tree farms, Aram managed to obtain access to Forest Service timber to cover logging needs until another stand of trees grew up, which takes some 50 years for Boise-Payette lands.

Forest Service priorities awarded most national forest sales to small operators, who already supplied Boise-Payette. But with a direct share of timber sales, Boise-Payette could grow on a more secure basis. Company lumber sales in 1949 exceeded $26 million and profits returned to close to 10 percent. When Aram went on to another Weyerhaeuser position in 1956, he left behind a strong corporation prepared to embark upon a far more dramatic expansion program.

Aside from forest products and construction, major Boise industrial concerns included food-processing companies. These developed out of the Boise Valley agricultural industry, which had undergone dramatic wartime expansion. Jack Simplot's onion dehydrator, which had begun in Caldwell in 1940, had added dehydrated potatoes as a wartime product to satisfy military contracts for 33 million pounds of annual production. Simplot specialized in an integrated operation. His large Caldwell box factory for product shipping got him into lumber production. In 1944, when fertilizer was unavailable for potato farmers, he expanded into phosphate mining to meet their needs. Dehydrated potatoes commanded a limited postwar market, but a shift into more palatable canned and frozen farm products tripled his wartime level of production in 1946 and 1947. At that point he moved his operational headquarters into Boise in order to have direct access to banking facilities adequate for a major industry. As his potato processing, dairy, fertilizer, mining, and lumbering empire continued to grow, Simplot's Boise operations gained local economic importance.

Retail marketing also underwent postwar changes, which matched advances in farm industry. In Boise, J.A. Albertson had started a local supermarket in 1939 that was grossing a million dollars annually only two years later. This departure from traditional small local grocery stores paralleled a national trend in retail distribution. Albertson's began an integrated operation with purchase of a Nampa poultry plant in 1946. After 1949 a Boise ice cream plant consumed 800,000 pounds of Boise Valley sugar production and 15 million pounds of local milk each year. Local fruit and berries also had a dependable outlet in this operation.

Expanded wholesale distribution services, for which Boise had been prominent for more than a generation, accompanied increased activity in retail outlets such as Albertson's. This kind of growth reflected general business expansion nationally and locally. Large new wholesale and retail outlets, such as Salt Lake Hardware and Sears Roebuck, which built substantial Boise centers in 1946, contributed to and benefited from a rapid increase in local construction. Major school additions in 1946 began an elementary and secondary educational program that continued for more than two decades. A new Union Pacific freight depot followed in 1948, along with more schools and plans for a new sewage disposal plant that came a year later. Joining the parade of progress were a new river crossing, fire department structures, hospital expansion, stadium construction, and other municipal improvements.

Boise's quiet, yet sustained development as a center of government and business services avoided any suggestion of the sensationalism that some Western communities endeavored to cultivate during this period. Bierne Lay, in a 1946 article for a *Saturday Evening Post* series on American cities, writes about Boise:

The city has no red-light district and police blotters seldom record darker deeds than loitering or overtime parking. For two years no killing has marred the peace. . . .

Boise is the richest city of its size in the United States; the buying power of its local pocketbooks is twice that of the $1160 national average. But Boiseans are not caste conscious. The well-being is evenly spread and the people don't care a hang how much dough you've got or who your old man was.

Lay explained that a pleasant climate and an attractive outdoor environment made Boise "a slumless, racket-free town." He added:

J.R. Simplot poses during World War II when his potato dehydrating plants were beginning to lay the groundwork for a diversified industrial empire that would include mining, phosphate fertilizer production, lumbering, and food processing.

Boise's backyard to the north is full of rugged mountains, forests, rivers, and lakes. The Sawtooth range, once known only to wild game and the Mountain Men, is now a National Recreation area that thousands of Boiseans visit every year. Courtesy, Arthur A. Hart.

"There just aren't enough jangled nerves and satiated appetites in Boise to make big-city vices pay off."

But Boise, in the postwar period, did encounter difficulty associated with legislative action to encourage Idaho resorts to try to compete with Nevada. Idaho had matched Nevada's divorce laws as they were liberalized more than a decade before, and Boise had served as a divorce residence for such notable figures as Sir Thomas Beecham, who obtained an Idaho divorce while he was conducting Seattle's symphony orchestra. Boise, however, had no desire to become another Reno and state legislative efforts to allow Idaho communities to compete with Nevada's slot-machine empire proved more troublesome. Because Idaho's state constitution forbids legislative authorization of lotteries—of which slot machines are a variety recognized by legal interpretation—any such attempts actually were void. But judicial tests were delayed for several years, so Boise outlawed slot machines by city action on April 5, 1949. To circumvent this restriction, Boise's slot-machine operators incorporated an adjacent village—which they called Garden City after earlier Chinese gardens of that locality—and moved their activities there. Legislation to get rid of slot machines, as well as a belated review by the state supreme court that confirmed their illegality regardless of legislative action, finally terminated such Idaho gambling enterprises on January 1, 1954. Except as a haven from Boise's municipal taxes and zoning laws, Garden City was left without much of a function. The uneasy relationship of Boise and Garden City has resulted ever since in ineffective and inefficient public administration, a problem common to many urban areas having small independent municipalities.

Regional and city improvements continued to encourage Boise's development during Garden City's slot-machine controversy. Mountain Home's air base was reactivated on December 8, 1948, with substantial impact upon Boise as well. Anderson Ranch Dam finally was completed at a cost of more than $26 million by the Christmas of 1950, and another $19.9-million flood-control dam, situated 10 miles above Boise, was erected in 1950-1952. Lucky Peak Dam contained no power-generating facilities, which were available at Anderson Ranch, but a large recreational reservoir was provided for boating and water sports. With adequate storage for irrigation as well as flood control, Boise Valley farmers had finally gained about as much security as could be expected, and production of high-value specialty crops, essential to justify and repay such large capital investment in farm development, contributed still more to Boise's economy.

Orchards and seed crops had special value. About 85 percent of national hybrid corn seed production—with 50 percent from George Crookham's enterprise alone—now came from Boise Valley. Alfalfa and clover seed also had become important. Sugar beets, potatoes, and onions continued as major crops in a commercial agricultural market with values far beyond subsistence farming.

Because of Boise's relative isolation, several amenities of national life reached the city later than they did most places. Dial phone service did not commence until July 26, 1952, when a large new plant went into operation. Television came still later. Boise had started radio broadcasting about as early as any community, but a national scramble for television channels led to a long delay in licensing for most stations. Boise's pioneer radio station finally began television testing on November 22, 1952, but regular commercial broadcasting had to wait several more months. Natural gas availability was delayed still longer, with construction bonds finally arranged for on September 14, 1956. (Boise had utilized a local gas system years before, but that had been abandoned as uneconomical.) With reliance upon electric heat and natural gas, a 1956 smoke-abatement campaign by the city council stood a better chance of success. A winter cloud of black smoke—typical for a generation or more—gradually ceased to mark Boise's location during periods of temperature inversion. An automobile-induced smog problem, however, developed to supplant coal smoke as a local nuisance, which assumed growing importance as a threat to community development.

Expanded hydroelectric power—to serve Boise and, especially, southern Idaho farmlands through pump irrigation—accounted for development of a greatly increased Idaho Power Company capacity. This Boise-based utility had developed a sequence of Snake River power dams, which were scheduled for completion in 1949 and 1950 to meet future demand. Another series of much larger Snake River power sites below Weiser were also available, but an extended national controversy, concerning a lower Columbia flood-control problem, attended their development. This complication had come into focus in 1948, when high Columbia water had wiped out Vanport. President Truman inspected the damage that spring and instructed R.J. Newell, United States Bureau of Reclamation regional director, to take measures to prevent future calamities. Newell returned to his Boise office and submitted specifications for a high Hells Canyon dam that would control the Snake River's share of lower Columbia

Top
Early canal development, which enabled irrigation of thousands of acres both in the valley and in the higher ground to the south, made Boise into a green oasis in a sagebrush desert. Ridenbaugh Canal flows through a scene that contrasts rich farmland below with dry hills in the background.

Above
Diversion Dam is a Boise landmark significant to all of southwest Idaho. Its construction in 1908 was part of the great Boise Project, which brought water to thousands of acres of sagebrush land. The U.S. Bureau of Reclamation maintains the 1912 power plant as an historic site. Courtesy, Arthur A. Hart.

Top
German architect John C. Paulsen's City Hall, demolished in 1953 and replaced by a drugstore, had an impressive interior.

Above
Boise's graceful Capitol dome rises above the treetops of Capitol Park. Like nearly all state capitol buildings, Idaho's is modeled after the national Capitol in Washington, D.C. Courtesy, Arthur A. Hart.

floods. This proposal also called for a major power plant and river stabilization that would increase electric output in lower Columbia generators. Idaho Power countered with a plan for another series of hydroelectric plants at superlative Snake River sites, rather than a single high dam.

After an extended battle, Idaho Power secured licenses for three dams, beginning with one almost 400 feet high at Brownlee. Morrison-Knudsen finished construction at Eagle Bar (Hells Canyon) in 1968. The dams greatly increased Idaho Power's capacity which with other smaller plants as well, rose from slightly over 100,000 kw in 1948 to 1.5 million kw in 1968) and also provided for increased downstream generation. Aside from offering a dependable source of power for commercial and residential purposes in Boise and other southern Idaho and eastern Oregon communities, Idaho Power specialized in encouraging industrial development of its service area. Boise's Chamber of Commerce joined in this effort, employing an industrial specialist for promotional purposes on July 10, 1956.

Accelerated industrialization also affected Boise's transportation concerns. An industrial foundation was incorporated on February 26, 1958, to induce enterprises to locate near Boise's airport. Idaho's Department of Commerce and Development was active in seeking industries that might be appropriate for interior Northwestern communities of limited population, and promising varieties were found. Recreational vehicles and mobile homes were most eligible for southern Idaho inducement. Boise's location was ideal as a recreational-vehicle center with a large intermountain and Pacific Northwest market. A fiberglass boat manufacturer started in Boise in 1956, with good local demand. A Long Beach company, which had expanded to Caldwell in 1958, managed a million dollars' worth of production there that year, and another California company started a Boise plant in 1960. For well over a decade, that kind of enterprise enjoyed a prospect for rapid growth. A more ambitious construction specialty also followed after 1960, when Harold Thomas and Art Troutner formed Trus-Joist on February 15. Their company produced experimental floor joists, which Troutner, an architect, had invented. Their 1960 sales of $49,000 were modest enough, but within two decades they were to exceed $100 million annually.

A variety of federal projects also stimulated Boise's growth at this stage. Bids were opened on February 5, 1960, for nearly $29 million to construct three Mountain Home airbase Titan missile silos, one of them not much more than 20 miles from Boise. After a long battle over location, a large new federal building was erected at a Fort Boise site close to downtown. Still more controversy attended a location study for Boise's Interstate Highway route. A design that would have transformed most of Julia Davis Park (Boise's original park resource with a community recreational focus since 1907) into a highway corridor, was proposed on August 14, 1960. After a storm of protest, an airport route was selected on November 19, 1961.

By 1960, after a decade of professionalization in government services, state employees had become an increasingly significant element in Boise's economy and community. Together with federal employees (about half as many) and industrial and commercial managers, they made up a major Boise occupational class, with over 1,400 engaged in public administration. Well over a thousand Boise

Left
Pioneer Boise business leaders C.C. Anderson and Harry Morrison take part in the First National Bank of Idaho's 90th birthday celebration in 1957. The huge cake features a new drive-in facility, the 1927 banking room, and the Empire Building (right).

Above
Boise's air terminal facilities were housed in these buildings in the 1950s. The enormous increase in air travel across the United States in the postwar years rapidly made these buildings (and those of most American airports) inadequate. The central core has been added to several times, and the 1981-1982 additions nearly doubled the size of the complex.

employees were engaged in construction and more than another thousand in manufacturing. Over 2,000 worked in retail trade, and a third that many more in wholesale trade. Finance, insurance, and real estate accounted for another thousand of Boise's core work force of nearly 14,000 employees. These census figures analyze only those living within Boise's city limits. By 1960 more than half of Boise's urban population resided outside those boundaries, so the numbers should be more than doubled to gain a more accurate impression of Boise's employment statistics.

Community concern for urban problems arising from a situation in which less than half of Boise's population supported and participated in city government, became more evident after 1960. With an overall population of nearly 40,000 in 1940, of slightly more than 50,000 in 1950, and of about 70,000 in 1960, Boise had been growing steadily. Some boundary adjustments in 1938 had helped raise Boise's city-limits figure to 26,130 in 1940, and modest additions in 1948 had helped account for a little over 34,000 (out of more than 50,000) in 1950. From then on, Boise's city-limits population remained stable, while Boise continued to grow more quickly. (Because of business expansion, Boise's 1960 boundaries contained little more than 30,000 in 1970, and included still less in 1980.) Tired of having to go through Idaho's legislature to get city charter amendments, Boise civic leaders finally arranged for an opportunity to make Boise into a traditional Idaho city with normal statutory powers. In a special election, held August 22, 1961, Boise's voters abandoned their 1866 city charter forever. After a few expansion efforts, a careful pro-

cedure for study and systematic planning of city boundary expan
sion was provided by ordinance on March 6, 1962. Boise, at last, was
prepared to incorporate a larger proportion of urban residents under
city jurisdiction. Arrangements for a professional public-service and
city-planning study followed on May 7. Boise's future growth would
be arranged for in a more orderly manner, and industrial expansion
could continue with fewer problems than had been encountered between 1946 and 1962. Boise could anticipate having a core population
in excess of the minimum 50,000 figure necessary for recognition as a
census metropolitan area. That designation, in turn, would help city
promoters bring about additional industrial growth, which they
regarded as essential for community prosperity.

Structural evidence of Boise's expansion accompanied population increases, which became more noticeable in 1960. New parks and
schools included Borah High School in 1958, after bond-issue problems discouraged construction of a single new riverside high school

Bishop Edward Kelly's funeral service was held at St. John's Cathedral in 1956.

Left
The Idaho State Historical Museum in Julia Davis Park opened its doors in 1950. The WPA project began in 1941, just before Pearl Harbor, and sat idle for the duration of the war. The Historical Society started as a pioneer association in 1881 and became a state agency in 1907.

Above
Swedish Evangelical Lutheran Church was built in 1905-1906 from the plans of State Capitol architect John E. Tourtellotte. Later called Immanuel Lutheran Church, it still stands at the corner of Seventh and Fort streets and is listed in the National Register of Historic Places for its architectural distinction.

on a large tract that became Ann Morrison Park on June 7, 1959. New buildings—such as a large new Methodist church, dedicated December 18, 1961—continued to mark Boise's growth as plans for a centennial observance were being formulated.

Boise's expansion in government business and industrial management had an increasingly visible effect upon community development by 1962. Boise Junior College received more adequate funding, as well as additional students, from the growing district. Boise's Little Theatre, which had commenced in 1948, offered increasingly improved dramatic seasons as population grew and more talent became available. A similar transformation was helping the Boise Philharmonic Orchestra offer superior concerts. Professional management and staffing of Boise's Municipal Gallery of Art and the Idaho State Library provided better quality service on an order already available from the Boise Public Library. A special grant, funded by Jack Simplot, provided for modernization of the Idaho State Historical Museum and a general Idaho State Historical Society professional operation after 1956. Winter sports, particularly a ski resort 16 miles from town at Bogus Basin, also gained crucial support. With excellent powder snow available on a nearby high ridge in an otherwise arid and, for skiing purposes, largely snow-free environment, Boise's commercial development profited from having diversified outdoor summer and winter recreation opportunities.

An expanding community with growing financial resources was able to support a variety of other services. Improved hospital facilities, appropriate in an area distant from major population centers, were maintained. Coordinated campaigns for building expansion and capital improvements for both of Boise's hospitals succeeded in raising a third more funding than their original postwar expansion goal, and advanced radiation treatment and similar medical programs became available about as fast as they were developed nationally. After almost a century of growth, Boise was continuing to realize some of the long-anticipated ambitions of gold rush pioneers, for whom no dream had seemed impossible.

AN ERA OF ADJUSTMENT AND CHANGE
1962-1982

*B*oise entered an era of adjustment and change, following its attainment of United States census status as a Standard Metropolitan Statistical Area late in 1962. The community's postwar concentration on governmental, business, and industrial management continued for another two decades on an increasingly larger scale. But new sources of controversy—by no means unknown in Boise's century-old history—accompanied greater professionalism in the search for solutions. Scarcely anyone foresaw just how frustrating Boise's efforts at civic planning and urban redevelopment would turn out to be. Traditional procedures in handling municipal and suburban development trends sometimes produced undesirable results. A bold new city rehabilitation plan resulted in a complicated process, for instance, in which laudable planning goals could not be easily reconciled with the political and economic realities. Boise's civic leaders have retained their confidence in a bright and promising municipal future, however.

City boundary expansion (December 4, 1962), made in order to attain metropolitan status, resulted from careful administrative planning. Urban and regional planning, with late 19th-century antecedents, had become well-established nationally by 1962, as had business planning for large corporations. Cooperative planning, sponsored by the Chamber of Commerce and other civic leaders, formed part of an arrangement to manage government according to sound business principles. Rapid expansion brought with it such problems as the unregulated commercial development of scattered business and residential tracts in irrigated farm lands, however. These and other prob-

Facing page
Although it is constructed over a framework of structural steel, the dome over the Capitol's rotunda exhibits the Roman Revival style favored by Thomas Jefferson for American public buildings. Courtesy, Idaho Statesman.

Built in 1903, the Hotel Boise (its sign is just visible at left) was downtown's tallest building before the Bank of Idaho built this 13-story structure in 1963. The occasion for this June photograph was the "topping out" ceremony for Idaho's new tallest building.

lems were recognized more clearly as Boise expanded more rapidly. But Boise's large corporations had extensive past experience with industrial and commercial planning, and their approach to civic growth guided municipal development along new lines. Little coordination went into site location of major Boise buildings prior to 1962, but when high-rise office and residential structures were built from 1962 to 1964, needs for more adequate location and design review became evident. New code requirements brought municipal planning and regulation into an already existing city zoning system. A new state Permanent Building Fund Advisory Council, served by a professional public-works administration, arranged for development of an eight-block Capitol Mall office complex, with construction extending over several decades. Compatible office-building design was a primary objective, along with careful planning of expansion in an important downtown area. A large new federal building was erected a few blocks farther away in 1967, and a new 1965 post office occupied a riverside site not very accessible to business-district patrons. But aside from federal aberrations that remained largely beyond local control, downtown structural design began to show commendable signs of planning that was responsive to community needs.

Boise's Chamber of Commerce decided, in 1962, to obtain a professional study of the community's potential for industrial expansion. Stuart P. Walsh's report to a Boise industrial conference, April 3, 1963, supported the Chamber's preference for an organized industrial-development program to bring in new enterprises. Walsh indicated that additional industry would increase Boise's population to about 100,000 in 1980, with Ada County rising to 150,000. (This projection proved conservative: while Boise's 1980 city limits included not many more than 100,000, Ada County gained 24,000 more residents than were anticipated.) In 1962 Boise's employment was about one-third wholesale and retail trade, one-fifth government, and less than one-tenth manufacturing. An unusually high governmental proportion appeared natural in a state capital, but a greater industrial share was recommended to conform to the balance typical of urban development.

An essential initial requirement to attract new industry was a four-year college. In 1965 Boise Junior College expanded from a two-year to a four-year program. Until legislative approval for a state-funded college could be obtained in 1967, Boise College was operated as an upper-division private institution in conjunction with Boise Junior College. Finally, in 1974, Boise State College was redesignated Boise State University. Rapid growth of the curriculum, particularly courses in business administration, had a substantial effect upon community development. Faculty enlargement brought in a greatly increased professional staff in all academic disciplines, and a variety of community cultural agencies and programs benefited from university staff support. A university public television channel, which commenced broadcasting in 1971, gained exceptionally widespread community acceptance and patronage.

In addition to satisfying needs for higher education, Boise civic leaders decided to organize in December of 1964 to rehabilitate their downtown business center. A more attractive community would benefit existing businesses as well as promote new enterprise. Concluding that an urban-renewal program would provide much-needed improvements otherwise unattainable, Boise's volunteer Planning and Development Committee obtained necessary state-enabling legislation that winter. Through city council action on August 23, 1965, Boise's Redevelopment Agency began as a board of five influential volunteers headed by Truman Joiner, Morrison-Knudsen's chief financial officer. A 1966 federal planning grant supported their efforts. Boise's city council adopted an urban-renewal proposal for an initial downtown project area on December 30, 1968, and selected a Pittsburgh firm, Urban Properties, Inc., to supervise redevelopment. Federal funding was obtained to support the initial phase on July 14, 1969. Urban Properties did not succeed in their redevelopment enterprise, however, and Boise Cascade replaced them in February of 1970.

After more than a decade of carefully planned company consolidations, Boise Cascade had reached an operating level far beyond that of other major Idaho lumber companies. Construction of a large headquarters building, designed for its compatibility to existing downtown structures, had begun July 18, 1969. Undergoing considerable diversification and anxious to expand into foreign operations, Boise Cascade looked for a company to acquire that had large capital-investment resources and international interests. Electric Bond and Share—which had organized Idaho Power in 1916 and had developed a vast utilities empire that had inspired New Deal regulatory legislation—became a Boise Cascade subsidiary on August 31, 1970. New varieties of company activity included recreational development as well as Boise's urban renewal. Boise's redevelopment objective was to introduce an enclosed downtown mall for a regional shopping center in order to balance a rapidly growing office complex. In addition to Boise Cascade and Jack Simplot's headquarters, a second large food-processing corporation—Ore-Ida, which became an H.J. Heinz subsidiary with local management and control—had moved its management to Boise on October 2, 1968. Not far from Boise's business district, Morrison-Knudsen and Albertson's were expanding their management operations rapidly. A retail marketing complex and a convention center to match their rapid growth was planned in an effort to bring more balance and downtown vitality into Boise's development.

Financial reverses in some of its nonforest products enterprises forced Boise Cascade to reconsider some aspects of its diversification policy in 1972 and to retract from development projects that no longer fitted company objectives. Activities that had to be abandoned at this point included Boise's redevelopment. A second urban redevelopment plan, responsive to problems encountered in Boise Cascade's redevelopment efforts, had been adopted on May 3, 1971. Federal funding for land and building purchases was obtained in order to consolidate ownership for unified development. A contract with a Detroit development firm, Dayton Hudson, was employed to create the regional shopping center with a redesigned enclosed mall. During this phase of redevelopment, efforts to preserve some of Boise's downtown architectural heritage led to arrangements for Idanha Hotel and Ada Theatre rehabilitation. A 14-story office building was completed adjacent to Boise's proposed downtown mall in 1974, and Dayton Hudson spent five years in a vain attempt to

Under the leadership of Robert V. Hansberger, Boise Payette Lumber Company expanded into a regional, national, and international corporation. It became Boise Cascade when it merged with Yakima's Cascade Lumber Company. After leaving Boise Cascade, Hansberger became involved in the redevelopment of downtown Boise.

In July 1978, J.A. Albertson celebrated the 39th anniversary of the founding of the first Albertson store at 16th and State streets. The chain now shares a regional market that covers several Western states, but many of the company's specialized production facilities are still located in the Boise area.

contract for the major retail outlets necessary to make the shopping center successful. Grove Street had been realigned around the project area, and extensive parking lots had replaced part of Boise's original business district, but completion of redevelopment remained an elusive goal.

Federal programs assumed an increasing significance in Boise's redevelopment after 1962. Transportation improvements included airport modernization and interstate highway construction, which more than compensated for Boise's earlier difficulties in obtaining rail service. Superior airport facilities brought in substantial federal operations, one of which grew out of fire hazards that had traditionally plagued southern Idaho's forest and desert borderland. During a big Elko range fire in 1964, United States Forest Service crews had had to be imported from Utah to assist Bureau of Land Management (BLM) forces, which had been overwhelmed in their attempts to contain that blaze. BLM and Forest Service officials recognized the need to coordinate their fire-control systems and, because of proximity to the major concentration of fires, Boise's airport was designated as the interagency fire-control center. Other federal agencies also participated, including the National Weather Service and, in 1976, the Fish and Wildlife Service.

Gradually enlarged over the years, Boise's Interagency Fire Center represented a $4-million capital investment when dedicated on July 25, 1970. An operating aircraft museum housed B-17s, Navy torpedo bombers (converted to air tankers capable of dumping 2,000 gallons of fire retardant), DC-3s, De Haviland Twin Otters for parachutists, an 80-passenger Electra prop jet, and a Convair 440 that offered effective service for smoke jumpers and ground crews. Overnight National Guard accommodations were available for up to 4,000 firefighters awaiting transfer. By 1974, when development was complete, a permanent staff of 110 employees offered logistical support, technical assistance, and training for 7,500 men. National fire-suppression management was provided, and crews from this center fought large North American fires in remote places such as Quebec and Alaska. Aside from operating a superlative modern fire department, Boise's airport also provided weekend and summer training for 8,000 to 10,000 Air National Guard pilots and support forces. By 1974 a staff of 571 employees operated this $17-million-a-year program, which contributed substantially to Boise's economy.

In addition to funding government installations, such as Boise's Veterans Hospital, federal programs helped support or improve schools, parks, housing, and municipal activities. After federally assisted sewage lines and disposal facilities allowed river rafting and tubing, a stream cleanup and greenbelt development transformed Boise River into a handsome recreational attraction. Boise's greenbelt improvement began on June 1, 1969, and the venture was programmed to extend more than a decade. By 1982 six miles of development had been completed, connecting all of Boise's river-area parks. Interior Department funding, made available under Idaho's comprehensive outdoor recreation plan (required for federal participation) by Idaho's State Department of Parks and Recreation, helped to develop an urban Veterans Memorial Park as a bicentennial project with additional federal funding in 1976. In 1980, Interior Secretary Cecil D. Andrus made a special Eagle Island state park grant available for downstream park development. Another variety of Interior Department preservation grant, administered by Idaho's State Historical Society in compliance with a required state historic preservation plan developed after 1969, assisted Ada Theatre rehabilitation and restoration and the preservation of Boise's old United States Assay Office. Preservation of Idaho's original penitentiary buildings, retained as a tourist attraction, was assisted by similar grants. Federal revenue-sharing and emergency-employment programs provided a much larger source for capital-improvement funds, which included civic structures such as Ada County administrative and law-enforcement buildings, Boise and Garden City halls, and other public works. On August 24, 1971, a federal wildlife reserve for eagles, hawks, prairie falcons, and other birds of prey was dedicated along Ada County's Snake River boundary.

Farther north, Forest Service lands were made available for a major expansion of Bogus Basin ski runs and facilities. Increasingly popular as a regional winter resort, this area had become overcrowded in 1954 and had served 10,000 skiers in 1956. A total of four ski lifts were made available, raising facility investment to $1.8 million. In 1973 a ski lodge, additional lifts, and night-skiing arrangements were incorporated into a $1.5-million expansion program. Another $2.5-million investment came in 1976, just in time for a snow shortage that caused difficult financial problems. Bogus Basin continued to contribute to Boise's economy, as well as to provide a local recreational attraction important for community expansion.

Federal involvement in Boise's development was matched by increased prominence of Boise participants in federal administration and legislation and in national affairs. After a term as governor of Idaho, Len B. Jordan headed a joint United States-Canadian commission that dealt with international boundary water problems, particularly with Columbia Basin development issues. Jordan joined Frank Church as a United States Senator, giving Boise added representation. Church, after his election in 1956, gained national recognition for sponsoring wilderness legislation in 1964, for his Foreign Relations Committee warnings against military embroilment in Southeast Asia, and for his success in gaining Senate ratification of the Panama Canal Treaty revisions. As chairman of the Senate Foreign Relations Committee, 1978-1980, he followed William E. Borah in an important post; only four other cities ever had two Foreign Relations Committee chairmen, and none had more. With a growing number of large international business corporations—including Jack Simplot's enterprises, which had gone into Dominican gold mining, worldwide dairy cow distribution, and South American lumbering—Boise had a strong constituency for interest in world affairs.

Besides United States Senators, Boise leaders in national affairs included Governor Robert E. Smylie, who presided over the National Governor's Council from 1963 to 1966; Hamer Budge, who, after a decade in Congress (1951-1960), had six years of Securities and Exchange Commission membership, including 1969-1971 as chairman; William D. Eberle, who had Cabinet status, 1971-1975, as special representative for trade negotiation; and Cecil D. Andrus, who relin-

Eighth Street, south of the Front Street railroad yard, developed into a substantial modern wholesale district shortly after the turn of the century. Large, brick warehouses were built to house grocery, hardware, and other distributors. In 1970, when this picture was taken, the neighborhood still retained its original character, but it has since been altered and expanded for shops and restaurants in what is known as Eighth Street Market Place.

Boise City desperately wanted a United States Mint, but settled for this U.S. Assay Office, which opened for business in 1872. Gold from Idaho mines varied greatly in value, depending on the amount of silver it contained, so accurate assaying was essential. Precious metals worth millions of dollars were treated in this National Landmark building. Courtesy, William G. Dougall.

quished his position as governor to become Interior Department Secretary, 1977-1980, in President Carter's Cabinet. A number of Boise business leaders, like Eberle, had gone from large local corporations into Eastern businesses. Charles McDevitt and William Agee (who, with Eberle, advanced from Boise Cascade), and J.L. Scott (who took over a large national supermarket chain, Atlantic & Pacific, after managing Albertson's), all made a similar transition. Peter Johnson of Trus-Joist became Bonneville Power administrator in 1981, bringing an interior Columbia Basin orientation to that important regional post.

State-government operations and employees assumed greater significance after 1962. As functions and professional staff expanded, Boise gained cultural benefits similar to those conferred by a rising importance of industrial and business management. A state budget increase in all funds, from a little over $100 million in 1962 to almost $1.4 billion in 1982, compared favorably with the growth of Boise's large corporations. But the expansion of federal and state agencies contributed to Boise's increased professional and clerical employment. Government employment, which was far less susceptible to business and market cycles and the sometimes abrupt shifts that made dependence upon major corporate payrolls an unreliable economic base, provided much-needed stability to Boise's economy. A systematic effort after 1969 to make state salary levels competitive with private business also proved important. A state employees' association was developed to help achieve hospitalization and similar benefits. State budgetary planning, developed after 1966 as governor's office and legislative fiscal staffs developed elaborate information and analysis procedures, matched the cost accounting and program planning typical of private corporations. Another decidedly important legislative reform, imposed by United States Supreme Court mandate in 1962, led to reapportionment of Idaho's legislature to reflect population in each new legislative district. States were required to give each citizen an equal voice in lawmaking. Prior to that time, Ada County's 45,043 voters had equal state-senate representation with Camas County's 574 and Clark's 448. Removal of that disparity in 1966 made Idaho's legislature somewhat more responsive to urban needs. Boise and other Idaho cities naturally began to benefit from their increased legislative influence.

Local governments assumed planning functions for their areas when Boise's expansion raised issues of growth management that required community attention. Boise obtained a California professional consultant's report, which was used as a basis for adopting a comprehensive management plan, on April 27, 1964. Ada County also accepted a comprehensive plan in 1964. Planners had to consider regulation of commercial and residential expansion that would prevent the replacing of farm land, irrigated at great cost, with development that could not use existing water rights and storage. Nonfarmers who acquired irrigated land were obligated to assume capital and project operating costs whether they could receive irrigation water or not. Complaints often arose from those who had converted farm land to other uses when they had to continue to meet irrigation charges, but without such protection the remaining farm lands would have been left with an uneconomical reservoir and canal system. In any event, planning was necessary to avoid excessive ser-

Idaho's State Capitol is dwarfed by recent additions to the skyline, as is the six-story Eastman Buildngm from the city's first "skyscraper" era, visible just over the low dome that marks the House of Representatives chamber in the Capitol. This view from the foothhills to the northeast shows USBank Plaza and Key Bank buildings. Courtesy, Arthur A. Hart

vice costs for scattered commercial and residential development, as well as to guard against the ruin of valuable irrigated tracts for agricultural purposes.

After comprehensive planning was completed, and a long series of area hearings held, a more specialized city-zoning system was adopted in 1966. Boise retained a specialized, professional planning staff to handle zoning problems and to produce a revised comprehensive plan in 1978. Ada County planning operated for a time through a council of governments, although some local units participated reluctantly and failed to provide financial support to meet professional planning costs. On June 27, 1977, a revised county comprehensive plan was adopted. Municipal-impact areas were identified and new Boise, Meridian, Garden City, Kuna, and Eagle municipal plans were submitted. Another revision, incorporating arrangements for the new areas, was adopted early in 1982.

Local municipal and county administration stood to benefit from more professional staffs in other departments and offices as well. Law enforcement, both city and county, was managed by and provided with better-trained staffs. Punch-card ballots, suitable for machine counting, replaced the large hand-counted paper ballots that had been traditional for city and county elections. The elections themselves were now managed by a single county agency. Professional property assessment also utilized modern methods, and fiscal

In 1982 the tallest building in Idaho is the Idaho First Plaza, home of the bank established in 1867 by B.M. DuRell, C.W. Moore, and Governor D.W. Ballard, among others. This 1978 photograph shows the steel work going up as the city of Boise undergoes yet another major change in its skyline.

management and tax collection were computerized along contemporary business lines. Business and governmental office procedures, which had undergone only a few relatively modest changes, were now transformed thoroughly, and Boise's city employees were absorbed into Idaho's state retirement program on March 1, 1966. Professionally staffed city and county park departments assumed far greater responsibilities over the expanded park systems, and Boise's City Zoo, which had had a hard time recovering from wartime neglect, was made into an important community attraction. Boise's public library, which had a long tradition of professional management and service, grew rapidly in expanded quarters after 1973. By 1982, Boise had 525 employees, down from 578 in 1979, while Ada County had 794. Moved into large, new adjacent office buildings, city and county administration had undergone remarkable changes in two decades of modernization.

Nongovernmental community services also were transformed by administrative, scientific, engineering, and technological advances. Boise had a long tradition of a single Community Chest fund drive each year. Consolidation in 1956 with national donation campaigns under the new name of United Fund (changed in 1974 to United Way), preceded an expansion to include all of Ada County in 1971. In 1982 Ada County's United Way was administering a $1.3-million budget to national and local social-and-health-service agencies. Medical insurance provided in Boise after 1945 by Blue Cross grew dramatically from 67,000 policy holders in 1962 to more than 222,000 in 1982. Boise's Blue Shield hospital insurance was added in 1978, with general Idaho coverage for both services. Because of Boise's large Mormon population, church-welfare services independent of public fund drives were particularly important. Together with federal and state social-service and public-welfare programs, these organized private efforts met a variety of community needs.

Improved medical facilities, designed to provide specialized services as rapidly as they became available in national centers, came more quickly after 1966, when Dr. A.M. Popma organized Boise's Mountain States Regional Medical Program. After establishing Idaho's only medical radiology service in 1938, he had developed a treatment center that provided a sound base for regional expansion. Boise's Mountain States Tumor Institute, funded out of that program, gradually developed after 1968 into a center that served more patients from other Idaho communities (and neighboring states) than from Boise. A million-dollar annual budget by 1974 came more from local fund raising and federal and private grants than from fees. By that time, more than a thousand patients were treated each year, justifying a two-year construction program, completed May 10, 1976, and the acquisition of important new equipment, including a $479,295 linear accelerator. Between 1974 and 1979, Saint Luke's Hospital and Mountain States Tumor Institute invested nearly $15.7 million in a joint expansion program, with about $2.3 million from local donations.

All of these efforts were coordinated, in 1968-1970, with a building project for Saint Alphonsus Hospital. Unable to retain its downtown facility, which dated back to December 27, 1894, and which had been expanded with $4.6 million in construction over 74 years, Saint Alphonsus had buildings that could no longer meet accreditation re-

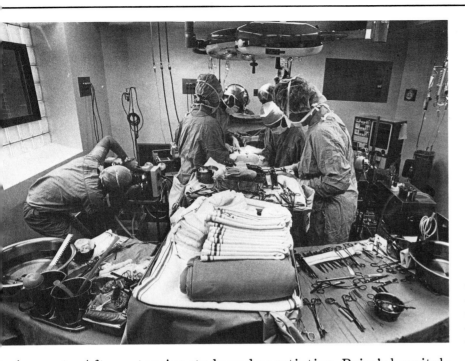

The Open Heart Surgery Program, one of the regional programs offered by St. Luke's, has been ongoing since 1968. Photo by Stormi Greener. Courtesy, St. Luke's Regional Medical Center, Public Information Office.

quirements. After extensive study and negotiation, Boise's hospitals agreed upon an assignment of responsibilities, and federal funds, which provided Saint Alphonsus with entirely new quarters on April 8, 1972, at a site with immediate access to Interstate Highway traffic for emergency cases. A helicopter landing was installed as well, so that all emergency services were provided there, while other specialties were assigned to Saint Luke's. This kind of cooperation made both institutions more efficient and cost-effective during an era of rapid inflation in medical expenditure. A Medical Arts Condominium, accommodating 65 physicians and surgeons, was constructed adjacent to Saint Alphonsus in 1972, while a similar group of facilities served Saint Luke's. With a psychiatric ward, dating back to 1953, and other specialties, such as kidney dialysis, orthopedic surgery, microscopic eye surgery, and a brain scanner, Saint Alphonsus abandoned intensive infant care and its maternity ward to avoid duplication with Saint Luke's, which continued to develop such specialties as open heart surgery. Together with a major Veterans Administration hospital that had been developed since 1922 at Fort Boise, these public hospitals and Boise's Elks Rehabilitation Center for crippled patients provided effective regional medical services for all but truly exceptional cases. Only in rare instances did patients have to be transferred to major cities for medical attention.

Campus-style commercial and industrial parks, with large office and production facilities, placed in an attractive open setting of broad lawns and trees, offered Boise firms a superior environment by 1976. Hewlett Packard, a large California electronics firm, had opened a Boise plant on September 1, 1973. The firm was housed in temporary quarters while an extensive suburban site, with adequate space for all future operations, was being developed. In a little less than eight years, Hewlett Packard's Boise operation grew to 2,600 employees at work at a 220-acre site occupied by $20 million worth of buildings. An eighth large building, increasing production space from 775,000 to a million square feet, was added in 1981-1982 to provide room for some 4,000 employees.

Morrison-Knudsen, which had decided in 1969 to centralize a larger part of its international management operations in Boise, had built a headquarters complex, which expanded greatly over a decade of construction. With 26,000 employees by 1975 (almost 12,000 domestic and more than 14,000 international), MK managed an operation well over double Idaho's state government in size. A development subsidiary of Morrison-Knudsen also began work on a 125-acre industrial park and office complex, which eventually housed such other important Boise concerns as Albertson's and Ore-Ida. Several other large office buildings were included in MK's Parkcenter development, and in 1980 another group of 28 single-level business buildings, with a total of 157,000 square feet, was started in an expansion program for a 13-acre segment extending into 1982. Other Boise firms had joined the tide of prosperity, and Idaho Power needed to undertake a billion-dollar construction program from 1977 to 1981. Diversification of major Boise industries continued to support a growing local economy, a trend that proved fortunate because, after 1972, high fuel costs restrained demand for some kinds of recreational vehicles, which constituted a significant share of Boise industrial production.

Livestock and dairy industries underwent a centralizing transformation after 1962. All of Boise's dairies were gradually consolidated into one company, Triangle Dairy, which had begun in South Boise in 1923. In 1967 the company absorbed a major Twin Falls dairy, providing service over much of southern Idaho. Triangle's main dairy herd had been moved out to Grandview years before and, in 1973, a subsidiary company was formed to convert Triangle's dairy pastures into Lakewood development. The 10-year project called for the construction of 1,900 homes in several planned development units, complete with six homeowners' associations and park and recreation amenities, which when completed would contrast greatly with a previous 304 acres of dairy pasture.

While dairy consolidation was proceeding, meat processing was under similar economic and governmental pressures to convert to large industrial units. Early in 1972, a large Midwestern meat-processing firm, Missouri Beef Packers, decided to build a Boise plant on a 160-acre tract that had Union Pacific mainline freight service. With a capacity of 250,000 cattle a year, this plant was designed to operate with 175 employees. After 1976 a still larger concern, Iowa Beef Processors, absorbed this facility into its Columbia Foods division at Pasco, but initial processing continued there. Boise and other valley communities had maintained meat-packing plants for many years, but not on such a scale. Similar centralization occurred in other agricultural industries, leading to closure of Meridian's cooperative cheese factory and Eagle's flour mill.

As a medium-sized state capital and business center, Boise enjoys cultural attractions usually associated with larger communities, without having to put up with many big-city problems. Any state capital has advantages that have become more pronounced with governmental expansion. A median city among state capitals in municipal population, Idaho's center of government exceeds those of New York, Pennsylvania, Illinois, and for that matter,

(continued on page 145)

A combination of preservation and progress has made Boise into a city in which development is tempered by an appreciation of natural and architectural features of distinction. Buildings spanning most of a century in architectural style—many of which are registered as National Historic Landmarks—represent early contributions to community heritage. Other important structures, old and new, offer glimpses of Boise's diverse history. Transportation, communication, art, and industry have shared in adding to Boise's civic and cultural identity. In schools and museums, along streets and in significant buildings, a discerning observer can interpret and understand Boise's visible past.

Boise takes its name from the river called by French fur trappers "La Riviere Boissee," or wooded river. Cottonwoods and willows make Boise River a green strip through an arid sagebrush desert, and even within the present city limits, it is possible to find secluded places. Courtesy, Arthur A. Hart.

Right
Early native inhabitants of Idaho gathered the bulbs of the beautiful blue camas every spring of their seasonal cycle of hunting and gathering. Camas was made into cakes that could be kept for months and comprised an important part of the Indian diet. Courtesy, Arthur A. Hart.

Facing page:
Top
Looking north from Table Rock, Boise's foothills appear as they have for thousands of years. Only in much earlier periods of cooler, moister climate could the vegetation have been richer and greener. Now seasonal changes from green to gold to brown recreate cycles that once took eons. Courtesy, Arthur A. Hart.

Bottom
Some desert plants thrive in the layers of volcanic ash laid down by ancient volcanic eruptions. As organic material gradually accumulates, the richness of the soil and its ability to retain moisture increases. After eons of such activity the soil has become rich enough for modern agriculture. Courtesy, Arthur A. Hart.

Facing page:

Top

Modern "Mountain Men" reenact a moment from the lives of the fur brigades that roamed Idaho at the beginning of the 19th century. On winter evenings men huddled around campfires to hear Shakespeare and the bible read aloud. Some learned to read and write in this primitive school dubbed the "Rocky Mountain College." Courtesy, Arthur A. Hart.

Bottom left

Thousands of people turn out each September for the Idaho Historical Society's "Museum Comes to Life" day. Featured are early crafts, such as spinning, weaving, blacksmithing, flint-napping, placer mining, and music-making on a variety of old-time instruments. In each of the museum's period rooms, costumed characters "live" their parts. Courtesy, Arthur A. Hart.

Bottom right

This collection of artifacts in the Idaho Historical Museum recalls election campaigns of long ago. The brass cannon was cast in a Boise foundry in 1876 for use at Democratic rallies. It was dubbed the "Sam Tilden" after the party's Presidential candidate Samuel J. Tilden, who won the popular vote but lost in the electoral college. Courtesy, Arthur A. Hart.

Left

Thomas E. Logan's adobe house, built in 1865, is now located in the Pioneer Village in Julia Davis Park. This rare building was moved to the park a decade ago, and its original red color and handsomely furnished interior have been restored. Logan served Boise City as postmaster and was elected mayor four times in the 1870s. Courtesy, Arthur A. Hart.

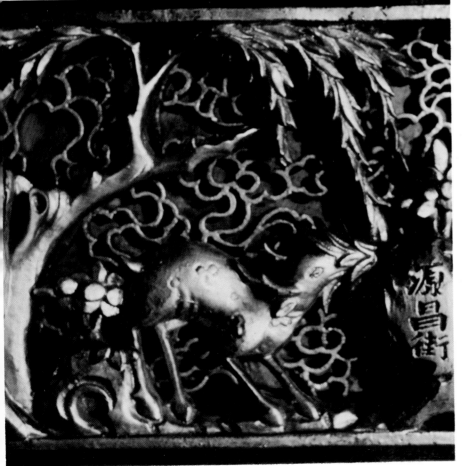

Facing page
This Chinese painting on glass was placed in a Boise temple in the late-19th century, and today it can be seen in the Idaho Historical Museum's recreated Joss House with other exotic artifacts of the same period. It personifies the attributes of power, wealth, long life, and healthy children prayed for by every generation. Courtesy, Arthur A. Hart.

Left
Boiseans bought their Fourth of July firecrackers from Chinese shops, and fireworks were also an important feature of Chinese celebrations in Boise. The colorful wrappings on the packages from China were so beautiful that many children could not bear to throw them away. Examples like this one from the Idaho Historical Society collection were framed and hung in many Boise homes. Courtesy, Arthur A. Hart.

Below left
At a time when original works of art were virtually unknown in Idaho, Chinese miners and merchants imported magnificent carvings from Canton to decorate their temples and tong halls. Teakwood animals covered with gold leaf contrast richly with the background of silvered mica. Courtesy, KAID.

N26 Idaho State Capitol
Boise, Idaho.

The people of Boise now own the historic
Union Pacific depot, completed in 1925
in time for the capitol city's first mainline
service. Courtesy, Arthur A. Hart

Facing page:

Top

This patriotic postcard view of Idaho's first Capitol building was made a few years before construction of the present Capitol began. The house of representatives wing of the new Capitol stands on the site of the old statehouse.

Bottom right

Among Boise's historic treasures are the stained-glass windows in the city's churches. This example from St. Michael's Episcopal Cathedral was designed by Charles Connick, and St. Michael's also has windows by Tiffany. Courtesy, Arthur A. Hart.

Left

Union Pacific's Mission-style depot became an instant landmark in 1925 when completed in time for the first mainline train into Boise. Its dominant position on the Bench overlooking the city, on an axis leading to the Capitol, gives it the kind of prominence the railroad and its New York architects hoped to achieve. Courtesy, Arthur A. Hart.

Above
*The Idaho Botanical Garden occupies a
site next to the Old Idaho Penitentiary
historic district. Prisoners quarried the
stone on the hillsides beyond from which
the walls and guard towers were built.
Courtesy, Arthur A. Hart*

Facing page
*Boise City Hall, built in 1893, was a red
brick castle designed by German architect John C. Paulsen, who also designed
the Natatorium and Columbia Theatre.*

Vaughan Price plays the banker in this 1973 reenactment of frontier banking at one of the historical interiors in the Idaho Historical Museum. During "The Museum Come to Life" annual open house in September, actors and actresses in period costumes perform in each interior. Courtesy, Arthur A. Hart.

Left:
Boise's great Egyptian Theater opened on April 19, 1927, displaying its elaborate mural decorations. This National Register landmark has been completely restored and renovated, and an endowment has been established to insure its continued preservation. Courtesy, Duane Garrett.

The Morrison Center for the Performing Arts was dedicated on April 7, 1984. Boiseans were dazzled by its spectacular spaces and superb acoustics. The local firm of Lombard-Conrad designed it. Courtesy, Ernest Lombard

The Grove Hotel and US Bank Tower (formerly Idaho First National Bank) crowd the view of the capitol planned in the 1920s when the City Beautiful movement was popular all over America. Courtesy Arthur A. Hart

Homeward-moving Boiseans paint headlight paths on Grove in this 1979 view of downtown made at dusk from the top of the Downtowner Motor Hotel. The intersection of Grove and Fairview is in the foreground, and prominent landmarks on the skyline are (from left to right) Boise Cascade, the Capitol, Bank of Idaho, One Capital Center, and Idaho First Plaza. Courtesy, Duane Garrett.

capitals of almost two-thirds of all Eastern states. Seven of those other smaller municipalities—almost all of them Eastern—have larger metropolitan areas, however. Yet smaller central cities have troubles of their own, which Boise began to overcome in 1962.

Concerned with difficulties attendant upon carelessly planned growth, John B. Fery, president of Boise Cascade since 1972, arranged in 1979 for funding of a Chamber of Commerce study of natural local population limitations. It was feared that excessive pressure on hunting, fishing, and mountain and wilderness areas, and boating reservoirs would nullify the attractions that entice new residents, as would smog from too many automobiles. Traffic sufficient to cause concern for Boise's air quality had materialized after 1962, but acceptable solutions had not been identified and employed. Large businesses, such as Boise Cascade and Morrison-Knudsen, had invested too heavily in their headquarters complexes to want to risk losing them, especially since they facilitated the recruiting of good managers. (Beginning employees just out of graduate school often preferred such locations as New York or San Francisco, but when they had advanced to higher management assignments, they were more likely to have families and want to transfer to cities like Boise.) An investigation of how much growth Boise could tolerate without sacrificing quality of life was therefore a worthwhile investment.

A larger than ordinary proportion of professional and administrative university, governmental, and business personnel has accounted for most of the cultural amenities that help make Boise attractive to new residents. Two decades of growth and improvement have helped improve Boise's philharmonic orchestra, Little Theatre, and other performing-arts organizations. Ambitious annual productions of Broadway musicals and occasional operas have offered other convenient outlets for local talent.

Schools and churches have also expanded to meet Boise's growing needs. In 1964 Boise had 30 elementary schools with 12,567 pupils, eight junior and senior high schools with 9,400 students, and a junior college with more than 3,200 students. By 1982 a more substantial share of Boise's school population was enrolled in Meridian's rapidly growing district, and the two districts together had 19,217 pupils in 48 elementary schools and 14,949 students in 14 junior and senior high schools. Five of these schools were private. Boise State University had grown to 10,366 students, almost 6,000 full-time by 1982. Comparable church statistics featured a growth from 113 churches representing 45 denominations to 192 of 50 varieties. Both in members (over 30,000) and in churches (40), Boise's Mormon population remained increasingly dominant. This remarkable growth, realized in only 80 years, was typical of southern Idaho. Yet Boise's Latter-day Saint organization had been perfected relatively late in Mormon expansion into Idaho. Older traditional denominations continued to have strong downtown churches in spite of suburban population growth: four of eight major downtown congregations moved to new nearby locations while half of them stayed on their original sites. With residential expansion, all of Boise's major Protestant denominations decided to have their new outlying churches occupy different areas to avoid duplication of services. Arrangements to organize an Idaho Council of Churches, which administered these comity agreements, were completed in 1964. A

Idaho Oldtime Fiddlers, an active group of musicians dedicated to the preservation of a significant Idaho tradition, performed at the annual "Museum Comes to Life" open house of the Idaho Historical Society in September 1981. Each year the National Oldtime Fiddlers Festival, held in Weiser, Idaho, draws contestants of all ages from across the United States. Courtesy, Arthur A. Hart.

decade later this council expanded into an ecumenical association with Roman Catholic and other judicatories cooperating in community-service planning and projects. Boise churches were responding to national religious trends. The Council of Churches became the Ecumenical Association of Churches in Idaho but was defunct by the '90s. Pentecostal and diverse conservative evangelical groups, some large, many quite small, provided a wide variety of religious experiences.

Like almost any sizeable community, Boise has had an array of fraternal and benevolent orders, but very few of the national orders found commonly in large cosmopolitan centers. Some fraternal organizations—Masons (June 20, 1865), Independent Order of Odd Fellows (January 24, 1868), Elks (January 11, 1894), and Shriners (December 15, 1898)—had 19th-century Boise origins. Others started later. But aside from Basque organizations, early national orders—German Turn Verein (1870), and some Chinese associations—had disappeared. A 1908 Basque mutual benefit society (Sociedad de Socorros Mutuos), comparable with a multitude of European immigrant national orders of that time, started in Boise then. Eazkaldunak followed in 1949, and a talented group of Oinkari Basque Dancers organized in 1960, in time to perform for Idaho's special contribution to the 1962 World's Fair in Seattle. The group also represented Idaho at New York's 1964 World's Fair. Boise's annual Basque Sheepherders' Ball has contributed cultural diversity to a community that has small groups of most nationalities, but few other organizations, old or new, aside from Japanese and Chicano groups and Scandinavian and Scottish societies.

Because of late industrialization and concentration of employees in traditionally nonunion occupations, Boise's 24 AFL-CIO labor locals represent a smaller proportion of workers than they did in a number of other Idaho areas. By 1982 about 15,000 Boise members belonged to food and commercial unions, or unions for carpenters, painters, plumbers, electricians, roofers, teamsters, operating engineers, bakers, or general laborers. Government and institutional employees, including firefighters, teachers, postal workers, and other federal and public-service employees also contributed to that total. Some of these unions were not AFL-CIO affiliates, but together they represented a considerable diversity of Boise occupations.

As a wholesale and retail distributing center with numerous federal and state offices, Boise in 1982 still faced problems of downtown development and community growth that had been subject to two decades of intensive planning effort. Boise's city council decided to assume responsibility for urban redevelopment, and contracted with Winmar Company of Seattle to take over design and management of their regional shopping center's enclosed mall. Progress had been made in construction of a parking garage and an office structure—Idaho First National Bank's 19-story tower—adjacent to the mall site. But Winmar's initial proposal made little provision for preserving Boise's downtown character. After a series of design review meetings, which the *Idaho Statesman* sponsored, a revised plan was developed. Commitments from major department stores again proved difficult to obtain, however, particularly after high national interest rates made financing much more difficult after 1980. But Boise's city officials remained committed to a strong downtown retail redevelopment, and Mayor Dick Eardley and his city council associates won reelection in 1981 as advocates of Winmar's program. Competitive efforts to substitute a suburban mall for a downtown regional shopping center met municipal resistance, but neither kind of project could be started until financial conditions became more favorable. Rehabilitation of Alexander's Store, designated for historic preservation as a mall component, proceeded early in 1982, but unavoidable delays blocked major construction efforts.

Aside from concern arising from obstacles to successful downtown redevelopment, Boise's governmental leaders encountered additional problems after 1978. By initiative legislation, a state limitation to local revenue collected through property taxes restricted the budgets of cities, counties, schools, and special districts, leaving important city and county agencies short of resources. Cutbacks were necessary in such important governmental or service areas as law enforcement, fire protection, and park and library programs.

Boise's Basque dancing group, the Oinkari, perform the "Ikurrina," one of the traditional dances that forms a colorful part of their national heritage. They have performed frequently, both statewide and outside Idaho, and the tradition is kept alive by training young dancers and musicians from early childhood.

In spite of an uncertain financial future, however, important civic improvements have continued in Boise. Completion in 1982 of a large university sports arena provided an important facility for major community functions. After two decades of frustrating problems and obstacles, Velma Morrison and a group of associates secured funding (with initial support from a $3.5-million Morrison Foundation grant) for a long-needed performing-arts center. Construction of this $15 million auditorium complex began October 4, 1981, on Boise State University's campus. As a monument appropriate for Harry Morrison, this project represented some of the most important business elements in Boise's long history, as well as future cultural promise.

As planning agents, the professional staff and administrators of government offices and of large corporations have exercised an important function in Ada County. Yet industrial, business, and government administrators can only facilitate activity of many thousands of people, most of whom do not work directly in government service or for one of a half-dozen major Boise businesses. By 1982 Boise had more than 6,000 business enterprises—mostly small, but some of them ranging toward large size. In addition, more than 1,000 attorneys, engineers, architects, doctors, and dentists offered essential professional services. About 46 veterinarians operated animal hospitals and, as noted by a distinguished returning missionary, provided Boise's dogs and cats with medical facilities and treatment superior to that available to more than two-thirds of the world's people. The Boise community maintained several country clubs, golf courses, and similar amenities characteristic of growing communities. Some were new, but others, such as Boise's aristocratic Arid Club, had continued for more than 90 years. Clubs and associations of every variety met community social needs in Boise just as they did everywhere else. Aside from strong Basque organizations, Boise had only a few national societies (Norwegian, Scottish, and similar groups) which have proliferated in areas with larger southern and eastern European populations. Yet almost every significant national group was represented at least in small numbers in Boise's increasingly diversified population. Excellent transportation service kept Boise business and society in close contact with cities everywhere. Five national and large regional airlines (United, Re-

The grinning lions' heads on the Eastman Building at Eighth and Main were a downtown landmark from 1905 until the building was destroyed by an arsonist's fire in 1987. The cornices were destroyed, but the lions' heads—chipped, broken, not a one intact—were saved and are still in storage.

public, Frontier, Wien Air Alaska, and Western) served Boise with about 40 flights daily in 1982, and several smaller commuter airlines offered additional connections to California, Oregon, Washington, Utah, Nevada, and Montana centers. Nonstop service to major cities—Chicago, San Francisco, Seattle, and Denver—provided fast convenient access to flights to European and Asiatic destinations.

Evidence of new community planning needs came from a variety of sources two decades after Boise staged a centennial celebration. Mormon plans to build a temple to meet religious needs of more than 80,000 Latter-day Saints indicated an important dimension of community growth. In less than a decade prior to 1982, some of Boise's large business enterprises underwent a startling expansion. A large contractor rose from one to almost two billion dollars in construction projects under way between 1974 and 1977. A similarly large Boise forest-products corporation had assets that increased to more than $2.7 billion in 1981. Boise's major banks had assets of about $2 billion in 1982, while another Boise bank had over $1.4 billion by that time. Boise's largest supermarket chain, with more than 400 stores in 1982, had a similar rate of expansion, with sales exceeding $1 billion in 1974, $2.2 billion in 1978, and $3 billion in 1980. That kind of growth, reflected in increased costs of government as well, had a dramatic impact upon Boise's economy and population. Industrial diversification also became more prominent. Aviation and railway locomotive rehabilitation plants, for example, brought a new dimension to Boise's economic resources. By 1982 Boise's industrial park had been filled, and a new one had to be started. With new legislation in to make Idaho a more attractive business location, Boise offered still greater economic opportunities.

By 1982 Boise's developers had accumulated almost 120 years of experience in dealing with obstacles to community progress. For almost two decades civic leaders had been active in planning a program of urban redevelopment intended to revitalize a century-old city that took pride in maintaining a modern, progressive approach to solving contemporary problems. To meet so difficult a challenge, they needed to cultivate patience that had been so typical of their Boise Shoshoni predecessors, whose Fort Boise land treaty of 1864 never had become effective and whose opportunity for obtaining any kind of relief appeared totally remote after passage of a final settlement deadline in April of 1982.

A reasonable amount of civic patience was being exercised. A national economic recession associated with exceptionally high interest rates deferred any success in development of a long-projected regional shopping center, regardless of location. Yet eventually, through planning or default, some kind of resolution to a series of shopping center development problems, coupled with arrangements for redeveloping Boise's business district, was inevitable. A time for decision was at hand. Several years of administration of a comprehensive community development plan, locating new residential areas to surround Boise's city center more adequately, had shaped a new settlement pattern that provided a modified geographical context for urban redevelopment. A greater sensitivity to community assets—including Boise's riverside greenbelt and other natural as well as cultural advantages—had emerged. But some local elements preferred to continue old, small-town procedures for operating a larger community. Others wished to conserve earlier values by inhibiting growth altogether, but population pressure had developed in spite of their reluctance to accept expansion. A more diversified economy was recognized as useful for insulating Boise from excessive dependence upon too narrow a commercial and industrial base.

Several important problems confronted Boise's municipal government in 1982. Mayor Dick Eardley identified these as related to transportation (both highway and mass transit), environment (particularly air quality), downtown redevelopment, and availability of low-income and middle-income housing. Business and governmental planners searching for effective solutions had to recognize some important—although perhaps short-term—obstacles. Revenue and budgetary restrictions imposed upon state and local governments after 1978 had impaired city and county capability to prepare for and manage community growth. Developmental pressures needed to be channeled into areas where schools, streets, sewers, parks, and police and fire services could be prepared in advance of settlement. Major governmental capital investments were needed to maintain and develop essential services and community amenities required for industrial expansion. Properly equipped government staffs were not available on a scale necessary to accommodate projected industrial growth. Revenue limitations after 1978 had provided partial (but perhaps temporary) relief by stagnating Boise's growth rate and thus reducing development pressure. In a state capital, with government employment a major economic factor, such an incidental result of curtailment of operations and services was to be expected. Yet over another decade or two, solutions to national economic problems and a projected resumption of Boise's commercial and industrial development offered prospects of renewed pressures that could not be ignored.

An essential component in any effective process for solving problems of community development is public awareness and understanding. Public participation in review of Boise's urban redevelopment planning led to important modifications of revitalization policy, as political leaders responded to their perception of public preference and demand. An increased tolerance of differing opinions concerning major local issues and improved communication to facilitate public comprehension of complex problems were available through activities of neighborhood associations and community study groups. Although some neighborhood associations responded only to special problems and then disappeared, others continued to function productively after a few successes in handling difficult matters. By 1982 Boise had professional planning staffs with a varied experience sufficient to produce effective community development programs. Gaining public acceptance was quite a different matter. Yet Boise's residents had become well aware of traditional values as well as of problems in adjusting to future developmental pressures. They still had to discover solutions consistent with Boise's special needs and appropriate for a community with a cultural heritage representing important regional values, rather than plans adapted to divergent localities and situations. But they still retained their long-established confidence in municipal development and urban revitalization.

Idaho's State Capitol, like most others is based upon the design of our national Capitol. Construction began in 1905 with the State Capitol Commission as contractor and was completed in 1920 at the modest cost of just over $2 million. A new Capitol Commission will oversee the building's restoration in time for its centennial in 2005.

Following page
Boise's Board of Trade traveled to other Western cities to boast their town's virtues. In 1916 this contingent paraded in downtown Seattle with banners that read: "Boise, Idaho, the garden spot of the world."

The view down Capitol Blvd. from a helicopter as 60 hot air balloons signal the start of the new millennium. Photo by Andrew Rafkind Studio. Courtesy, City of Boise

Chapter 10

DRAMATIC GROWTH IN AN ELECTRONIC AGE

1983-2000

Boise's 20-year struggle to secure a large retail mall downtown, using federal Urban Renewal grants, ended in May 1985, when the Taubman Co. of Troy, Michigan, pulled out. Like four previous developers, Taubman had been unable to secure commitments from major department stores as anchors for their project. Dick Eardley, who had been mayor for 12 years, longer than any other, was perceived by 1985 as the tenacious backer of a plan that could not work. City leadership had repeatedly rejected amendment of its Metroplan to allow rezoning for a suburban mall at Cole and Franklin Roads, then known as Westpark. The city's Planning and Zoning Commission had told the council it would cost taxpayers between $5.7 and $8.5 millions, primarily in road construction, plus an additional $1.5 million in annual operating costs if a mall were built at that site.

By 1985 an impatient public was ready for a change of direction. Dirk Kempthorne, Public Affairs Manager for FMC corporation, announced his candidacy for mayor on April 10, promising to open the Boise Redevelopment Agency land to individual developers on a parcel by parcel basis. He also urged that a suburban mall be built on the most feasible site within the city limits. Mayor Eardley, who had led Boise through some of its most trying times, decided not to seek reelection. Councilman Glenn Selander who had, like Kempthorne, declared in favor of a suburban mall, lost to him in the November election. By that time new council members had approved rezoning of the Westpark location, allowing Salt Lake City developer John Price to proceed with his Towne Square Mall.

Mayor Dick Eardley held the position through some of the city's most trying times. Revenue shortfalls due to a natural recession stalled urban renewal and forced cuts in fire, police, and library services. Courtesy, the Idaho Statesman

Bob Loughrey, executive director of the Boise Redevelopment Agency (BRA), guided the effort to revitalize downtown after the mall concept was abandoned. The Grove, the convention center, and parking garages were built during his tenure. Courtesy, the Idaho Statesman

Right
Boise's historic Eastman Building burned on the night of January 23, 1987. A developer for the long-empty structure had just been found when it fell victim to arsonists. Photo by Tom Shanahan. Courtesy, the Idaho Statesman

Abandonment of the downtown mall concept allowed for preservation and renovation of historic buildings there that have long given the city its identity. Although everything south of Main Street between Capitol Boulevard and Ninth Street had been leveled in the '70s, developers on the edges of the BRA blocks had begun earlier to invest in landmarks like the Idaho Building, 1911, the Elks Building, 1913, the Turnverein Building, 1906, Eagles Hall, 1912, and Pioneer Tent Building, 1910. Leaders in this renaissance in adaptive reuse of historic buildings were Joan Carley, who developed the Old Boise district, and Ken Howell who continues to find viable ways to keep significant landmarks alive and functioning. Before he developed the Idaho Building, Howell renovated the Alaska Building in 1984 and took over the 1902 Union Block that earlier developers had called beyond saving. In 2000 he is renovating the towered chateauesque Idanha Hotel, 1900, one of the city's most beloved landmarks. Within the BRA area the Egyptian Theater of 1927 was purchased and restored by Earl Hardy in 1981, and the white terra cotta-faced Alexander Building of 1924, was renovated in 1988.

As national prosperity replaced the depressed economy of the early 1980s Boise continued to grow at an unprecedented rate. This brought opportunities for business expansion but created headaches for planners and elected officials. Throughout the '80s and '90s the issue of how to manage the city's growth, while maintaining the quality of life Boiseans were used to, dominated public policy discussion and debate. Downtown redevelopment, using federal Urban Renewal funding, was stalled for nearly 20 years before an improving economy and the choice of a new direction got things moving again.

Between 1980 and 1990 the city's population grew at the rate of 1.4 percent a year. Between 1990 and the present, the rate of growth has more than doubled to 2.9 percent. The Metropolitan Statistical Area, which includes Ada and Canyon counties, was estimated in mid-2000 to have 408,817 people, with about 170,000 within Boise City limits. The designated market area, including

population surrounding Ada and Canyon counties, was estimated at more than half a million.

The Boise Redevelopment Agency (BRA) had started as a citizens advisory committee made up of business leaders. Its responsibilities were then taken over by the city council and it was again modified in April, 1984, to be a citizen's panel with council representation. The election of Ron Twilegar, Brent Coles and Mary Tate in November, 1983, helped create a new approach to redevelopment. Coles, with degrees in Political Science and Public Administration, had worked as a Boise City planner before his election. Twilegar was elected chairman of the BRA in January 1984, and continued in that position after the council approved again adding citizens to the panel. Mayor Eardley appointed four prominent business leaders who had been members of a group sponsored by Boise Cascade Corporation to continue the push for a downtown mall. "Uptown Boise," as it was styled, was formed later that month at a meeting to which no elected officials were invited. Its goal was to secure 750,000 square feet of new retail space downtown. Fifty-three of the 80 people invited pledged $50 each for operating expenses.

With the downtown mall plan dead, the BRA board continued to renew downtown in other ways after Dirk Kempthorne took office on January 1, 1986. The shape of the new downtown was largely determined by an effort of the Boise chapter of the American Institute of Architects to bring a Regional Urban Design Assistance Team (RUDAT) to Boise. The team recommended creation of a pedestrian mall on Eighth Street between Idaho Street and the Greenbelt, construction of a convention/trade center, leasing of urban renewal blocks rather than selling them, and the creation of "common areas" with places for sitting, strolling, biking, eating and sunning. The team found Capitol Boulevard "sorely lacking in visual organization and urban amenity."

The BRA board adopted the RUDAT plan on October 28, 1985, and in November hired the Portland firm of Zimmer Gunsul Frasca and Don Miles of Seattle as consultants. By May, 1986, the pioneer local architectural firm of Hummel La Marche & Hunsaker was chosen as prime design contractors. Mayor Kempthorne appointed architect John Rummel and historian Arthur Hart to the BRA board, and re-appointed Marilyn Shuler.

Meanwhile, John Price's Boise Towne Square Mall was moving ahead rapidly. The Bon Marché, while agreeing to keep its downtown store, committed to the mall as did J. C. Penney. Mervyns and Sears were both signed before the year was out. Ground breaking took place December 4, 1986 and the mall opened in October 1988. The new downtown plaza, named The Grove after a contest open to the public, was dedicated on December 6. Regular performances by local

British Columbia Premier William R. Bennett answered questions on Canadian-American trade at the National Governors Conference in Boise, 1985. Idaho Governor John Evans moderated the session. Courtesy, the Idaho Statesman

The city's historic north end includes several residential districts with a variety of architectural styles and magnificent old street trees. Courtesy, Arthur A. Hart

Opposite page
Union Pacific's grand old steam loco-motive 8444 pulled the centennial train into Boise as thousands waited to greet its arrival, July 3, 1990. Courtesy, the Idaho Statesman

Below left
Boise celebrated the centennial of Idaho statehood in July 1990, with parades, laser light shows, fireworks and pageantry. Courtesy, the Idaho Statesman

Below right
Thousands thronged to the brightly festooned capitol on July 3, 1990, to hear patriotic speeches. Idaho celebrated the centennial of its becoming a state on July 3, 1890. Courtesy, the Idaho Statesman

school choirs and other musical groups were scheduled throughout the holiday season. A central fountain for the plaza was donated by United Water Corporation and installation of public sculpture of a realistic kind met with general approval. This was in sharp contrast to the outcry that had greeted artist John Mason's abstract "Point of Origin," a $32,000 piece of sculpture funded by the city arts commission. First installed in front of City Hall, the large steel rectangles were later moved to a site at the Boise Art Museum in Julia Davis Park.

In March 1989, the BRA was renamed Capital City Development Corporation (CCDC), in part to remove the stigma that lingered from the agency's unsuccessful efforts over two decades to secure a downtown mall. Federal urban mass transit funds had been used to install bus lanes and waiting shelters on Idaho and Main Streets. Mayor Kempthorne later received permission from HUD to narrow bus lanes on the two streets to allow three lanes of other traffic without loss of an additional $1.8 million in mass transit funding.

In August the National League of Cities presented Boise with the James C. Howland Urban Enrichment Award for its renewal efforts. Among the continuing improvements in the downtown was the opening of the convention center, Boise Centre on the Grove, on January 27, 1990. The inaugural celebration drew 2,500 people. The city received another boost in February when *Parenting Magazine* rated Boise one of the top 10 cities in America in which to raise children. The centennial of Idaho statehood later that year was celebrated with many projects expressing the city's pride in its legacy.

Unfinished business for CCDC was to find a hotel developer for the land on the corner of Capitol Boulevard and Front Street. West Coast Hotels was chosen as builder of the convention hotel. The plan included Bank of America Center, with an indoor hockey rink and seating for 5,000 people. In November a *New York Times* feature about Boise was headed "Boomtown U.S.A.," citing the fact that the city's job growth in 1992 had led the nation at 6 percent.

In February 1994, Washington Mutual Bank's Capitol Plaza tower was able to proceed with construction. All 40 condominiums in the building's top floors were spoken for at prices ranging from $160,000 to $360,000. Architect Neil Hosford's design featured a multi-gabled top and a lightness that would be a refreshing visual contrast to the dark and massive appearance of the 1970s Idaho First National Bank and the soon-to-be built Grove Hotel.

In January 1997, expansion of Boise Towne Square Mall was approved by city design review. The major construction included a 180,000 square foot Dillards department store, a two-story 90,344 square foot retail expansion, and major additions to Sears and Bon Marché stores. In 1997 CCDC

"Streets for People" is enlivened by sidewalk sales. This one was offered by The Book Shop—voted the city's most popular bookstore by a wide margin in a 1990 poll of Statesman *readers. The Book Shop and all other independent bookstores that placed in the poll have since been forced out of business by national chains. Courtesy, Arthur A. Hart*

Governor Cecil D. Andrus was dressed for the occasion as he rode in the Centennial parade from the depot to the statehouse on Statehood Day, July 3, 1990. Courtesy, the Idaho Statesman

Micron Technology of Boise is now the largest American producer of computer chips. Its southeast Boise plant has grown dramatically in the past 20 years. Courtesy, Micron Technology

approved plans for a 25-story Boise Tower to be built at the corner of Eighth and Main. Construction has yet to be started as of mid-2000.

The expansion and consolidation of Boise's major employers contributed greatly to the city's prosperity between 1982 and 2000. Worldwide demand for affordable personal computers significantly aided the growth of Hewlett-Packard and other Boise companies. HP's laser printer, designed and manufactured in Boise, was the first in the world that sold for less than $100,000. HP Boise conceived of a low-cost printer for use with personal computers. The "HP LaserJet" was introduced in May 1984, at a list price of $3,499. This and subsequent models revolutionized PC printing and established HP Boise as the world leader in laser printing—a position it still holds. Today an HP LaserJet printer can be bought for under $400. Hewlett-Packard has about 100,000 employees worldwide, of which 60,000 are in the U.S. and 5,000 in Boise.

Micron Technology, founded in 1978 with personal backing from J. R. Simplot, began production of dynamic random access memory chips (DRAMs) in 1981 with 50 employees. After 1982 sales of $5 million jumped to $21 million in 1983 the company began major expansion that has continued almost unbroken to the present. With 8,000 Boise workers, Micron is the city's largest employer. When foreign companies began dumping chips on the American market below cost Micron filed an anti-dumping petition with the International Trade Commission in 1985. The ITC ruled in Micron's favor and the U. S. Commerce Department got Japanese companies to agree to sell chips at their fair value. Micron was able to rehire laid-off employees and begin a climb that led *Forbes Magazine* to say in 1991 that the company was the only profitable DRAM maker in the world, and the third largest. With profits of $104 million in 1993, Micron moved to 402nd on the *Fortune* 500 list.

By 1995 Micron had diversified and was building computers and selling network access through new divisions. Asian companies, led by Samsung of Korea, led the world in sales, but Micron was the U.S. leader after buying Texas Instrument's Memory Division.

Morrison-Knudsen Corporation, once the second largest construction company in the world, suffered serious reverses in the period 1982-2000, but is now on its way back to its former profitability. Washington Group International, Inc. was formed in July 2000, following acquisition by MK of Raytheon Engineers & Constructors. Washington Group has about 38,000 employees at work in more than 40 countries. Boisean William Agee was hired as CEO in 1988 after controversial tenures as chief fiscal officer at Boise Cascade and CEO of Bendix. The company's loss of $53 million in 1987 had led to his appointment. In 1994 he reorganized operations to include divisions MK Rail and MK Transit that were later abandoned. During the seven years of Agee's tenure as CEO the company's debt had grown to $264 million, and by February 1995 he was fired. This occurred during years when other Boise companies prospered and *USA Today* had published a story headed "Booming City of Boise is No Longer a Secret."

The J. R. Simplot Company, a privately held agri-business, with headquarters in Boise, continues to grow around the world with about 12,000 employees in the U.S, Canada, Australia, and Mexico. Its annual revenues are about $2.8 billion derived principally from food processing, fertilizer manufacturing and agriculture. The Food Group delivers billions of pounds of frozen and fresh potatoes, frozen vegetables and fruit, and avocado products. Most are sold

Mayor Dirk Kempthorne congratulates Morrison-Knudsen CEO Bill Agee August 3, 1990, on the corporation's purchase of the historic 1925 Union Pacific depot. MK would later sell the landmark to the city. Thousands of citizens contributed money for the purchase. Courtesy, the Idaho Statesman

Morrison-Knudsen (now Washington Group) world headquarters is spread across the urban landscape between the foothills and Boise River. Courtesy, Washington Group

to the food service industry to customers like McDonald's, Burger King and Kentucky Fried Chicken. Simplot got into the cattle-feeding business as a way to utilize large quantities of potato waste generated in its processing plants. Today its Land & Livestock group is one of the nation's top ten suppliers of beef.

The S-Sixteen Simplot Family Limited Partnership owns and develops commercial real estate. Its Boise holdings include 8th Street Marketplace, Boise Factory Outlets, Columbia Village, and The Grove Hotel and Bank of America Centre.

Extended Systems, founded in 1984, is headquartered in Boise with subsidiaries in Germany, France, Italy, the Netherlands, Singapore, and the United Kingdom. It specializes in mobile management technology and engineering, and has sold more than a million hardware and software units worldwide.

Trus Joist, a Boise manufacturer of steel and wood open-web trusses for commercial construction, grew into an industy giant in the 1980s. In 1991 the company formed a joint venture with Canadian forest products company MacMillan Bloedel. Trus Joist MacMillan's revenues were $778 million in 1998. On January 7, 2000, TJM was purchased by the Weyerhaeuser Co.

Boise-based Albertson's, Inc., after steady growth throughout the 1980s and '90s, tried to become the number one grocery chain in the nation in August 1998, by a merger with Salt Lake City-based American Stores. The combined companies had more than 2,470 stores in 37 states, topping Kroger as number one. But in June 1999, the Federal Trade Commission ordered Albertson's and American to divest themselves of 144 supermarkets in California, Nevada, and New Mexico. The Commission ruled that the merger would substantially lessen competition in those states, possibly resulting in "higher prices or reduced quality and selection for consumers." The divestiture, agreed to by Albertson's and American, was the largest ever required by the FTC in the retail industry. Costs associated with the merger caused the company's stock values to fall, but market analysts and Albertson's CEO Peter Lynch were optimistic that after a period of adjustment the company, still second largest in the country behind Kroger, would return to its former long-time profitability. Kroger, mean-while, strengthened its local competitive position by buying Fred Meyer, Inc. of Portland, which has two stores in Boise, one in Meridian, and one in Nampa. Costco and Walmart also present new challenges for Albertson as they expand operations in southern Idaho and elsewhere. The grocery business has become a battle of giants, but Albertson's seems sure to remain near the top.

Boise Cascade Corporation, as it enters the new millennium, is still a major producer and distributor of pulp and paper and a leader in business-to-business office products

sales. It owns or controls more than two million acres of timberland to support its lumber and other manufacturing operations. In April, 1993, John Fery, long-time CEO of the company, retired and George Harad took over.

As air travel continued to increase in the last decades of the century and truckers took over more of the nation's freight hauling, rail service was consolidated to reflect the times. Branch lines that were no longer profitable were discontinued all over Idaho, and the tracks taken up. In 1984 the Interstate Commerce Commission gave the Union Pacific Railroad permission to abandon downtown trackage along Front Street that had served the city's wholesale district for 90 years. In January 1993, billionaire J. R. Simplot bought the property from the railroad for a planned development that could resemble a "city within a city," with a mix of housing, retail, and entertainment.

Amtrak passenger service on the Pioneer route across southern Idaho, first cut in 1971, and revived through the efforts of Idaho Senator Frank Church in 1977 was finally discontinued on May 10, 1997. Morrison-Knudsen Corporation bought and restored the landmark Union Pacific depot in the '90s, and sold it to the city at a significant loss after the company suffered serious reverses and had to retrench. Thousands of citizens contributed to the purchase of the handsome 1925 Mission-style structure, and Mayor Brent Coles expressed hopes that light rail might be established as a commuter link between valley towns. The hope was to establish regular rail service eventually between Micron Technology in the east and Nampa in the west. Light rail could serve thousands, many of whom now drive as many as 50 miles to and from work each day.

Covered wagons rolled down Capitol Boulevard as the sesquicentennial of The Oregon Trail was celebrated in 1993. Courtesy, the Idaho Statesman

Boise Urban Stages, (BUS), the mass transit system, posted significant shortfalls in 1997, even though it carried 1.9 million people in 1996—up from 774,000 in 1992.

Automobile traffic continued to increase at a rate that astonished and annoyed long-time residents, despite major road construction designed to alleviate it. In September 1985, the U.S. House of Representatives passed a bill to fund construction of a Broadway-Chinden connector and Idaho Senator Steve Symms pushed funding for the project and construction began in October 1988. When completed in 1994 the three-mile elevated approach to downtown from the west had cost $90 million.

The Eighth Street bridge across Boise River, built in 1911, was closed to automobiles after completion of a new bridge beside it on the west. The landmark Memorial Bridge on Capitol Boulevard, built by Morrison-Knudsen in 1931, was widened and restored. Features of the original design were preserved, including ceramic and bronze panels commemorating the Oregon Trail. The structure was listed in the National Register of Historic Places in December, 1990, the first bridge in Idaho to receive that recognition.

Major expansion of Interstate 84 and its connectors with the city have been continuous throughout the '90s and will no doubt continue into the new century. Idaho in the year 2000 has far more licensed motor vehicles than people; Ada County alone has more than 320,000 registered vehicles.

The 150th anniversary of the opening of the Oregon Trail was celebrated in 1993 with commemorative signage along its routes across Idaho. A covered wagon train passed through Boise on July 24—part of a national recreation of the pioneer trek. The old trail had passed along the bench to the south before Boise City was platted in July 1863. From then on it moved down Main Street.

Boise air travel grew dramatically during the 1980s and '90s. Deregulation of the airlines in 1978 had created a "musical chairs" of carriers coming and going in a newly competitive market. Increasing numbers of passengers in and out of the terminal necessitated major expansion. In 1983 a $7 million voter-approved revenue bond allowed construction of a new concourse. Final cost of the 80,000-square-foot expansion was $10 million. Increased international air traffic into the city, primarily by Boise-based corporate employees, led to the opening of a U.S. Customs Office at the terminal the following September.

Airlines that served Boise briefly after deregulation were: Air West, Hughes Air West, Republic, Cascade, Frontier, Gem State, Key, Mountain West, Pacific Express, Pacific Southwest, Sky West, Western, Transwestern, Air Idaho, Big Sky, Columbia, and Continental. Many of them went into bankruptcy or were absorbed by other companies. Delta Airlines began Boise service in 1987 after merging with Western. United Airlines, formed in Boise in 1931 out of Varney and other companies, still serves the city as it has for nearly 70 years. Delta, Alaska, American, Horizon, Northwest, and Southwest all fly out of Idaho's capital city today.

In 1994 Morrison-Knudsen Corporation unveiled the first American freight locomotive to run on 100 percent liquified natural gas. Union Pacific bought the 5000-horsepower unit, built in MK Rail's southeast Boise shops. Caterpillar was a partner in the venture and MK bought five other railroad-related firms in anticipation of future sales of 100 to 150 locomotives a year. Losses in other areas forced the company to sell MK Rail, along with the Union Pacific depot it had just bought and restored at a cost of over $3 million. The Boise railroad repair and construction shops are now owned and operated by Motive Power Industries of Pittsburg.

Boise church membership remained stable for Roman Catholics and long established Protestant denominations between 1983 and 2000. The area's growing Hispanic population, traditionally Catholic, led to more bilingual or Spanish language services. Although Methodist and Presbyterian membership grew only slightly during the period, Southern Baptists now outnumbered each of them.

Boise Mormon membership increased to nearly 40,000 by the mid-nineties and was growing at a faster rate than any other denomination. This growth was acknowledged by the church's Salt Lake City leadership with construction of a Boise temple on North Cole Road next to Interstate 84. The striking gray marble many-spired structure opened for public viewing on May 10, 1984.

Union Pacific locomotive 1298 was built in MK Rail's Boise shops in July, 1994. Courtesy, Morrison-Knudsen, Inc

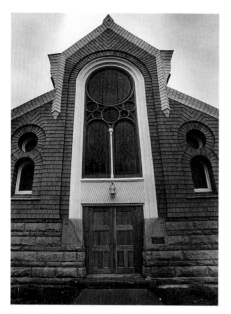

Temple Beth Israel, built in 1895 by pioneer Boise Jewish families, is on the National Register of Historic Places. Its style is considered Moorish—not unusual for 19th Century synagogues in America. Photo by David Brookman. Courtesy, the Idaho Statesman

The Basque Museum and Cultural Center was dedicated in June, 1987, with music and dancing. Nicole Lejardi-Coleman, 3, scolded her partner Josu Zubizarreta, 2 ½, for not following her dance instructions. Photo by Teri Davis. Courtesy, the Idaho Statesman

St. Paul's black Baptist church moved to the building formerly occupied by Capital Christian Center. Their former home on Broadway Avenue was moved to Julia Davis Park where it has become the Idaho Black History Museum, the first such museum in the Pacific Northwest.

By century's end 62 Christian denominations in the city were represented by 260 individual churches. There were two synagogues and one mosque.

The city's ethnic diversity also grew dramatically over the last two decades of the 20th century. Refugees from Southeast Asia and former Iron Curtain countries were joined by those fleeing the war in Bosnia and other Balkan countries. The 1990 census revealed that the growth rate of ethnic minorities in Ada County since 1980 was Hispanic, 45 percent; Asian, 93 percent; American Indian, 54 percent and Black, 40 percent. The rest of the population over the same period grew at the rate of 18 percent. During the same years 87 persons from the former Soviet Union moved to Boise, 27 from the Pacific islands, and 23 from South America. More revealing of Boise's new diversity is the number of languages other than English spoken in homes. Spanish, not surprisingly, was number one in total numbers, followed by German, French, Slavic, (of several kinds), Chinese, Japanese, Vietnamese, Scandinavian, and Korean. Italian, Portuguese, Arabic and Hungarian were also spoken. The 1990 Census takers recorded more than 100 languages spoken in Idaho households.

Idaho's Basque population, centered in Boise, is the largest in the United States. The Basque Center on Grove Street was built in 1950 as a social club and to preserve Basque culture through dance and language classes. In 1987 and 1990 the center sponsored an international Basque festival called Jaialdi held at the Old Idaho Penitentiary, a National Register historic site. Thousands enjoyed Basque food, music, dance and sports. In 1985 the Basque Museum and Cultural Center was incorporated and began operations next door to the Basque Center in the Jacobs-Uberuaga house,

the city's oldest surviving brick building, once a Basque boarding house. In addition to a museum the Cultural Center houses Basque Center language and dance classes, a Basque pre-school, and one of the largest libraries of Basque materials in the United States. In 1995 and 2000 Jaialdi was held at the Western Idaho Fairgrounds. The 2000 four-day festival attracted about 30,000 people.

On July 1, 1983, police chief John Church resigned after serving longer in the position than any chief before him. Since his appointment in January 1968, the department had grown from 60 sworn officers to 140. His innovations had made the Boise Police Department one of the most progressive in the nation, recognized as such by the International Association of Chiefs of Police. In November 1984, Boise policeman Vaughn Killeen was elected Ada County sheriff, the sixth former Boise police officer to hold the position. In 2000 Killeen was reelected for a record fifth term.

Perceived revenue shortfalls caused the layoff of policemen in 1985. City councilmen Brent Coles and Ron Twilegar alone voted unsuccessfully to stop the cuts; a budget surplus discovered later allowed rehiring of the officers and raised questions about the city's accounting procedures. A nationwide depression was blamed for Boise's tight budgets in the early '80s. City services had been cut back ever since a one percent property tax initiative was passed by voters in 1978—a tax revolt modeled after a similar initiative passed earlier in California.

The war on illegal drugs continued to have top priority throughout the '80s and '90s under police chiefs Jim Montgomery, 1983-88, James Carvino, 1988-93, and Larry Paulson, 1993-2000. On January 31, 2000, former Bellingham chief Don Pierce took over the department. A community ombudsman was hired to investigate complaints of police misconduct—a response to a series of fatal police shootings in the '90s. In every case extensive investigation by independent agencies had cleared policemen of wrongdoing. Officer Mark Stall was killed in a shootout on September 27, 1997, the first Boise policeman to die in line of duty.

Most of those killed in confrontations with police were under the influence of alcohol or drugs—facts revealed by autopsy. Tough enforcement of the law, which citizens expect and demand, increased problems for government in Idaho as elsewhere in the nation. Jails were over-crowded and costs of maintaining them and building new ones escalated. Statistics released in April 1997, showed that 25 percent of those incarcerated had been convicted of motor vehicle offenses: DUI, suspended licenses, reckless driving, or eluding police officers.

Mayor Brent Coles, elected on November 2, 1993, following former Mayor Dirk Kempthorne's election to the U.S. Senate,

Mayor H. Brent Coles. Courtesy, Office of the Mayor.

Boise's Chinese community paraded its traditional dragon in a display of Idaho's ethnic diversity on the evening of July 3, 1990. Boise State University's Bronco Stadium was packed for a spectacular four hour show. Courtesy, Idaho Statesman

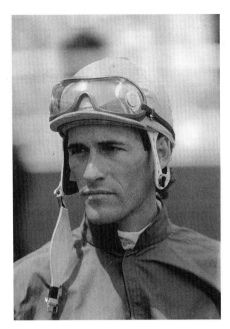

Hall of Fame jockey Gary Stevens of Boise won the first race he ever rode at Les Bois Park when he was 16. He won the Kentucky Derby three times, the Belmont Stakes twice, and the Preakness once, in a career that saw him become the youngest jockey to win $100 million. He retired in 1999. Courtesy, the Idaho Statesman

The Ore-Ida Women's Challenge bicycle race attracted top competition from all over the world. This 1985 photo shows the pack headed for Idaho City on Highway 21. The 21 kilometer race had some steep climbs and exhilarating downhills. Photo by John Blackmer. Courtesy, the Idaho Statesman

took an active lead in the fight against drugs, co-chairing the U.S. Conference of Mayors Drug Control Task Force, and originating in Boise the *Enough is Enough* anti-drug campaign. His prominence in the fight against drug abuse in the nation's cities contributed to his election to the presidency of the U. S. Conference of Mayors in June 2000.

After an absence of nine years professional sports returned to Boise in 1987 when Diamond Sports, Inc. of New York bought the Tri-cities franchise in the Northwest Baseball League. The Boise Hawks opened the 1989 season in a new Memorial Stadium on land leased from the Western Idaho Fair. In 1990 the Hawks became affiliated with the California Angels of the American League, and the skilled young players this brought to Boise led to immediate success. The Hawks won three of the next four Northwest League championships.

Diamond Sports also brought World Team Tennis to Boise in 1994 with the formation of the Idaho Sneakers. Professional boxing, hockey, and arena football followed. Boise's Steel Heads played in the West Coast Hockey League, the privately owned Idaho Stampede in the Continental Basketball Association, and the Idaho Stallions in the Indoor Professional Football League.

Boise State University left the Division 1AA Big Sky conference in 1996 to join the Division 1A Big West Conference. In 1997 the NCAA-sanctioned Humanitarian Bowl football game was awarded to Boise and played for the first time, and Boise State University beat the University of Louisville in 1999. The annual game was a spin-off from Boise's World Sports Humanitarian Hall of Fame, founded in 1994 to honor athletes who are role models and who serve their communities. The first inductees were golfer ChiChi Rodriguez, Olympic decathlon champion Rafer Johnson, and Wimbledon tennis champion Arthur Ashe. In 1995 baseball stars Roberto Clemente and Dale Murphy were inducted, along with basketball hall-of-famer Julius Erving. Later inductees include, 1996: Kip Keino, Pat McCormick, Bonnie Blair; 1997: Mel Blount, Billy Mills, Kevin Johnson; 1998: Jackie Joyner Kersey, Pele, David Robinson; 1999: Tom Landry, Wilma Rudolph, Tony Gwinn; 2000: Mary Lou Retton, Nate Archibald, and Kirby Puckett.

Boise's concern for preserving and enhancing the environment is reflected in continuing efforts to fight air and water pollution, to acquire open space and wetlands, to enlarge the park system, including the Boise River Greenbelt, and in the creation by citizens of new nature-oriented institutions. The river itself, while increasingly appreciated as a prime amenity and recreational resource, can still flood occasionally, despite engineered efforts over the years to control it. The city's river protection ordinance was amended in December 1983, to restrict building along the river. The

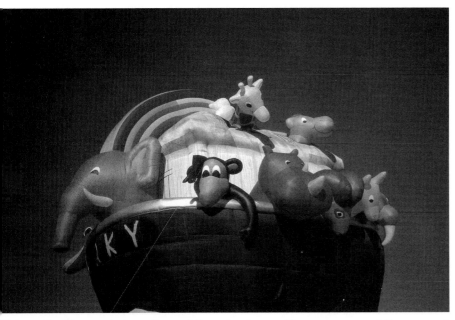

Hot air balloons come to Boise from all over the west to take part in the annual River Festival. This whimsical creation depicts Noah's Ark. Courtesy, Arthur A. Hart

Greenbelt, a strip of parkland along its course with paved pedestrian and bicycle paths, has been extended from the center of the city to Lucky Peak dam in the east and to beyond Glenwood Avenue in the west. It is now more than 20 miles long. Greenbelt Appreciation Day was inaugurated in 1983, and has evolved into an "adopt the river program" in which individuals, groups, and businesses volunteer to keep sections of the route cleared of litter. A Boise River Resource Management and Master Plan was adopted by the city council in early 1999. Even in the coldest of winters hundreds of people walk the Greenbelt to view the spectacular annual gathering of Bald Eagles, and bicyclers and joggers use it all year.

Although Boiseans who attended a series of public meetings in the '90s expressed themselves strongly in favor of more neighborhood parks, a bond issue seeking to fund them in February, 1994, fell far short of the two-thirds needed to pass. More than half of those voting said no. Wanting and paying are two different things. Boise's park system now encompasses 2,388 acres and 80 individual parks. The system was enhanced significantly with the October 17, 1989, dedication of Katherine Albertson Park. It was grocery king Joe Albertson's 84th birthday, and part of his legacy to the city where he opened his first store in 1939. The land, valued at $3.1 million, was developed with an additional gift of $1.5 million. Its use is limited to walking and nature-watching. Dogs are banned during the wildfowl nesting season.

The Idaho Botanical Garden had its beginning in 1984 on 50 acres of land leased from the State of Idaho next to the Old Idaho Penitentiary historic district. Botanist Christopher Davidson was the founder and first executive director of the non-profit organization that now has more than 1100 members. The Friends of the Garden auxiliary organization has

Above left and right
The Idaho Botanical Garden occupies a site next to the Old Idaho Penitentiary historic district. Prisoners quarried the stone on the hillsides beyond from which the walls and guard towers were built. Courtesy, Idaho Botanical Garden (left) and Arthur A. Hart (right)

raised an average of $20,000 each year. Hundreds of volunteers work thousands of hours planting, weeding, and doing other maintenance tasks from early spring to late autumn. Regular tours and special events are offered year round. Boise State University has established its Center for Horticulture Technology at the Old Idaho Penitentiary and works with the Botanical Garden in ways that benefit both institutions. Judy Ouderkirk, present director of the garden, was honored on January 1, 1994, as the *Idaho Statesman's* Citizen of the Year for her leadership in saving wildlife habitat in Hulls Gulch from development. She and Ann Hausrath, working through the Wetlands Coalition, organized March 21, 1989, eventually raised $320,000 to buy over 300 acres in the gulch for a nature preserve. The gulch and Boise foothills are home to more than 6,000 mule deer, foxes, coyotes and other mammals, and are occasionally visited by elk and moose. More than 200 species of birds have been recorded between the valley and the evergreen summit.

The World Center for Birds of Prey opened in 1984 in new headquarters south of the city. The Peregrine Fund, dedicated to saving falcon species endangered by DDT contamination in the food chain, moved to Boise from Fort Collins, Colorado, bringing the entire captive breeding population of Peregrines and other rare species with them. Boise's Morley Nelson, worked with raptors for more than 30 years. Seven films he made for Walt Disney were seen by millions of Americans. His efforts stopped government agencies from paying bounties on eagles, hawks and falcons, and led eventually to the establishment of the Snake River Birds of Prey National Conservation Area, passed by Congress August 4, 1993. This 482,000-acre reserve on both sides of the Snake

River canyon south of Boise contains the nation's highest concentration of nesting raptors. A 1940s survey found 15 species and more than 1,000 nesting pairs. Golden Eagles, Prairie Falcons, and Redtail Hawks are the best known of these birds. Cecil D. Andrus, Secretary of the Interior during the Carter administration, issued Public Land order 5777 in 1980 designating what became the National Conservation Area 13 years later. He was governor of Idaho before going to Washington, and was reelected on his return.

Boise's valley setting, between mountain foothills on the north and high benchland on the south, creates a natural pocket susceptible to atmospheric inversion. Historically it was coal smoke that darkened the sky in winter, but increased wood burning, following the national energy shortages of the early '80s, along with increased automobile traffic, led to bans on wood burning during critical periods and mandatory vehicle emissions testing. The testing is credited with increasing the city's compliance with Environmental Protection Agency standards significantly. The elimination of leaded gasoline has also had a positive effect on air quality. In August, 1993, the city put into operation the first of a fleet of non-polluting buses fueled with natural gas.

Ada County Highway District faced major cuts in federal funds in 1983 when county commissioners repealed a mandatory vehicle emissions testing law. The Environmental Protection Agency threatened to withhold up to $27 million earmarked for roads and sewers until the county reversed its position—which it did.

An urban, people-friendly plaza was built in 1990 to replace the fortress-like approach to city hall. Trees, shaded seating, colorful flags, and a fountain enhance an area that was little used before. The $500,000 park was named for Velma Morrison, its principal donor. At the MK Nature Center east of downtown, winding footpaths follow a fast-flowing mountain stream where several species of trout can be observed from windows set below water level. Thousands of school children learn natural history in an outdoor classroom where they can watch wood ducks and other birds nest

Falconer Morley Nelson shows off his magnificent Arctic Gyrfalcon. Nelson, through films and television appearances, led efforts to make Americans aware of the need to preserve endangered birds of prey. Courtesy, Morley Nelson

167

and raise their young. Museum exhibits indoors enhance the learning experience.

Boise has a long history of support of cultural activities. In the last decades of this century significant enhancement of the arts has taken place. The opening of the Morrison Center for Performing Arts in early 1984 provided a regular home for performances of the Boise Philharmonic Orchestra, Ballet Idaho, Opera Idaho, and national touring groups and noted artists. The Esther Simplot Performing Arts Academy, housed in the Eighth Street historic district, provides rehearsal space for these organizations and offers training for young artists. Excellent facilities were created by thoroughly remodeling two turn-of-the-century brick warehouse buildings.

Boise Little Theater, now in its 52nd season, has performed at least six plays annually for the past 43 years. In addition to its regular season, BLT offers summer one-acts, a Junior Little Theater, and Christmas shows for children. Other community theater companies offer a wide choice of performances year-round: The Idaho Shakespeare Festival, now 20 years old, the Stage Coach Theatre company, Boise Actors' Guild, Knock 'em Dead dinner theater, Idaho Theater for Youth, and Boise Contemporary Theater. Boise State University offers live theater and musical performances open to the public. The Shakespeare Festival opened a new outdoor theater in 1998.

Boise Gallery of Art was renamed Boise Art Museum in April 1988. Three major building expansions, the last in 1997, have provided 16 galleries, a sculpture garden, an interior skylighted sculpture court, and a classroom wing. The arts of many cultures and eras are presented through traveling exhibits. Annual events include Art in the Park, a holiday sale, a wine festival, and a monthly Museum After Hours featuring music and refreshments.

The Idaho Historical Museum, neighbor to the art museum in Julia Davis Park, tells the story of Idaho with scores of exhibits and recreated historical interiors. Major expansion in the 1980s allowed creation of large new exhibit areas, an impressive foyer, a gift shop, and improved handicapped access. The "Museum Comes to Life" annual fall celebration attracts thousands to see demonstrations of pioneer crafts and costumed performers in historic interiors.

Several commercial art galleries in the downtown area participate in a regular First Thursday event, with transportation provided throughout the evening.

Appreciation of the city's architectural heritage has been advanced by the Boise City Historic Preservation Commission and the non-profit Idaho Historic Preservation Council. The council gives annual Orchids and Onions awards. The on-going efforts of the Idaho Historical Society's Historic Preservation office, located in the National Landmark U.S. Assay Office, assist all Idahoans with survey information and listing of sites in the National Register of Historic Places, upon approval of a statewide Historic Sites Review Board.

Boise Public Library opened a branch in Towne Square Mall in February, 1989, and celebrated its centennial in April, 1995. Kathy Hodges wrote its history *A Light in the Window*. A new library building is in the planning stages.

The Discovery Center of Idaho is a hands-on science museum founded in 1988. It has 150 exhibits in a 26,000 square foot building and an expanding educational program for children and adults.

Among other significant additions to the cultural scene in recent years is the Log Cabin Literary Center on Capitol Boulevard next to the library. An historic forest-industries building has become headquarters for seminars, readings, and an annual Book Fest in mid-September featuring local and guest writers in panel discussions and book signings. The event has grown spectacularly since its founding in 1999.

Planning is underway to create a 30-block cultural district to include museums, galleries, public art, theater, restaurants and night clubs. The Flicks, an alternative movie house that regularly shows classic and foreign films, has operated in the area for more than 20 years. The Idaho Black History Museum and the Basque Museum, described earlier, are part of the proposed district. The Idaho Anne Frank Human Rights Memorial, the only such project of its kind in the nation, will be completed in 2001 on the banks of Boise River near the library.

As the new millennium begins, Boise is experiencing steady growth and facing issues similar to those of other growing cities. Its citizens continue to seek ways to protect the foothills that form the city's scenic backdrop, avoid over-development and maintain the quality of life that they have grown to love.

Bottom right
Rafting and innertube float trips on the Boise river are favorite summer pastimes. This team with its mascot is racing others against the clock. It doesn't really matter who wins—it's all fun. Photo by John Blackmer. Courtesy, the Idaho Statesman

Bottom left
The Idaho Shakespeare Festival has presented an annual season of live performances for more than 20 years. In 1998 it opened its season in a new outdoor theater off Warm Springs Avenue. John Irwin and Geoff Lower are shown in a 1983 rehearsal for Henry IV, Part One. Courtesy, the Idaho Statesman

Chapter 11

CHRONICLES OF LEADERSHIP

No record of Boise is complete without a glimpse of the people and pursuits that forged its commercial development. The following chapter, therefore, offers insight into many of the companies and institutions that helped Idaho's capital flourish.

In part, the history of Boise's business community is an account of happenstance. The city, like most, was founded upon an accident of nature. In the beginning, its place on the river made Boise an accessible trading post. An Army fort was established. And, when the surrounding mountains yielded gold and silver, a commercial district emerged to serve miners and soldiers alike. The Oregon Trail came right along its Main Street. Travelers, too weary to push on to the coast, settled down to farm the valley.

The rugged Idaho interior north of Boise Basin provided abundant timber. But carving roads through the wilderness was treacherous labor. So the loggers devised innovative means of reaching the backwoods trees, and their resourcefulness and determination spawned a vital heavy-construction industry. Timber, mining, and agricultural entrepreneurs also relied on the city as a center of trade, transportation, and culture.

Boise's sophistication increased throughout the 20th century. A junior college was founded in the throes of the Depression. It evolved into a four-year institution, a member of the state university system. The territory's original bank grew to rank among the nation's 100 largest. The construction, wood products, and food processing and marketing industries combined with government agencies as the city's major employers.

World War II sparked the city's most remarkable period of advancement. Boise's population and its retail trade were bolstered during the war years by Army troops stationed at Gowen Field. The war effort also fueled local industry's output. With peace, many soldiers returned to the Boise Valley to stay. Developers and construction firms went to work building a booming city. Retailers, many enduring for decades, eventually followed their market to suburban shopping centers.

Some Idaho endeavors, fired by hard work and innovation, have grown to international dimensions, (The fact that they continue to base their headquarters in Boise attests to the city's quality of life.) Other enterprises have found success serving the Boise market, an area that includes most of southern Idaho and eastern Oregon. Regardless of their size or the nature of their activities, they are all partners in the ongoing progress of the City of Trees.

ADA COUNTY HIGHWAY DISTRICT

Progress of growing communities is marked by the emerging presence of new roads that intersect with the roads of the past. The routes we travel provide a roadmap to the history of Ada County.

Boise City's founding planners laid the street grid in a rectangular pattern somewhat parallel to the Boise River, probably incorporating a path of the Oregon Trail. The first 10 blocks, laid out in 1863, grew to 136 by 1885 (*right*) as some Oregon Trail travelers stopped in Boise rather than continue west.

The first "addition" to the city north of Fort Street, turned the street grid to a more traditional north/south orientation. The first bridge across the river was at Ninth Street. The "Valley Road" headed west as the forerunner of State Street and the east-bound "Road to Penitentiary" later became Warm Springs Avenue.

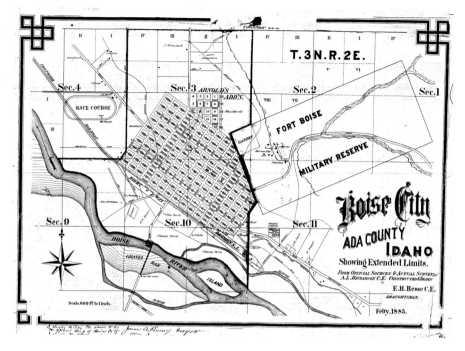

The 1885 Map of Boise City.

Horses, wagons, and the occasional bicycle occupied the roads of Ada County towns (*below*). Surfaced with dirt or gravel, the streets balanced the comfort of horses with the convenience of pedestrians—a balance still sought today, long after autos replaced the horses. Street and road maintenance was the responsibility of each town's city council or, in the unincorporated parts of the county, of the Board of County Commissioners. A substantial service industry shoed and cared for horses, built wagons and wheels, and fabricated accessories of wood, metal, and leather.

Pictured (*top, page opposite*) is a trolley rounding the corner at 10th and Idaho Streets. As the Boise Valley agricultural economy matured with the arrival of irrigation reservoirs and complex water distribution systems in the early 20th century, the region's transportation arteries became more sophisticated. Two rail services evolved. One connected the towns of Middleton, Caldwell, Nampa, and Boise in a convenient "interurban" loop; the other provided urban and suburban service within the city of Boise.

Pioneer Freight. Inset is the Estes Wagon Works. Courtesy, Idaho State Historical Society

In the early years of the 20th century, automobiles gradually crowded horses, wagons, bicycles, and even the trolleys off the public roads. The Ada County Road Department had to adapt the roads to the requirements of the auto—which in turn required innovations in its own fleet of operating equipment. The photo (*below right*) shows a flat-bed dump truck. Blacksmith shops and wagon works gave way to gasoline filling stations and auto dealerships. A few years after their invention in 1923, automatic traffic signals began to appear at street intersections in Boise.

The photo (*below*) shows Overland Road, one of the east-west roads in a system of road sections. The first Idaho land survey began in Ada County at Initial Butte in 1887. The survey identified one-mile squares called "sections." Thereafter, roads along the section lines became the customary location for farm-to-market roads, a pattern that later set the stage for converting the resulting one-mile grid to arterial highways.

Trolley car at 10th and Idaho streets. Courtesy, Idaho State Historical Society

Overland Road. Courtesy, Idaho State Historical Society

Ada County Road Department. Courtesy, Idaho State Historical Society

Fairview Avenue paving. Courtesy, Idaho State Historical Society

The automobile performed better on paved surfaces. Fairview Avenue (*above*), which connected Boise and Meridian, was paved for the first time in 1910. Volumes of traffic were sufficiently low that highway authorities had no need to build multiple lanes or specialized left turn lanes.

With a booming agricultural industry in the Boise River valley, Boise City and the smaller towns in the county grew rapidly after 1900. New bridges across the Boise River symbolized the region's progress and its potential for even greater opportunities. The Capitol Boulevard Memorial Bridge (*below left*)—the most artistic in the

Memorial Bridge. Courtesy, Idaho State Historical Society

state—completed a project to connect the Union Pacific Railroad Depot and the Idaho Statehouse in fine style. The bridge honored the pioneers of the Oregon Trail who settled the West and Idaho. A crowd of 25,000 attended the three-mile parade, speeches, picnics, and a public dance in a Varney Airlines hangar on the day of dedication in May 1931.

The old Broadway Bridge (*below right*), built in 1892, was inadequate for the needs, or ambitions, of Broadway Avenue businesses. The South Boise Booster Club headed the drive to build a new bridge. When the new bridge opened in 1956, Broadway merchants sponsored a parade and

then held street dances in their parking lots.

In 1913 the Idaho Legislature created a State Highway Commission, asking it to lay out a state highway system. Another 1913 law required all motor vehicles to have good brakes, a horn, headlights and taillights. Driving over 30 mph was considered unsafe and imprudent.

"Route 1" the Idaho Pacific Highway, followed part of the Oregon Trail and connected the cities of eastern Idaho to Boise, Meridian, Nampa, and Caldwell before turning north to Sandpoint. The federal government began supplying "aid" to states for road building. By 1926 it had identified a national system of numbered and connected roads. Ever since, highway construction often involves the joint effort of three levels of government.

Here, Federal Way (*opposite page top*)—U.S. Highway 30—comes down the hill and turns north into Capitol Boulevard in 1936.

Ada County voters decided on May 25, 1971, to consolidate all of the county's individual street and road departments into one

Broadway Bridge. Courtesy, Idaho State Historical Society

Federal Way. Courtesy, Idaho State Historical Society

administrative and governmental district—the Ada County Highway District. The new district gathered up all of the snow plows, road repair equipment, and other highway gear and went into business on January 1, 1972. The decision coincided with a new wave of population growth in the region and pressure for better planning and more coordination of government services.

Capitol Boulevard. Courtesy, Idaho State Historical Society

The new district implemented the transportation policies of county and city general plans. In addition, the district was in a position to standardize highway, sign, and right-of-way requirements all across the county, providing a consistent and predictable environment for the traveling public.

In 1968, the Old Oregon Trail permuted once more, this time into Interstate 84. The controlled-access, high-speed highway served its inter-state function and also contributed to the growing commerce between Ada County and the towns in Canyon County to the west. Meanwhile, old Highway 30 through Boise City and Ada County came under local jurisdiction once more.

The Oregon Trail, beautiful bridges, and farm-to-market roads are only

part of the transportation legacy that history has brought to the citizens of today. Now that the communities are old enough to have a history, this legacy invites preservation, restoration, and respect. It is still possible, for example, to look south to the old Depot (below left) along modern Capitol Boulevard, to detect in the medians, the street-lights, and the restored concrete railings of the bridge, the continuing influence of the original vision for the boulevard. The pioneers who rode in the parade on that day in 1931 would easily recognize the place.

An excellent civic life involves appreciating the gifts of the past as well as the possibilities for the future. The transportation network linking people with each other has always been a basic element of that shared life. The Ada County Highway District, having accrued nearly 30 years of its own history, expects to preserve the historic paths we travel while adapting them for the opportunities that lie ahead.

Artist's conception of the West Park Center Bridge. Courtesy, W&H Pacific Engineering

AGRI BEEF CO.

In the early 1950s Bob Rebholtz, founder of Agri Beef Co., was a young boy in San Francisco, dreaming of cowboys and round-ups. It was a dream he shared with many young boys around the world. Most abandoned the idea once they outgrew their toy pistols. But not young Rebholtz.

Growing up, Bob Rebholtz spent every summer "cowboying" around the West, soaking up as much as possible about the cattle industry. Not a year went by that Rebholtz didn't spend furthering his knowledge of beef production.

As the Rebholtz boy grew, so did his dream: from riding horseback and roping cattle, to owning his own livestock business. After sharpening his business skills at the University of California-Davis and Stanford Business School, Rebholtz set out to turn his dream to reality.

In 1968, the chance he was waiting for arrived when Snake River Cattle Feeders in American Falls, Idaho became available under a lease-purchase option. Rebholtz seized the opportunity and,

Rebholtz, the "executive cowboy," in the 1980s.

A professional cowboy oversees a field of grazing cattle. Feedlots and ranching are still the lifeblood of Agri Beef's business.

under his direction, the cattle-feeding operation grew quickly.

As the dream turned to reality, Rebholtz continued to expand the scope of his vision. In 1975, he purchased El Oro Cattle Feeders in Moses Lake, Washington.

Within three years, he was ready to make a major move.

In 1978, Rebholtz moved his family to Boise and joined with a friend and fellow feedlot owner to incorporate a new livestock feeding business. They named it Agri Beef Co.

When the Rebholtz family moved to Boise, Robert Rebholtz Jr., who is now the president of Agri Beef, was just 11 years old. But he was not too young to understand that his dad was a little more progressive than other dads.

"We moved to Boise because it was a thriving environment for technology," says Rebholtz Jr. "My father recognized that Boise offered the ability to develop state-of-the-art information systems." And thus, you could say Bob Rebholtz was a cowboy ahead of his time.

More than a decade before the Information Age hit its stride, Rebholtz was building his business on data. He believed that the more information Agri Beef had—

about everything—the cattle, the competition, the agriculture, the environment, the weather, the customers—the more successfully it could be managed. It was an innovative philosophy to say the least—managing an agriculture business from a mainframe computer was virtually unheard of at that time. It was this break with traditional feedlot strategies that set the tone for Agri Beef's passionate pursuit of innovation. Rebholtz nurtured an environment in his company that encouraged people to question everything, to continually create better ways of working. And it continues to pay off.

Today, the company that began with Rebholtz, his young wife Dorothy, and two employees on a feedlot in eastern Idaho has blossomed into a formidable force in the agriculture industry, with nearly 700 employees and gross sales of $400 million a year.

Unfortunately, Rebholtz is no longer able to enjoy the success of his Company; he died in 1997 after a courageous nine-month battle with cancer—but his vision

In 1992, Rebholtz chaired the Beef Industry Council's promotion committee that named Cybill Shepherd (shown facing him) their official spokeswoman.

lives on in this family-run, employee-focused company.

If someone had given Bob Rebholtz a nickname during his illustrious career, perhaps a good one would have been "the executive cowboy." Rebholtz was as comfortable in boots and a 10-gallon hat as he was in a New York City boardroom. He possessed the ideal combination of professionalism and charisma to help Agri Beef flourish.

"Dad loved being around people," says Rebholtz Jr. "He tried to get others involved in making every aspect of the company and the community better—and he'd get people involved in both the decision-making and the accountability for the decisions." This ease with people was a catalyst for Agri Beef's growth and its impact on Boise.

By 1978, the company had a large enough customer base to pursue further opportunities. It was the strength of Rebholtz's working relationship with MWI Veterinary Supply founder Millard W. Ickes, that cemented the deal, when Agri Beef Co. purchased

MWI in 1981. And it was a solid friendship with Rich Rawlings that helped make PerforMix Nutritional Systems a success when Agri Beef built the company in 1985.

"Soon after my dad was diagnosed with cancer," says Rebholtz Jr., "he talked with us about his long-term goal of making Agri Beef an ag-based, natural-resource type company—very much relationship focused. Whether we were with employees, customers, or outside stakeholders, he wanted us to develop the strongest possible relationships that we could ever build."

Agri Beef has accomplished this goal not just by providing products and services, but by providing products and services in a "fair and honest fashion."

"Those are words my dad continually used: 'fair and honest fashion,'" says Rebholtz Jr. "To him that meant, a) that our products and services are a result of the hard work and dedication of everyone involved in the company, and b) that a handshake is a handshake. If we represent the company to do X, it will do X *plus* something."

Agri Beef Co. today looks a little different than it did in 1978. The

company now consists of five major business segments: feedlots, ranching and breeding, veterinary supply, nutritional supplements, and a growing export business. And Agri Beef is recognized nationally as a leader in each of these industries.

The company is ranked among the top 25 cattle-feeding operations and the top 10 animal-health distribution companies in the country. In 1999, the National Cattlemen's Beef Association named Agri Beef the "Cattle Business of the Century." And, in line with the original force that brought Agri Beef to Boise, the company has the largest AS400 computer system and one of the most sophisticated Internet order-entry systems in the state of Idaho.

Despite its tremendous growth, many Boiseans don't even realize what Agri Beef Co. does. But that's not to say they haven't heard of the company.

"Whenever I tell someone I work at Agri Beef, they say, 'Oh! I've heard that's a great place to work,'" says KayT Matheson, who's been with the company for seven years. "I guess people can't keep quiet about how valued we feel, how much our leaders invest in our individual success, and how empowered we are to really make a difference in this company."

"I see a very bright future for Agri Beef," says Barry Kane, one of the newest leaders in the company. "This company will grow because everyone is having fun and working toward common goals. With this happening, there is no limit to the success we can attain."

One gets the feeling that if the executive cowboy himself were here, that's *exactly* what he'd want to hear.

ALBERTSON'S

Joe Albertson's first inkling of entering the grocery business came when he was still a student at the College of Idaho in the late 1920s. Running short of money, he told his future wife Kathryn McCurry that he was going to leave college and embark on a career with a local Safeway grocery store. "In good times or bad, people have to eat, so I figure it's a good business," he told Kathryn. Six decades later, Joe's original theory continues to hold true, and his company has evolved into the second-largest food and drug store chain in the United States.

Joe's career with Safeway spanned 10 years, and he quickly moved up the ranks until he was supervising more than a dozen stores. But Joe wanted more. He wanted his own store, built to his specifications and managed his way. With $5,000 of his own money and a $7,500 loan from his wife's aunt, Joe formed a partnership with L.S. Skaggs, a former Safeway division manager, and Tom Cuthbert, Mr. Skaggs' accountant. On July 21, 1939, Joe Albertson opened the first Albertson's food center at 16th and State streets in Boise, Idaho. Their operating philosophy was simple: "Give customers the products they want at prices they can afford, with lots of tender, loving care."

Joe's first store was revolutionary for its time. Never before had shoppers been treated to in-store services like a scratch bakery with an automatic doughnut machine. Joe's store also featured one of the first magazine racks in the country. Shoppers plunked down a nickel for homemade, double-dipped ice cream cones called "Big Joe's." They could even eat fresh roasted nuts and hot buttered popcorn while doing their weekly

Joe Albertson, founder.

shopping. The services were a hit, as was Joe's customer service philosophy. Joe personally met as many customers in his first store as he could, and called them by name when they stopped in to shop.

The store's location was also revolutionary. Joe deviated from the traditional main street locations that other grocers had cho-

sen and placed his store in a local neighborhood. Joe's philosophy was that clothes drying on clotheslines and tricycles in driveways were sure indications of people who would need a grocery store close by. That was his method for site selection, and it worked. His customers appreciated being close to home, and the neighborhood Albertson's became the preferred place to shop.

All of the hard work and personalized customer service paid off. The new company earned nearly $10,000 in profits its first year. New stores were opened in neighborhoods in Nampa and Caldwell outside of Boise the following year, and sales topped $1 million in 1941. The expansion of Albertson's had begun.

In 1944, the partnership with Skaggs and Cuthbert was dissolved, and in December 1945, Joe formed Albertson's Corporation. In 1959, 20 years after the

From the products they carry to the interior and exterior decor, Albertson's stores are designed to best meet the needs of the neighborhoods they serve.

Joe Albertson's first store, #101, at 16th and State streets in Boise, Idaho.

first Albertson's store opened, the company had 62 stores and 2,667 employees. That same year, the company went public with its stock. It was a timely move for the company and its investors. The company continued to grow across the country throughout the 1960s, with sales and earnings following suit.

Albertson's stores were opened in neighborhoods in Southern California, the Pacific Northwest, across the Intermountain states, and into the South. By 1964, Albertson's had grown to the 25th largest food and drug retailer in the nation, and it climbed steadily upward throughout the next three decades. It was the fourth-largest food and drug chain in the nation in 1998 when it announced that it would merge with American Stores Company, based in Salt Lake City, UT.

Albertson's and American Stores Company already shared a history. The two entities had crossed paths more than once in the development of the retail food and drug industry. American Stores Company founder Samuel M. Skaggs founded Skaggs Cash Store in 1915, and in 1919 created Skaggs United Stores with four of his sons—the predecessor of today's Safeway, Inc. One of Joe's original partners L.S. Skaggs

was also one of Sam's sons. Sam and six of his sons helped to shape the industry, founding Osco Drug stores and Skaggs Drug Centers. Financial strength and operational excellence into the 1960s paved the way for both Joe and Sam to forge bold paths into the future of the retail supermarket industry, and in 1969 the two formed the first food and drug combination stores in the nation.

Although the partnership was dissolved in 1977, with the shared stores being divided equally, both companies continued to grow. In 1979, Skaggs Drug Centers acquired American Stores Company and the Acme stores under its umbrella, and adopted the American Stores Company name. Albertson's continued to build new stores through the 1980s and 1990s, and American Stores Company grew through acquisitions of Sav-on Drugs, Jewel Companies, and Lucky Stores. The partnership between Albertson's and American Stores Company was renewed when the merger between the two companies was approved in June 1999, creating the second-largest food and drug company in the nation.

Joe's original philosophy still holds true today at the more than 2,500 stores in Albertson's, Inc. Divided among eight operating regions, the company employs more than 235,000 associates, making it one of the largest employers in the United States.

Albertson's prides itself on being a good corporate neighbor, and focuses its corporate giving efforts on three critical areas: hunger relief, education and development of youth, and health and nutrition.

In 1999, the Company contributed over $48 million in cash and in-kind donations to help meet the needs of the communities in which their stores are located. The Albertson family has also given back to the Boise community; they donated 41 acres of land along the Boise River below their home for a peaceful walking park. Kathryn Albertson Park is maintained as a natural environment and bird sanctuary. The J.A. and Kathryn Albertson Foundation has also made significant contributions to Idaho education, donating millions of dollars.

It's been said of Joe Albertson that he did a common thing uncommonly well. Joe himself said that one man is limited in what he can accomplish as an individual. His contribution to the retail industry and Idaho prove that it only takes one man to do great things. The organization that bears his name continues to thrive today, and much of Albertson's current success lies with his standard philosophy--providing people with the products they need at prices they can afford, with lots of tender, loving care.

From 1969 through 1977, Sam Skaggs and Joe Albertson partnered to form the first combination food and drug stores in the United States.

AMERICAN ECOLOGY CORPORATION

American Ecology Corporation is one of the nation's premier providers of safe, environmentally sound services for hazardous and low-level radioactive waste treatment and disposal. Local legend Jack Lemley, American Ecology's chairman and chief executive officer, played a key role in bringing it to Boise.

Having managed mega-construction projects on every continent, Lemley is a true international manager—someone who's equally at home building mines in the jungles of New Guinea as he is negotiating with bank officials in a Paris board room.

Lemley capped an impressive construction management career in 1989 when he became chief executive officer of Transmanche-Link, the British and French company that built the Channel Tunnel, to date the world's most logistically difficult and expensive construction project. For that, Lemley was made an Honorary Commander of the Order of the British Empire.

But for all his renown, Lemley is a down-to-earth son of Idaho, committed to living in its capital. How American Ecology became a successful part of Boise's dynamic

American Ecology laboratory personnel analyze waste to verify requirements are met.

Jack and Pam Lemley at American Ecology's first location in Boise.

business landscape was less predictable. In 1995, just as the Chunnel project was winding down, Lemley agreed to join the board of a then Texas-based firm that was hemorrhaging red ink.

For decades, American Ecology had successfully operated major facilities in Texas, Nevada and Washington State. A facility in Tennessee later joined the fold. When Lemley joined the board, however, the company's financial condition was so poor that experts recommended shutting it down. Fortunately, the board chose a better solution. Management asked Lemley to become chairman and CEO. Lemley agreed, so long as he could move the company's headquarters to his beloved Boise.

Brought up in Coeur d'Alene, Lemley earned a degree from the University of Idaho in 1960 and em-

barked on a construction career. A decade rising through senior management ranks at Morrison-Knudsen Co. allowed him to cut his teeth internationally. Lemley's career there included rescuing the King Khalid Military City Project, a $1.3 billion project to build a city for 70,000 in Saudi Arabia. He also supervised an $800 million mine development in Papua, New Guinea, and a $1.9 billion mine, railroad and port facility in Columbia. These complex projects prepared Lemley for the challenges he'd face with his latest turnaround.

American Ecology's origins date back to 1952, when a predecessor company opened to manage radioactive materials for the U.S. government. Over the years, the company grew steadily by serving both government and industry. In 1962, it opened the nation's first disposal facility for low-level radioactive waste in Beatty, Nevada, and in 1964, opened a second site on the U.S. Department of Energy Hanford Reservation. American Ecology operates at both sites today. Expansion into other states followed.

Profitable for many years, American Ecology ran into trouble in 1993 after a Texas-based management group assumed control and made a series of ill-advised acquisitions. When Lemley took over, the company was in dire straights. Lemley quickly cut costs and moved corporate headquarters to Boise. At first the turnaround team operated out of a trailer parked in the driveway of Lemley and Associates consulting in the historic Hyde Park neighborhood. American Ecology later moved into more comfortable space at the J.R. Simplot Co.'s former offices in the Boise National Bank Building,

Placement of the Trojan Nuclear Power Plant Reactor Vessel in a disposal trench at the Richland, Washington disposal facility. The vessel is positioned for permanent burial with an overhead crane and mobile platform.

a downtown landmark on the National Historic Register.

A revitalized American Ecology next focused on shedding unprofitable operations and streamlining the remaining, profitable businesses. And Lemley re-negotiated a large bank debt that had tied the company in financial knots, turning the obligation into stock purchase warrants and a financial stake in one of the company's business development projects.

Four years later, the effort paid off. American Ecology was back in the black by 1999, reporting a profit of $4.4 million on revenues of $34 million. The future is again bright, with a seasoned, experienced management team and an optimistic growth outlook.

American Ecology is actively marketing its services and keeping the investment community informed via its Internet site at www.americanecology.com.

American Ecology, through its US Ecology subsidiary, has safely managed more than 100 million-plus cubic feet of low-level radioactive, hazardous and PCB waste. It is well positioned to take advantage of new opportunities and society's emerging waste management needs for decades to come. Here's a snapshot of its environmentally protective operations and services:

Richland, Washington: This desert site—one of only two full-service, low-level radioactive waste disposal facilities in the nation— has been operating safely since 1965. It has more than 40 million cubic feet of unused disposal capacity, sufficient to safely handle large quantities of waste well into this century.

Oak Ridge, Tennessee: Here the company employs multiple processing techniques to reduce the amount of radioactive materials requiring land disposal. Skilled workers also refurbish and rebuild large nuclear power plant motors and other expensive equipment for re-use.

Beatty, Nevada: Hazardous, PCB and other industrial waste are treated and disposed at this geologically superior desert site.

Robstown, Texas: Located along the Gulf Coast industrial belt, this site treats and disposes of hazardous wastes from chemical and agricultural companies. In 2000, the company successfully opened a municipal waste landfill adjacent to its existing operations.

American Ecology also performs environmental clean-up services nationwide, using trained professionals based at its operating sites.

Publicly traded on the NASDAQ exchange, the company's stock symbol is ECOL.

US Ecology workers seal and cap Engineered Concrete Barriers within a low-level radioactive waste disposal trench at American Ecology Richland, Washington site.

BOGUS BASIN SKI RESORT

Bogus Basin is one of few, successful non-profit ski resorts in the nation. It got its humble start in the late 1930s when a group of hearty individuals realized their dreams of a ski hill above Boise. Many of them worked by hand, clearing brush and timber to cut out the first of the resort's 49 runs. They named Bogus Basin after the fool's gold that was found in the hills below Deer Point. Many old-timers will give a wink and a nod as they embellish the lore of "Jughead Jake" and "Pan Handle Pete." Legend has it, the two used the fool's gold to "whoop it up" in the valley, and then left town before their secret was learned, leaving many Boise businessmen nothing to show for it except "bogus gold."

These days, there is a bounty of treasures at Bogus Basin. The year-round resort is located just 16 miles from downtown Boise. It caters to more than 300,000 skiers and snowboarders each winter season. During summer months, Bogus is host to concerts, weddings and reunions.

In 1998 Bogus Basin created a buying frenzy for winter recreationists. Management and the Board of Directors decided to slash prices on season passes. Families and individuals came in droves to purchase the deeply discounted passes. At $199 for a regular pass, $29 for a child's pass (age 7-11) and $800 for a family pass, Boise was turned into a ski town! Bogus Basin issued more than 25,000 passes for the 1998–99 season. No other ski resort in the country had ever done such a thing. Many skeptics waited for the other shoe to drop—but it didn't. The 1998-99 season went off without a hitch. In fact, Mother Nature helped out by delivering one of the biggest snow years in Bogus Basin's history. Bogus Basin continues to offer ultra affordable season passes so that everyone can enjoy "The Best Local Ski Resort in the Country."

The area's development all started in 1938, when a 24-month WPA road project "paved the way" for the development of Bogus Basin as a recreation site. A handful of Forest Service experts were called in, including Alf Engen, founder of the Alta Ski Area in Utah and Corrie Engen, of Brundage Mountain in McCall, both of whom played major roles in site selection and early run design. Three years later, in October 1941, the non-profit Bogus Basin Recreational Association (BBRA) was incorporated to raise funds and oversee the maintenance of the ski area. An all-volunteer Board of Directors was formed. The Board was chosen from the Association, which was made up of members of the community. The Bogus Basin Ski Club sold $25 memberships and put up the first rope tow in the Bogus Creek Area. However, the official opening of the area was postponed as priorities changed on December 7,1941, with the start of World War II.

On December 20, 1942, a 500-foot rope tow opened for public use. The National Ski Patrol was also established as Bogus Basin opened. In 1946, the T-Bar surface lift was installed with help from the Morrison-Knudsen Co. Kingcliffe Corporation owned the T-Bar. The company leased the rope tows to the Ski Club.

Several years later, in 1953, The Kingcliffe Co. experienced financial difficulties. J.R Simplot stepped in to purchase the lifts. Simplot later sold back the lifts to the BBRA for $1. The BBRA hired William "Coach" Everts as the volunteer general manager of the weekend ski area. Everts also directed the Boise City Recreation Department.

Early Bogus Basin skiers wait in line at the Poma Lift.

Bogus Basin, 1948.

In 1957, the Poma surface lifts were installed, easing the 45-minute lift lines at the popular ski resort. The next season, in 1958, Bogus Basin made the jump to a seven-day a week operation. General manager Bill Everts stepped down to serve on the Board of Directors, which he did for 30 years and Robert Loughrey was hired as general manager. By 1959, the Deer Point Chairlift was constructed.

During the early-to-mid 1960s the Bogus Basin road was improved and paved, construction of the Bogus Creek Lodge completed, the longest illuminated ski slope in the world installed and the Shafer Butte skiing complex developed. The Superior Chairlift and the Morning Star Chairlift were also constructed.

In the 1970s the resort continued its fast-paced growth with the Showcase Chairlift replacing the upper Poma lift. In 1973 skiers watched the development of the Pioneer Area, which included a new lodge, parking, the Pioneer Condominiums and a new chairlift

serving the Bitterroot Basin. Three years later, installation of the Pine Creek chairlift opened up additional advanced terrain on the "backside" of the mountain.

"High tech" was the buzz word in 1981 when the Deer Point Lift was replaced by a "state of the art" YAN chairlift. Skiers enjoyed a smoother, faster ride to the top of the mountain. In 1984, Robert Loughrey retired and Terry Lofsvold was selected as the general manager. Two years later the Bogus Basin Nordic Facility was constructed with a trailhead warming hut and 17 kilometers of trail.

The 1990s saw even more changes for Bogus Basin. In 1991, the Bogus Creek Lodge was upgraded and expanded. Michael Shirley was appointed as general manager when Terry Lofsvold retired. In 1994, the resort celebrated the completion of an extensive 20-year Resort Area Master Development Plan. Two years later, the new Master Plan and Environmental Assessment was approved by the U.S. Forest Service. Implementation of the new master plan began, which included a high-speed detachable quad chairlift to replace the Deer Point double chairlift, while crews constructed a new beginner facility and chairlift called "The Coach," as a tribute to Bill Everts.

In February 1998, management announced the new season pass pricing program. Bogus Basin Road was resurfaced and paved in its entirety. The Showcase Yurt was constructed. The final year of the century witnessed the construction of a new, high speed, detachable quad chairlift which replaced the Pine Creek double chairlift. The Morningstar lift was converted from a double to a triple chairlift. Frontier Point Nordic Lodge was constructed. The $199 season pass sale continued with more than 25,000 sold.

In 2000, Idaho Power and Bogus Basin installed an additional power source to the mountain, enabling Bogus Basin to continue improvements planned for the mountain. In the coming years, contingent upon skier visits and continued success with the season pass pricing, there will be more changes on the mountain. The new projects include: a new, high speed lift directly to the top of Shafer Butte, conversion of other lifts to high speed quads, continued improvements to terrain and lodges and plans to improve snowmaking abilities.

The rich history of Bogus Basin proves that everyone had a stake in the resort's success. That is still true today. That is why every dollar of cash flow generated in operations goes into improvements on the mountain. As Michael Shirley says, "Please enjoy your resort and we'll see you during our season pass sale!"

BOISE SAMARITAN VILLAGE HEALTHCARE AND REHABILITATION CENTER

The Collister area of northwest Boise has a rich and diverse history bound together by three perpetual strands: place, persons and capacity to care. This area, the location of Boise Samaritan Village, was once the center of the Collister area's growth, due to the life activities and philanthropic interests of Dr. and Mrs. George Collister. The Collisters' 160 acres, five miles from Boise, were planted with 11,000 fruit trees, including some of the first peach orchards in the Treasure Valley. There they built a 20-room mansion in 1912 referred to as Collister Station, located on the interurban railroad. A Boise physician for 54 years, Dr. Collister helped establish St. Alphonsus Hospital, was physician at the state penitentiary, and experienced success in treating Rocky Mountain Spotted Fever. He pursued exhaustive civic and social interests and responsibilities, including two terms on the city council and membership in the Elks Lodge. Dr. and Mrs. Collister helped build two churches near their home, which are still in use today. They also provided the land for Collister Elementary School and Dr. Collister was instrumental in its development and design. On his birthday, a few days before his death in 1935, many Collister School children carried flowers to

Boise Samaritan Village Healthcare and Rehabilitaion Center.

Collister Mansion.

Dr. Collister's patient room at St. Alphonsus.

The Collisters' legacy of service was revitalized in 1947 when the Collister mansion was acquired and named the Idaho Elks Convalescent Home for Children, treating polio patients during the epidemic in Idaho, as local hospitals overflowed. Ten years later the program had grown to provide regional rehabilitation services, which required a larger facility. One was built and occupied in 1957 at its location off of Fort Street in Boise. Recently a new facility was constructed, and it continues as the Idaho Elks Rehabilitation Hospital today.

Vacant, the mansion was again acquired for community service later in 1957. The Association of Lutheran Churches remodeled the facility to accommodate 16 elderly residents and named the facility Boise Lutheran Sunset Home. Only months after its opening, the Association of Lutheran Churches contacted the Evangelical Lutheran Good Samaritan Society to assist with the facility's operation. The Good Samaritan Society, a Christian non-profit organization located in Sioux Falls, South Dakota, was becoming well-known nationally as innovative in healthcare for elderly and disabled persons. August Hoeger, founder and then president of the Good Samaritan Society, met with the Association to develop a new relationship.

Under new management the facility grew to serve 29 people and after several months it was decided that The Good Samaritan Society should own and manage the facility. Eight nurses, several nursing aides and a kitchen staff assisted the residents in their new home. The newly-arranged organization was named Boise Valley Sunset Home. The program was guided by the following mission statement: "We endeavor in every way to

Relationships: Sam and Marci sharing a moment.

provide for the total care of each resident in our center, based on the individual needs of each. One of our greatest aims is to give all of our residents a chance to maintain or regain their individual dignity by an effective rehabilitation program...We want our center to be a place where people are truly living."

The Christian orientation and guiding vision of the Good Samaritan Society expressed in its motto, "In Christ's Love Everyone Is Someone," provided the leadership of Boise Valley Sunset Home the vision to change with the needs of Boise's elderly and disabled people. Over the next 42 years community volunteers served on the Advisory Board to the Village providing valuable insight into community needs. Changing has included many "firsts." In 1970 Boise Valley Sunset Home was the first skilled nursing facility to designate a portion of its facility to accommodate young disabled

people in a then new wing. An organization of disabled persons interested in independence grew from this living community and was named The Idaho Association of Physically Handicapped Adults. The group was active in the Idaho legislature regarding disability issues and for 20 years operated a small, community transit service from the facility, serving residents of the Healthcare Center and the community. Sam's Day Care Center, established in 1979, was the first day care in a nursing home, in the state. The dental program developed in 1988 with Dr. Clay Wilcox, was the first, and only, on-site dental program in a nursing home in the state.

Boise Valley Sunset Home changed its named to Boise Samaritan Village in 1983 with the addition of two 50-unit apartment buildings for independent, low income, elderly people. The buildings, called Samaritan Village Apartments and funded through HUD, were constructed to satisfy a growing need in the community for affordable housing. The nursing home/healthcare and rehabilitation center had grown to accommodate over 200 people, and was reorganized into distinct levels of care with specialized staff meeting the specific needs of the residents on their unit. Specialties were Alzheimer's Disease, the young adult population, post-hospital/ subacute care and degrees of care to elderly people with chronic illnesses or disabilities. In 1988 another facility was added, The Cottage, an assisted living facility serving young disabled people in a more independent environment. On opening day of the Cottage seven young people were able to move from Healthcare and Rehabilitation Center to The Cottage.

The Village was now a campus of facilities situated where the Collister Mansion and orchards had been.

Three extensive construction and remodeling projects over the past 17 years have refreshed and modernized Boise Samaritan Village. The need for change continues as the facility creates more private space for residents and extends its brain injury program into the community. In 1999, four young brain- injured men moved from the Healthcare Center to their own apartments in the community, where the Center continues to provide support services. Expanding the music therapy program and adding massage therapy and reflexology are the newest changes to complement healthcare. The place, the people and the capacity to care continue to yield to the needs of people in this community.

Music therapy: Dean enjoying bell-choir.

BOISE STATE UNIVERSITY

Economically, the depths of the Great Depression may have been the worst of times to begin a venture in higher education. But to Idaho Episcopal bishop Middleton Barnwell, it was a time of opportunity, for he believed that a good education made even the poorest person rich in spirit. So, in September 1932, Barnwell opened Boise Junior College at St. Margaret's Hall, previously a girls' school the church had operated since 1892. The college began with 70 students and eight full-time faculty members.

The bishop would be stunned to see how the tiny junior college has evolved into Idaho's largest institution of higher education. Today's Boise State is a major, metropolitan university serving the region through an array of academic and technical programs and services. Located in Idaho's dynamic capital city and in the midst of an unsurpassed natural environment, Boise State is a place where students receive a "real education for the real world."

Barnwell founded the junior college to provide a low-cost option where Depression-strapped local students could attend college. The community quickly embraced the school. The Boise Chamber of Commerce provided financial assistance and helped form a nonprofit corporation to govern the college. In 1934, Boise Junior College was officially incorporated with a seven-member board of trustees. Five years later, Boiseans voted to create the Boise Junior College District, putting the school on a more solid foundation of revenue from property and liquor taxes.

The growing school needed more room, so in 1940 the trustees relocated the campus across

This early 1940s photograph is of the campus of Boise Junior College.

the Boise River to the site of the abandoned Boise Municipal Airport. At the center of the otherwise vacant campus was the brand-new red brick administration building, which for years contained most classrooms, offices, and the library for the junior college.

Almost closing during World War II, the school rebounded when students returned to campus in record numbers after the war. The campus skyline changed dramatically throughout the 1950s and 1960s as citizens of Boise supported bond issues to construct several new buildings. In 1956, enrollment topped 1,000 for the first time.

By the early 1960s the demands for education in the growing region had outstripped the resources of the junior college.

It was time for a four-year college in Idaho's largest city. In 1965 Boise Junior College became Boise College and offered bachelor's degrees for the first time. Enrollment jumped 40 percent, straining the school as it struggled to upgrade its faculty, curricula, library and buildings.

In 1969, Boise College joined the state system of higher education as Boise State College. Only five years removed from junior college status, Boise State had become a state-supported school with statewide responsibilities.

Enrollments increased at a heavy pace during the 1970s. Under state support, new academic programs were added, more faculty were hired, and the campus family of buildings continued to grow.

Recognizing the school's new status, in 1974 the Idaho Legislature changed the name of the institution to Boise State University.

In the 1980s Boise State University continued to expand, with the addition of several master's degree programs, a public radio station and the construction of two major buildings in partnership with the community, The Pavilion in 1982 and the Velma V. Morrison Center for the Performing Arts in 1984.

The 1990s was another decade of change. The University offered its first doctorate degrees, added a College of Engineering to meet the needs of the region's technology-based industries, became a member of the Big West and later the Western Athletic conferences, laid the groundwork for a satellite campus—Boise State West in Canyon County—and became the first university in Idaho to top the 16,000 enrollment mark.

Boise State offers its students many unique educational opportunities because of its setting in the governmental and commercial heart of Idaho. The University works closely with businesses, health-care institutions, schools and government agencies in the Treasure Valley to provide "real world" internships and work experience for students. Boise State also has the largest evening and summer session programs in the state.

The University meets the needs of the region through a "distributed campus" that provides courses at a variety of locations using a variety of technologies. More than 16,000 full- and part-time students attend Boise State, and another 30,000 people are served through non-credit courses, workshops and other programs. Each year the University opens its doors to 800,000 people who attend concerts, athletic events, lectures and other cultural and entertainment events.

Boise State offers more than 200 major fields of interest, with 91 baccalaureate, 36 master's, two doctorate, six associate degrees and 26 technical certificate programs.

Boise State is accredited by the Northwest Association of Schools and Colleges. Programs in engineering, education, business, nursing, chemistry, music, respiratory therapy, theatre arts, social work, dental assisting and construction management, among many others, are also nationally accredited.

The University's 154-acre campus includes more than 60 buildings. Boise State facilities include the Special Events Center (capacity 435); the Grace Jordan Ballroom in the Student Union (1,000); Bronco Stadium (30,000); The Pavilion (12,380); the Centennial Amphitheatre (800) and the Morrison Center (2,000).

To prepare for the future, the University has recently added two new engineering buildings, a parking structure, new athletic facilities and a student recreation center. In addition, it is drafting plans for Boise State West, a satellite campus in Canyon County.

As Idaho's metropolitan university, Boise State offers students a blend of cultural, recreational, social, and educational opportunities not found elsewhere in the state. Its traditions of academic excellence and community service, along with an enthusiastic faith in the future, make Boise State University one of the West's most dynamic institutions of higher learning.

The campus of Boise State Univesity today.

DAVIES AND ROURKE ADVERTISING

Davies & Rourke Advertising, Inc. officially opened its doors in 1973, in order to serve the communication needs of businesses in Idaho and the Pacific Northwest. But the roots of what today is still one of Idaho's most respected advertising agencies go much deeper.

In 1953, John Givens and Kenneth R. Davies teamed up to form Givens-Davies Advertising Agency, Inc., serving clients from offices in the Yates Building in Boise, Idaho.

John Givens was educated in journalism, political science, and economics at Boise Junior College, St. Olaf's College, the University of Washington and the University of Idaho. He changed to a career in advertising after a half decade of working in retail sales and promotion.

Ken Davies was schooled in advertising and business administration at the University of Oregon and co-founded the agency after working for three and a half years with the *Idaho Statesman* daily newspaper and radio station KBOI in Boise. Davies was an accomplished musician and composer, which made his decision to seek a career in advertising all the more noteworthy. Fresh out of military service, he was earning his way through Boise Junior College arranging music and playing piano at area clubs. While playing one evening at a rowdy Boise nightclub, a beer bottle hit his piano, and he immediately turned to advertising as his new career.

Givens and Davies promoted their agency on the ability to provide a variety of marketing approaches to meet the needs of a growing, competitive market. Early agency sales literature called advertising "the power tool of marketing and most effective

when based on sound motivational research and sparked with a variety of creative approaches that go right to the target."

This positioning strategy worked. Within a few years, the staff grew to almost two dozen and the agency had secured a number of prime advertising accounts. In 1959, the company moved to new, larger offices in the Columbia Building on Washington Street in Boise. Givens and Davies provided advertising services to the area's first television station, NBC affiliate KTVB-TV; Bank of Idaho, the state's largest financial institution at the time; rapidly expanding Intermountain Gas Company; and fast-growing timber and wood products giant Boise Cascade Corporation. Of particular note—Givens-Davies was the first agency to provide advertising services to Joe Albertson as he established the foundation for Albertson's supermarket chain.

Ken Davies oversees film-editing project in the 1950s

Ken Davies (left) and Mike Rourke formed Davies & Rourke Advertising, Inc. in 1973.

After 20 years working shoulder to shoulder building Idaho's most powerful and best-known advertising agency, differences in business and financial philosophies between the principals prompted a breakup of the company. Givens left to form John Givens Advertising, taking the Bank of Idaho as a primary client. At the same time, Ken Davies enticed Boise Cascade communications director Michael Rourke to join him as an advertising agency partner. In 1973, Davies & Rourke Advertising was officially incorporated. The new company opened its doors with an impressive client roster including Boise Cascade, Albertson's Supermarkets, Home Federal Savings, KTVB Television, and Intermountain Gas Company.

Prior to his partnership with Davies, Mike Rourke had 12 years of advertising and public relations experience with Boise Cascade and Weyerhaeuser companies, as well as two years working with A.C. Nielsen Market Research Company in Chicago.

As the country prospered, sales competition increased as expanding companies recognized the need for solid marketing and advertising programs. Over the next several years, Davies & Rourke continued to expand its services to a growing

John Givens, original partner, in 1950s.

list of clients. The company had long since earned a reputation as the premier advertising agency in the region.

With growth came change. In the 1970s, the country's business was booming. Albertson's, the agency's largest client, was rapidly expanding through the purchase of supermarket chains in California, Texas, and Florida. Ironically, while Albertson's was looking to a national advertising agency to serve its growing media buying needs, eastern-based Atlantic & Pacific supermarket chain was recruiting Albertson's chairman, president, and key executives to move East and breathe new life into a floundering A&P supermarket chain. As Davies & Rourke's account supervisor for Albertson's advertising programs, Rourke's talents and expertise were well recognized, and he resigned from the agency to be a part of the new A&P management team in Montvale, New Jersey.

During this same period, Bob Hofmann left his position as a vice president of Gillham Advertising in Salt Lake City to return to Idaho and joined the account services team at Davies & Rourke. A native Idahoan, Hofmann attended the University of Idaho and worked with Boise communications com-

panies Henry G. Curtis Public Relations and L. E. Johnson and Associates before joining Gillham Advertising in 1970.

Because the Albertson's account was shifting to national media buying agencies, Davies & Rourke was in a period of downsizing. Ken Davies turned to Hofmann to help bring stability and fiscal responsibility to the company. It was 1977 when Davies and Hofmann formed a new partnership to re-engineer Davies & Rourke Advertising as the leader in their marketplace.

Through a combination of realistic marketing and sales strategies, innovative creative campaigns, and special attention to client service, Davies & Rourke Advertising opened a new chapter in its long history. To help serve the company's continued expansion, in 1981 Jeffrey Nielsen joined the Davies & Rourke account service team. Following graduation from the University of Iowa, Nielsen moved to Salt Lake City where he worked for KUTV Television and held several corporate advertising positions with Utah-based companies. His talents and contributions to Davies &

Davies & Rourke moved to its newly constructed offices in Boise's Lake Harbor area in December 1998. Receptionist Carrie Henley discusses the day's project list with partners Jeff Nielsen (left) and Bob Hofmann.

Agency office site built in 1973 at 16th and Franklin in Boise.

Rourke were soon apparent, and he accepted an ownership position and was named vice president of the agency in 1982.

With his management transition team in place, Ken Davies was just days from retirement from the agency when he was diagnosed with cancer in 1990. Advertising lost an icon when Ken Davies passed away in June 1991.

In 1992, the agency moved to new quarters in southeast Boise's River Run Business Complex. The agency was rapidly refining its cyber-based communications capabilities, and Ernie Monroe moved to Boise from Milwaukee to serve as creative director for the agency in 1994.

Davies & Rourke continued to attract new clients who recognize the value of solid market strategies and an innovative creative product. To better serve its clientele, in 1999 the agency constructed a new building in northwest Boise's Lake Harbor Business Park, which was specially designed to serve the communications needs of Davies & Rourke's clientele.

With roots close to 50 years old, Davies & Rourke Advertising continues to meet the challenges of the communications revolution and is poised and ready to tackle the next generation's advertising needs.

DEBEST PLUMBING

One of seven children abandoned by his parents, Milford Terrell learned about challenge early in life. Living in the Children's Home in Boise, then being adopted, but separated from his siblings and moving from one family member's home to another, Milford's will to succeed and strong work ethic were born. Given a chance, Milford believes anyone can and will succeed.

In 1973, with a $1,000 loan, the purchase of a used van and a desire, Milford Terrell began DeBest Plumbing. Working from his garage, he had one part time employee and serviced four building contractors. Twenty-three years later, situated on three acres, with a fleet of trucks and 72 employees, DeBest reflects on many challenges turned to successes.

A major economic downturn occurring in Boise from 1979-1983 prompted DeBest Plumbing to accept new challenges. Rather than focusing on problems, Milford Terrell saw a change to diversify. He began doing small commercial jobs. Primarily a residential plumbing company until then, Milford expanded into government work at Mountain Home Air Force Base. The small

commercial jobs provided opportunities for personal and professional growth and education, good preparation for things to come.

Economic downturns don't last forever. Each job gave DeBest a foundation and reputation that would be the basis for handling the economic upturn. When Boise was ready to begin building in a big way, DeBest Plumbing was ready. Two major projects, The Boise Convention Center and Boise Town Square Mall, put DeBest Plumbing on the map in 1987. With these two major projects under its belt, DeBest Plumbing became one of the largest plumbing contractors in the State of Idaho.

Improving economic conditions between 1987 and the present, and the recent diversification within the company, presented new challenges. Now a growing company, the need for dedicated, qualified workers became a top priority. To keep and attract this work force, DeBest implemented many additional employee ben-

efits. These weren't being offered by most other mechanical and plumbing contractors. Employees and their families now enjoy health and dental insurance and a retirement package as well as a savings program. Mental health and substance abuse programs, financial planning seminars, weekly safety meetings, and quality circle management meetings all add to the productivity of employees today. DeBest Plumbing participates in federally- approved apprenticeship training as well as supporting its employees through the four-year licensing process to become a state-licensed journeyman plumber.

Increased government regulations and more competition in the marketplace necessitated better tracking of jobs. Computers were added to aid with the bidding process, job costing, accounting procedures, and correspondence. A state-of-the-art computer system tracks jobs from bidding to completion.

In 1993, Milford diversified his

business interest even further by opening a fire protection business. DeBest Fire Protection has been awarded contracts for some of the largest projects in the Boise area and the State of Idaho.

A service department was established in 1988, ensuring that there is always someone available to answer questions and handle problems as they arise.

The greatest competitive edge remains high quality work and service to customers. Employees are encouraged to maintain the "DeBest attitude." Offering the best service to customers, the best products, the best efficiency and the best price, DeBest Plumbing holds fast to the belief of treating people fairly and equally while getting the job done. Long-time employees Rick Garrett, Joe Carleton, and Lynn Healy contribute to the ongoing quality of service, with each having devoted 26 years of service to the company. Believing strongly that, "you're only as good as the people who surround you," Milford Terrell

credits DeBest's success to a great accountant, positive relationship with the bank, bright and dedicated employees, and the Lord working in great and mysterious ways!

Milford Terrell believes in giving back to his community. Milford's many civic-minded pursuits include serving as president of the Boise State University's Bronco Athletic Association; chairman of the Humanitarian Bowl; member of the Mayor's Code Committee; chairman of the State Plumbing Board; vice-chairman of the Western Idaho Fair Board; vice-chairman of the Garden City Planning and Zoning Committee; state leader for Idaho Conference of Seventh-day Adventists Pathfinders youth organization; and chairman of Camp Ida-Haven Governing Committee; serving on the White House Conference for Small Business; being a member of the Epilepsy League; being a long time member of the Boise Chamber of Commerce; and being a supporter of the Boise River Festival. His most recent awards include 1995 Small Business Person of the Year, the 1999 Blue Chip Enterprise Award for Small Business, Small Business Man of the Year for the State of Idaho, Associate of the Year from the Building Contractors, National Society of Fund Raising Executives Award, and the BSU Athletic Association Bronze Bronco.

Milford Terrell is well-known in his community for his philanthropy. Not one to just give "lip service" to his favorite causes, Milford puts his "money where his mouth is," by financially supporting at least 15 charitable or civic organizations on a regular basis. Milford's success can truly be measured by the opportunities he has given others, as much as by his own achievements.

Milford Terrell, founder of DeBest Plumbing.

COSHO, HUMPHREY, GREENER & WELSH, P.A.

Cosho, Humphrey, Greener & Welsh, P.A., today a 45-person law firm, has a long history in Boise, Idaho. The firm's 17 lawyers make it a medium-sized firm for this city, and the practice has evolved with the fast changing business and economic climate of Idaho. Today, the firm counts among its clients Boise Cascade, a stalwart of the state's timber industry; Micron Technology, the state's largest private employer; and numerous other high-tech businesses. The firm also continues to represent numerous other private and public entities, both in complex transactional work and before a myriad of federal, state and local agencies and every court. The firm's core practice area continues to be civil trial and appellate work in a wide variety of fields. Because of the particular history and varied talents of its lawyers, the firm regularly litigates on behalf of plaintiffs and defendants—this so in recognition of the principle that the experience as plaintiff's lawyers greatly enhances the effectiveness and strategy utilized as defense attorneys. Particular areas of the law most often reflected in the firm's practice are business, real estate, bankruptcy, estate planning and family law.

The firm began when Louis H. Cosho and Howard Humphrey formed the partnership of Cosho and Humphrey in 1961, later joined by R. Michael Southcombe. The firm's other branch is Clemons, Skiles and Green, which began in 1963. In 1964, the firm relocated to and became one of the first tenants in the state's first "skyscraper," the Bank of Idaho building.

In 1972, Cosho, Humphrey and Southcombe merged with Clemons,

Skiles and Green and became Clemons, Cosho, Humphrey and Samuelsen. In 1976, Stanley W. Welsh joined the firm, and in 1977, Richard H. Greener and Fredric V. Shoemaker also joined. In the tradition of its founders, the hard work and talents of these lawyers continue to drive the firm today. These and other members of Cosho, Humphrey, Greener & Welsh, P.A. are recognized leaders in their legal specialties. In addition, the firm's members are regular contributors to their profession and serve the civic interests of the Boise community. Both Howard Humphrey and Lou Cosho were presidents of the Idaho State Bar.

Typifying the tradition and history of the firm, its shareholders formed a partnership to purchase the historic Carnegie Library Building. The building, now on the National Historic Registry, was the result of the collaborative effort of Boise City, the Columbian Club and the Boise School Board, which donated the site.

The Carnegie Building, August 2000.

The building was completed in 1905, the same year construction began on the State Capitol Building located on the adjoining block and designed by the same architect. The Carnegie Building served as the capitol city's public library for 68 years.

Cosho, Humphrey, Greener and Welsh, P.A. spent a year-and-a-half renovating and remodeling the premises to suit the firm's needs, and took occupancy of the Carnegie Building on January 24, 1987. A portion of the lower level was rented to another firm for several years until Cosho, Humphrey growth required the entire building.

Today, Cosho, Humphrey, Greener & Welsh, P.A., firmly rooted in the community's history and mindful of the heritage of its founders and the building it occupies, looks to Boise's future in its delivery of top-notch legal services.

EMPLOYERS RESOURCE MANAGEMENT COMPANY

Employers Resource Management Company is America's administrative employer, providing service to hundreds of small and mid-sized business owners across the country. Headquartered in Boise, Idaho Employers Resource ranks among the top 25 employee leasing companies in the United States, serving over 800 businesses and 10,000 co-employees. The family owned business has co-employees in all 50 states.

Mr. George Gersema, CEO, states, "Administrative employment enables a company to "unload the routine human resource operations that have nothing to do with their primary focus." Essentially, the client divides and shares the responsibilities of being an employer with Employers Resource. Employers Resource helps with governmental compliance, handles human resource issues, manages every aspect of workers compensation, and provides companies with expanded and enhanced health insurance and employee benefits. In addition, the company assists in fairly resolving employee complaints without the threat of lawsuits.

Since its creation in October 1985, Employers Resource has been on the cutting edge of the employee leasing industry. Started by George Gersema, his wife Mary, brother Duke and Mr. Ray O'Leary, the company helped pioneer the operations design of employee leasing. As the first employment leasing company to operate in all 50 states, Employers Resource set the pace for the industry. Employers Resource was first in the industry to embrace the co-employment concept. Its mediation and arbitration services and its innovative medical savings account programs broke new

George Gersema - CEO.

ground in the employee leasing industry.

Employers Resource opened its first offices in Concord, California and Richmond, Virginia. Two years later, in 1987, the Garden Grove California office opened. In that same year, Employers Resource reached the "1,000th employee" mark. The company grew quickly, opening the Boise, Idaho and Dallas, Texas offices in 1988. The company headquarters moved to the Boise location shortly thereafter. Offices in Indianapolis, Maryland and Florida opened in 1989,1990, and 1991, respectively. In December 1991, *Inc.* magazine listed Employers Resource as the 26th fastest-growing private company in the United States.

Employers Resource continued to grow, offering clients solutions

Mary Gersema–COO.

Douglas "Duke" Gersema, executive vice president.

to a variety of human resource problems. In 1997, Employers Resource was honored as part of the "Idaho Private 75," listed as the 15th largest private company in the State of Idaho. The company has been ranked in the "Idaho Private 75" each year since.

A dedicated staff with a clear vision of the company's future promises continued growth. With innovation as its hallmark and excellence in customer service its standard, the company promises to be a national trendsetter in the employee leasing industry well into the future.

Born and raised in Idaho, Mr. George Gersema attended William and Mary College in Williamsburg, Virginia, earning bachelor's degrees in both business and economics. Nationally-recognized for his achievements and contributions to the employee leasing industry, Mr. Gersema has

served in many leadership positions. He presently chairs the National Association for Alternative Staffing (NAAS) National Affairs Committee and is the immediate past president of the organization. Mr. Gersema has published numerous articles for industry trade journals and frequently serves as spokesperson for NAAS.

Mr. Ray M. O'Leary serves as president of Employers Resource. Mr. O'Leary received both his B.S. and M.B.A from the College of William and Mary in Williamsburg. With over 20 years of entrepreneurial experience, Mr. O'Leary has served in numerous functions in the administrative employee industry. He has served on the National Affairs Committee of the Nation Association for Alternative Staffing (NAAS). Within Employers Resource, Mr. O'Leary is responsible for providing management expertise to local offices; management projects and corporate

development; and overseeing sales efforts.

Mr. Douglas Gersema serves as the executive vice president and a director of the company. He is also the administrator for the employee Welfare Benefit Plan. Mr. Gersema has Bachelor's degrees from both the University of Oregon and Northwest Christian College in Eugene, Oregon and his Certified Financial Planner designation from the College of Financial Planning in Denver, Colorado.

Ms. Mary Gersema, chief operations officer, is a director and a founding member of the Employers Resource Management Company. Ms. Gersema holds a bachelor's degree in Accounting from John Tyler College and is a Certified Payroll Professional. She also has a certification from the Society of Human Resource Management as a Human Resource Generalist.

FEARLESS FARRIS STINKER STATIONS

"Fearless Farris is the Stinker"— was a cry heard on many radio stations throughout the 1950s, '60s, '70s, '80, and '90s. What kind of a message is that? Who would carry that kind of message, anyway? Farris Lind *is* the Stinker, and to know him is to love him. He is the man who brought independent gas stations and lower priced gasoline to the public of Idaho. He is the man who would pay anyone in his family 50 cents for a new slogan or saying to be placed on a billboard sign on old Highway 30, an otherwise dreary, boring, and monotonous drive across southern Idaho. Signs like:

"If you lived here you would be home now,"

"Don't just sit there, Nag your husband,"

"Sagebrush is free, put some in your trunk," and

"Watch out for white horses in a snowstorm."

And, of course, the most famous saying of all, "Petrified watermelons, take one home to your mother-in-law," referring to some glacial boulders that resembled watermelons. This sign and many

others were editorialized in major newspapers across the country, including the *San Francisco Chronicle* and *Examiner*, Los *Angeles Times*, *Chicago Tribune*, *Washington Post*, and others.

Farris Lind, born in Twin Falls, Idaho to a farming family, who slept in a lean-to attached to the main house, and whose adventuresome spirit continually brought him to the face of danger, excitement, and success, was quite an extraordinary man.

He did not have enough money to attend college after graduating from high school, but he did have enough to pay for flying lessons. He loved the idea of flying, and loved the art of flying even more, when he took the lessons. He spent every free moment and every penny he could earn flying. This put him in good company when World War II came along, since the government needed not only every able-bodied man, but especially valued those with flying experience.

Farris enlisted in the Navy, became a flight instructor, and served until the end of the War. During that time, he received the nickname "Fearless" and was referred to as "Fearless Farris."

At the end of the War, Lind founded a crop dusting company in Twin Falls, Idaho, which he called Fearless Farris Pest Control Service. True to his name, he was able to get jobs that no one else could or would even try to do. In the business with him were some of his Navy service buddies, but when one was killed doing airplane acrobatics. Farris closed the

Fearless Farris' Boy Scout Service Center, 1996.

business and went on to other adventures.

He worked for a radio station in Canada selling advertising for a while, but then came back to Twin Falls to determine his future and to chart his course. During this time, he recalled the satisfaction he felt when he worked for his brother at a highway gasoline station, talking to the travelers, telling stories, and inventing promotional ideas for merchandising that would appeal to the traveling motorist.

Lind traveled to Boise, called unannounced on then governor Chase Clark, and two hours later walked out of that office with a lease on a state-owned, but closed weigh station along with financing for two gasoline storage tanks. He built a small gasoline station, which he called Fearless Farris Savin' Station, and began running ads in the local newspaper. With the same wit and charm he was to use throughout his career, these ads were for the common everyday consumer and made fun of the large major oil companies and their "big city ways." He played up his role as the defender of the common man, doing battle and trying to survive against the huge oil companies. The people loved it. And they loved the promotions that Lind constantly ran.

Over the course of the next couple of years, Lind built several more stations and his sales volume grew dramatically. An editorial in the local newspaper suggested that, "Farris Lind is a real stinker to the major oil companies," because he was outselling them by a significant amount and had such strong consumer appeal. In a second article written in the same newspaper about a month later, the

writer suggested that Lind actually call himself "the Stinker." A few weeks later the new name was formed, Fearless Farris Stinker Stations, and the logo with the skunk wearing boxing gloves (fight against all odds and all comers), the exaggerated tail, and the stripes down the front of the skunk instead of the back.

Growth was steady and strong, and the appeal to the consumer was great. However, the biggest fight of all came during the spring of 1963, when Farris Lind was stricken with polio. From one of the most aggressive, charismatic outdoorsman, hunter, fisherman, entrepreneur, and businessman, he found himself in an iron lung, unable to breathe by himself and totally paralyzed from his neck down his entire body. He had his wife and family, four sons and a

daughter, in addition to his business that demanded his attention, and he couldn't even breathe, let alone move.

But, rather than succumbing to self-pity, anger, or frustration, he collected himself and began another great chapter in his life. He continued to pilot the business, to provide council and stewardship for his family, and provided inspiration to thousands of people. In 1972 he was awarded the President's "Outstanding Handicapped Citizen of the Year" award. He began his Washington, D.C. acceptance speech, "I feel badly that I am qualified for this award, but since I am...." He then continued to deliver an address to the audience that again demonstrated the courage, the wit, and the determination of this very exceptional man. And *never* could he draw even his own breath.

Farris Lind passed away in January 1983 after setting an appointment with his son Scott to review his new Stinker Station convenience store for the following day. As was always the case, the meeting was set to review the performance of the store and find new ways to make it even better.

A Boy Scout center located in Boise, Idaho bears his name. Forty Stinker Stations are now located around the Idaho business community, as well as two restaurants and a small motel. But the words, phrase, and sound that everyone recalls and which will live for generations to come, is "Fearless Farris is the Stinker."

GIVENS PURSLEY LLP

The Givens Pursley law firm was created in 1977 by four of Boise's more experienced attorneys. They came from very diverse backgrounds and political philosophies, but shared a belief that a law firm should consist of attorneys who were all actively engaged in the practice of law and active participants in the community's political, civic and cultural affairs. Two had served in the Idaho Legislature and all in appointed positions at the City and State levels while developing and maintaining extremely active private practices. They also shared the belief that their clients deserved to be served directly by attorneys experienced in areas relevant to the clients' needs. This concentration allowed them to understand their clients' business and, therefore, to serve the clients' needs more effectively and efficiently.

The primary practice areas of the founders have remained the core of Givens Pursley's business.

City Hall and the Police Station, 1975, where the City's business was conducted until the early 1980s, including the debates in the early '70s over establishing a setback for the Boise Greenbelt.

Founder Ken Pursley (left), who played a major role in the development of Boise's Greenbelt, walking the Greenbelt adjacent to a major office project developed by W.H. Moore (right).

Those practices consisted primarily of business and real estate, commercial litigation, health care, water law, and legislative and governmental affairs. Those practice areas have grown as the City of Boise, and the needs of the City's business community, have grown. This growth, along with the work in related business practice areas brought to the firm by attorneys who joined Givens Pursley from other firms and positions, has resulted in more than 30 attorneys, and one of the largest, and perhaps most diverse, of the law firms headquartered in the State.

One of the founders, Ken Pursley, has served as the managing partner since the inception and has been the principal architect of the firm's organizational structure. He has been one of the driving forces behind the firm's growth. He had practiced with a large Chicago law firm and then a larger Boise law firm before deciding to create a new firm with what was then a novel organizational approach. It was his belief that the traditional law firm structure, which revolved around

seniority, was not likely to provide the right incentives for optimizing service to clients. Believing that an organizational structure ought to be designed to focus on service to clients, he concluded that the internal financial and other incentives ought to be designed primarily to motivate its members to serve clients, not reward longevity. As a result, Givens Pursley has internal structures that reward the attorneys for working hard in the service of clients and for concentrating their practices, learning as much as they can about the particular businesses in which their clients are engaged. These internal incentives which cause firm attorneys to be uniquely client service-centered have contributed significantly to its success.

Givens Pursley's growth has been most evident in the business and transactional practice which is now managed by two partners,

City Hall and Police Station after renovation for Givens Pursley law offices, 1991, modernized while retaining a visual connection with past uses.

Ed Miller and Chris Beeson, who have been with the firm since near its inception. The firm has been a major participant in Boise's growth, having handled or been involved in most of the significant real estate developments chronicling Boise's dynamic growth over the last two decades. These include many of the significant new shopping centers and office complexes in the area; major, planned, unit residential developments; prominent historic renovation projects; and a major public/private joint venture involving the construction of a new Ada County Courthouse with substantial private development. This practice has also expanded into a set of associated practice areas including tax, securities, land use, financing and entity work. It has evolved to a more general commercial practice serving a large variety of business enterprises, recently including emerging businesses and technology companies.

Health law has always been an important part of Givens Pursley's practice. The firm has represented Saint Alphonsus Regional Medical Center since its inception. That area has grown with the increasing complexity of the health care delivery and has evolved into a very demanding practice involving several regional medical centers, rural hospitals and other health care facilities. These facilities all require detailed knowledge of the rules and regulations affecting the health care industry as well as considerable experience in real estate, business organization, governmental affairs, contracting and other skills. That practice is now managed by two partners, Pat Miller and Stephanie Westermeier, who have been with the firm since they entered private practice and is supported by David Lombardi, Judd Montgomery and other members of the firm who have other concentrations.

Other practice areas have grown through the addition of experienced attorneys from outside the firm. In 1984, Ken McClure joined the firm

from the State Attorney General's office and soon took over management of the legislative and governmental affairs work. Roy Eiguren, who had previously served in the Bonneville Power Administration and as a principal partner in the Boise office of a West coast law firm, joined Givens Pursley in 1994 and added not only a major energy practice, but also an extensive legislative and governmental affairs practice. In 1990, Senator James McClure retired from the U.S. Senate and joined the firm, bringing with him a wealth of experience, relationships and uncommon wisdom. This group is now regarded as one of the strongest legislative practice groups in the State.

Jeff Fereday came to Givens Pursley in 1985 after working in the U.S. Secretary of the Interior's office and a Denver law firm. He brought significant experience in water law, natural resources and environmental issues, and immediately began expanding the firm's water and environmental practice. The water practice originally involved the representation of the entity governing the operation of irrigation reservoirs on the Boise River, which have supplied the water for much of the area's agricultural development. The firm's water practice now includes a wide range of water rights issues and clients from around the State, and focuses particularly on serving municipal and industrial water providers and ground water irrigators. Mike Creamer and Christopher Meyer arrived in 1989 and 1994, respectively, and have enhanced the firm's strong environmental, natural resources and water fields practice.

In 1987, Conley Ward resigned his position as Commissioner of the Idaho Public Utilities Commission and joined the firm, bringing with him a substantial involvement in the telecommunication industry, as well as familiarity with a wide range of energy issues and litigation experience. Shortly thereafter David Lombardi, an experienced Boise litigator, took over management of the commercial litigation practice from one of the founders who accepted an appointment to the Idaho Supreme Court. The commercial litigation practice has since grown with the needs of the firm's clients and now includes a wide range of health care, business and employment law issues.

Later in the 1990s, Givens Pursley was the beneficiary of the transfer of a group of experienced attorneys from the Boise office of a major West Coast firm. That group included Hugh O'Riordan and Gary Allen, who in 1994 brought a significant environmental practice, and Deb Kristensen and Kelly McConnell who in 1999 brought substantial media/First Amendment, lender representation and bankruptcy practices.

While maintaining extremely active practices, members of Givens Pursley have always placed a high value on being active in the community's political and cultural affairs. Several have served in elected positions such as the U.S. Senate, Idaho Legislature and the Boise City Council and others have held various appointed leadership positions at both the City and State levels, including the Boise City's Parks and Recreation Board and the Idaho State Capitol Commission. One of the founders, Ken Pursley, played a key role in an important development in Boise's recent history, the creation of the Boise Greenbelt, which is today one of Boise's crown jewels and an important part of its wonderful living en-

vironment. He served as chairman of the Greenbelt Committee during the critical early years when many of the major land acquisitions were accomplished. His efforts set the stage for the later full-development of the Greenbelt by championing a setback ordinance which allowed the balance of the property on both sides of the Boise River to be developed as a continuous greenbelt path system.

Givens Pursley has also had a commitment to helping preserve visual connections with Boise's history while it has grown and modernized. Members of the firm were investors, and the firm was a principal tenant, in the preservation and conversion to office use of the old Boise Hotel (Hoff Building). Subsequently, the firm acquired buildings that had served as the Boise City Hall and the Boise City Jail and converted them to offices while preserving the important visual reminders of their historical use.

Givens Pursley is a law firm with a diverse group of experienced lawyers serving a very diverse client base. The firm is at the center of many of the most exciting and challenging

Ken McClure (left) and Roy Eiguren (right), who lead Givens Pursley's government affairs practice, discuss a client's concerns with Governor Dirk Kempthorne.

business, health care, natural resource and governmental policy issues. Its lawyers are recognized regionally and nationally as leading lawyers in their fields. That recognition is reflected by many of the firm's attorneys being the listed in *Best Lawyers in America*. As described in the *Idaho Directory/Yearbook*: "This firm covers the waterfront on legal specialties and may be the single most important firm in the state in policy development."

Givens Pursley water lawyers Ray Givens (right) and Jeff Fereday reviewing some of the Treasure Valley's irrigation history.

DELTA DENTAL PLAN OF IDAHO

Idaho has experienced many turning points since it attained statehood in 1890. One such milestone was set in place in 1971 with the creation of Delta Dental Plan of Idaho, headquartered in Boise.

Under the direction of the Idaho State Dental Association, Delta Dental Plan of Idaho was brought into existence. It is an autonomous Idaho corporation with its own board of directors. It is affiliated with Delta Dental, U.S.A., the pioneer and premier provider of group dental coverage in the United States since 1954. Delta Dental's only focus is oral healthcare. It has developed a unique cost management system, referred to as the "Delta Difference."

This "Delta Difference" offers many benefits for employers, patients and dental professionals. It has a high standard of excellence, yet is economical and efficient in monitoring expenditures and providing service. Almost 90 percent of Idaho's dentists participate in Delta Dental Plan of Idaho. Even though it is not necessary to see a participating dentist, there are advantages in doing so. Non-par-

Delta Dental Plan's mission is to provide an exceptional level of service, while agressively acquiring maximum market shares and maintianing a stable financial position.

ticipating dentists anywhere in the world will be paid by Delta Dental of Idaho, but the benefits of using a participating dentist are innumerable.

A simple philosophy propels the organization. Delta Dental is dedicated to increasing the availability of dental health care coverage plan to the people of its state. To that end, all the activities and programs provided by Delta Dental Plan of Idaho must simultaneously meet the needs of its subscribers, its corporate clients, and the state's dental professionals.

Delta Dental Plan of Idaho takes a hands-on approach. They work closely with dental office personnel by offering frequent training seminars held either at the Delta Dental of Idaho headquarters or at other central locations throughout the state. This assures a better

Delta Dental moved into its new headquarters on Parkcenter Boulevard in April, 2000.

understanding of the claims submission process as well as timely, accurate claims processing and prompt problem resolution.

Community is important. Delta Dental Plan of Idaho is committed to education and quality of life. As charter members they are actively involved in the Idaho Oral Health Alliance. The focus of the Alliance is access to dental health care and statewide fluoridation. The David F. McCune scholarship has been established in memory of Dr. McCune, a past board member of Delta Dental Plan of Idaho. The scholarship is granted each year to two students who wish to enter the dental hygienist program at Idaho State University. Their tuition is paid in full for the two-year program.

Delta Dental Plan of Idaho does one thing and does it well. Paying close attention to quality, value and service is the reason Delta Dental Plan of Idaho is the leader for dental care coverage in the market place since 1971. Delta Dental maintains that position by using its extensive network, utilization database, and ingenuity to design cost-effective dental programs.

HANSEN-RICE, INC.

The vision and dream of Dan Hansen and Ivan Rice was realized in 1983 when they established Hansen-Rice, Inc. Both men brought expertise to the company with their many years of experience in the construction industry, primarily with metal buildings. They knew the business which allowed them to see a need and an opportunity to create a building system that would better serve their clients.

Essentially, they combined the best elements of three related but independent worlds: the structural steel industry, the joist and girder industry and the pre-fabricated metal building industry, resulting in a unique building system. This system provides the inherent strength and performance of structural steel hot-rolled mill shapes, combined with the spanning strength of joists and girders and the economies and "fast track" ability of a pre-engineered metal building package. Utilizing the building package and HRI's "design-build" general contracting abilities, HRI clients work with one company, versus a more traditional method of building construction which independently

Daniel B. Hansen and Ivan F. Rice, founders, Hansen-Rice, Inc. (HRI).

involves an architect, an engineer and a contractor.

The company was incorporated on January 6, 1983. The first office was located at 123 South Second Street in Nampa and had approximately 800 square feet of space on the first floor of a renovated house. There were four employees in addition to Dan and Ivan when they opened their doors. Dan and Ivan both wore many "hats" in the start-up years—including hard hats—setting steel and hanging sheeting, etc., on the job sites, in addition to their responsibilities as sales representatives and project managers. The other "departments" included: an estimator-designer, a bookkeeper-receptionist-secretary and two project superintendents. The first year they employed approximately 25 field personnel.

Within a short period of time they expanded their

500,000 square foot manufacturing facility located in Utah.

offices into the additional 800 square feet of available office space at the Second Street location. In 1988 Dan and Ivan began planning for a larger facility by purchasing land from the Union Pacific Railroad in an industrial park on the north side of Nampa. This current site on Chisholm Drive was chosen because of its proximity to Interstate 84 and also because Nampa is centrally located in the Treasure Valley. In 1990 they built a 4,000 square foot facility. Since then, there have been two additions, and a major interior remodel. The building is now over 15,000 square feet and has 50 office personnel with 10 separate departments. The number of field employees can be as high as 450, depending upon the workload.

In 1985 an affiliate company, Golden Empire Manufacturing, Inc. (GEM) was formed to provide the structural design, engineering,

HRI obtained patents in the U.S. and Canada on its raw product storage design in 1993. The building design has been used for potato storage as well as onion and sugar beet storage.

fabrication and integration of all steel components into the "GEM Building System." Hansen-Rice retained the design-build general contractor portion, providing in-house design plus construction management and construction superintendents. Coupled with GEM's engineering abilities and a select group of consultants in specialty disciplines, HRI offers their clients a distinct cost-saving advantage in engineering and construction expenditures with a complete design-build package.

Customer service has been the heart and soul of both companies since their inception. When writing their company goals and philosophy, Dan and Ivan began by stating, "Customers are our greatest asset." They have been true to their convictions, confirmed by the fact that on average, 75 percent of all Hansen-Rice business is repeat and many of their new clients are referrals from existing customers. HRI is most proud of this statistic; it is the cornerstone of their suc-

cess. They provide service above and beyond the norm and define a successful project as one that is safely built and completed on schedule, within budget, with quality and customer satisfaction.

From the very beginning, the company's client base has been diversified. HRI has built fully- integrated meat and potato processing plants, freezer/cooler facilities, distribution warehouses, corrugated container plants and industrial warehouses in addition to office complexes, automobile dealerships and various retail and commercial buildings. The company is licensed to do business in all 48 contiguous states and has completed projects throughout most of the U.S., as well as foreign countries. The largest facility built to date is a 1.2 million square foot (nearly 28 acres) distribution center.

HRI has both a United States and Canadian patent on its building design for raw product storage. This building is used for the potato industry, as well as for storage of onions and sugar beets. Targeting the potato industry has moved the company into foreign countries for domestic clients. When the worldwide potato industry looks for ad-

vanced technology, they look to the United States and specifically to Idaho. HRI has received inquiries from all over the world regarding their advanced storage technology.

Dan and Ivan have assembled a solid group of employees who play a tremendous part in the success of the company. Many of the office and field personnel have been with the company for ten years or more, due in large part to a strong "family" atmosphere within the company, garnering employee enthusiasm and loyalty. All employees are committed to "do whatever it takes to get the job done," providing a high level of customer service.

Hansen-Rice has had a significant impact on the local economy by employing hundreds of people from the Treasure Valley. The company has also impacted many other communities throughout the U.S., Canada, Mexico and Argentina by providing new plants and facilities for companies who in turn employ thousands of people.

The future looks bright for Hansen-Rice, due to a great customer base, its dedicated, hardworking employees, sound fiscal management and a growing economy. The company holds firm to its motto "Dedicated to Excellence and Quality."

Hansen-Rice, Inc.'s corporate offices.

HAWLEY TROXELL ENNIS & HAWLEY

The firm of Hawley Troxell Ennis & Hawley LLP was organized in Boise in 1964, more than a third of a century ago, and traces its roots back to the days of Idaho's early territorial years, over a century ago. The firm is Idaho's oldest and largest law firm with 54 attorneys and 10 paralegals with locations in Boise, Pocatello, and Ketchum. James Hawley, Idaho attorney and governor in the early 20th century, was joined in practice by his son Jess in 1917. Hawley Troxell Ennis & Hawley LLP was formed in 1964 when two of Jess Hawley's sons, Jess Hawley Jr. and Jack Hawley, joined forces with Robert Troxell and Paul Ennis.

The headquarters of the firm extends over three floors of the Wells Fargo building in the heart of Boise. The Pocatello office opened in 1985 to provide service to the southeastern area of the Gem State, and expansion into Ketchum took place in 1992. The Ketchum office serves the Wood River-Sun Valley area. Former colleagues of the firm now sit as Idaho Supreme Court Justices, Court of Appeals Judges, and a United States District Judge for the District of Idaho. The firm's attorneys have served and continue to serve on a variety of civic boards and governing bodies, including the Boise Metro Chamber of Commerce, Idaho State Historical Society, Boise Area Economic Development Council, the Idaho Law Foundation, Opera Idaho, the Boise Philharmonic, the Boise family YMCA, and Bannock Regional Medical Center, to name a few. In addition to Governor James Hawley, several of the firm's partners have served in public office, including the Idaho Legislature, and have actively partici-

James H. Hawley on day of Main Line Celebration April 16 – 1925

pated in the organization and management of a number of political campaigns.

The roots of the firm begin with James H. Hawley. By the time Idaho achieved statehood on July 3, 1890, James Hawley had been a citizen of the territory for 28 years. As a 15-year old miner, Hawley had traveled to the Idaho gold fields in 1862 to seek his fortune, and remained to make a mark in the new rugged area. He participated in the Boise Basin strike where $24 million in gold was recovered in four years in the mid-

Hawley Troxell Ennis & Hawley traces its origins to the colorful career of James Hawley, the first Hawley to make a mark on the Gem State. Courtesy, Idaho Historical Society

1860s. With his mining proceeds, Hawley moved to San Francisco to earn a college degree, returning to Boise in 1868. Hawley continued to mine for gold (he and his mining partners took $145,000 in gold out of two mines in Quartzburg) while he studied law. He received his Idaho law license in 1871 and on July 4, 1875 he married Mary Elizabeth Bullock,

who had traveled to Idaho along with many others in covered wagons. He was elected to the Idaho Territorial Legislature in 1871 and served in both the lower and upper houses. He introduced a bill for women's suffrage in the 1874-75 session. In 1886, Hawley was appointed U.S. attorney and he and his family settled in Boise. Together, James and Mary had eight children. In the 1890s, James H. Hawley was a central figure in two major conflicts in Idaho, often as a defense attorney: labor unrest in the northern mines and

the sheep and cattle war in Cassia County. One of his most famous cases was his defense of "Diamondfield" Jack Davis, who was charged with murdering two sheepmen on behalf of cattle barons. Hawley was the prosecutor in the Boise murder trials of Big Bill Haywood and George Pettibone in 1907, with Clarence Darrow as defense attorney. Hawley served as mayor of Boise as well as being elected governor of Idaho.

The firm of Hawley Troxell Ennis & Hawley continues in the tradi-

The base of Thunder Mountain was the initial location of the firm's first law "office," then known as Hawley Puckett. Courtesy, Idaho Historical Society

tion established by James H. Hawley, of energetic and valued legal service matched with dedicated public service. Visit the firm's web site at www.hteh.com for additional information.

HOLLAND REALTY, INC.

Holland Realty celebrated its 20th anniversary on April 1, 2000, with news from the Southwest Idaho Multiple Listing Service and Ada County Association of Realtors that the company had finished its year topping all other brokerages. Holland Realty completed 1999 with a productive first place in sales, listings, total volume, and number of top producers in the Circle of Excellence. With sales in excess of $350 million for 1999, Holland Realty enjoyed the most successful year in its history.

In the mid-'70s, John and Janet Holland obtained their real estate licenses to further their mutual hobby of buying, restoring, and reselling "fixer-uppers." Though both had chosen other careers utilizing their accounting degrees from The College of Idaho (now Albertson College), their real estate endeavors developed into a love they chose to pursue full time. Within a short time, the Hollands negotiated the purchase of a small real estate company and changed the name to Holland Realty on April 1, 1980.

With just four sales agents and interest rates hovering around 13 percent, the determined new company, with John's expertise as former Caldwell City Treasurer and Janet's as a legislative auditor, strived to turn a profit while other real estate companies were struggling. In an era that preceded computers, cell phones, and fax machines, John Holland and his agents spent their days and evenings knocking on doors, making telephone calls, and forging strong friendships with each other, as well as with land owners, builders, and developers. Many of the relationships formed while helping builders and devel-

John Holland, president and owner of Holland Realty, Inc.

opers through those tough times continue today.

John's first philosophy, a simple one which was strengthened by the lean times, is still in place today. From agents to staff members, he hires people he likes, trusts, and who share his work ethic. "If you don't enjoy the people you work with, how can you possibly look forward to going to work each day?" he says with a smile. "My goal from the beginning was to build a strong company with intelligent, hard working people I wanted to spend time with. So far, it's worked very well."

Indeed, Holland Realty's Broker, Greg Coursey, was a good friend from college, as well as Best Man at the Hollands' wedding 27 years ago. Greg's assistant has been with the company over 16 years and began as the babysitter to Hollands' son Eric, now a senior at Bishop Kelly High School.

As Boise began to grow, so did Holland Realty, venturing into new construction and assisting developers in community design. In 1983, with nearly 20 sales agents and an office bursting at the seams, John Holland moved from the little house on State Street to the Emerald Professional Building

at 4720 Emerald Street and set his sights on making his company the best in the valley.

With the help of good friend and mentor Max Boesiger Sr., one of the Treasure Valley's most successful developers, John studied the art of building neighborhoods. "People don't want just a house," Holland says. "They want to be part of a community; they want to know their neighbors and feel that their kids are safe. The more our area grows, the more important these things become. Our goal is to help developers design subdivisions that meet the needs of the people who will live there."

Through the years, Holland and his agents have done just that. Working with a multitude of developers, Holland Realty has helped design, market, and sell over 5,000 home sites and many, many more homes. In fact, Holland Realty helped pioneer residential developments along Boise's Park Center Boulevard and Eagle's Floating Feather Road.

Developers come to Holland Realty for assistance on everything from locating appropriate property to planning layout and design, reviewing lot sizes, recommending signage and landscaping, marketing the lots, and overseeing lot sales. For the builders, Holland Realty provides the lots, listens to ideas, suggests home plan changes and improvements, and then sells the homes.

While Holland Realty is very active in new construction, just over 50 percent of the company's business comes from existing home listings and sales. "You can't build a strong company without providing complete service to the existing home market," John says. "We have our existing home specialists, and we have our new construction specialists, but we strive to hire and continue to train well-rounded, full-time and full-service Realtors."

In keeping with that goal, the Hollands try to provide "scheduled relaxation," as both feel that being the best is a fine balance between work and play. Each year they host company golf tournaments, ski parties, bowling tournaments, and other social functions. The comraderie built during the fun times makes for a more pleasant working environment.

John and Janet both believe that being successful in business also carries with it the responsibility of being active and contributing members of the community. John sits on the Children's Advisory Board for St. Luke's Hospital. Holland agents and staff participate in activities such as the Boise River Festival, American Red Cross Blood Drives, and Toys for Tots. Boise's Community House, the Idaho Food Bank, Idaho Special Olympics, and a host of other worthwhile programs benefit from

Janet Holland stands before Holland Realty's first office at 1940 W. State Street in Boise, circa, 1980.

the generosity of Holland Realty and its sales force.

The Hollands purchased their office building on Emerald Street in 1990 and now, with over 100 agents, occupy all 16,000 square feet, as well as several onsite offices in developments and an office in Nampa. Each spring, all locations are adorned with the trademark red and yellow tulips, which have become a symbol for the company and the annual "Spring Home Festival," the largest new home show in the Treasure Valley.

As John and Janet look toward the future, both believe they have built an organization strong enough to withstand the changing face of the industry. In a time of technological advancement, they have employed a full-time specialist to assist staff and agents with computer training classes and to implement the Holland Realty website, from which all Multiple Listing data is now accessible.

"Our future endeavor is to expand Internet sales, relocation sales, and commercial real estate sales," Holland says. "We consis-

Holland Realty's main office at 4720 Emerald Street in Boise. Over 1,500 red and yellow tulips, a Holland Realty trademark, grace the building each Spring.

tently study national housing trends, and our agents routinely take courses in real estate to earn additional designations (Associate Broker, New Home Sales Specialist, Accredited Buyers' Agent, Graduate Realtor Institute, Certified Residential Specialist, etc.). We believe our future is built on our continued learning." John's additional education has earned him a Certified Real Estate Broker designation, one of only a few in Idaho.

As franchises lure other companies into their fold, Holland Realty remains independent and has become the largest of its kind in the Treasure Valley. "Our success is mainly attributed to our being a locally-owned and operated company that can adapt to opportunities much faster than franchises," states John. "We feel we can offer a higher level of service to our customers by being local." The Hollands feel their company is better able to service their clients when they don't have to consult the franchise manual or a far-away corporate entity. "It's worked for the past 20 years, and we are committed to making it work for the next 20. We work hard, have some fun along the way, and are devoted to improving our customer service each and every day."

IDAHO SPORTING GOODS COMPANY

More than half a century ago, just following World War II, Idaho Sporting Goods Company began in Boise. C&S Sporting Goods, a Spokane corporation, opened a store in Boise in 1947 at 10th and State streets. The original Boise C&S Sporting Goods had three full time employees and one part time employee. Jack Kimmel and Walter Cranston purchased the C&S Sporting Goods Boise outlet on November 16, 1953 and renamed it the Idaho Sporting Goods Company. Idaho Sporting Goods has remained at the 10th and State Street location in Boise since 1947. They are the oldest sporting goods store in the area and have serviced schools in Idaho, Nevada, and Oregon for 46 years.

In 1953, as Idaho Sporting Goods Company was begun, the building at 10th and State Street was occupied by five businesses: a real estate office, a restaurant, an insurance agency, Morlers Cyclery, and Idaho Sporting Goods. Idaho Sporting Goods purchased the 12,000 square foot

Standing in the shoe department in 1994, (left to right): Pat Brady, Tim Brady, Cherie Brady, Hugh Brady, Kelly Brady and Nick Brady.

Employees of Idaho Sporting Goods Company in 1970, (left to right): Dick Peterson, Larry Howerton, Mick McConnell, Bob Dethman, Gus Barrett, Hugh Brady, Pat Brady, Ralph Brady, Dave Delisio, Tom Smock, Connie Dewitt, Vi Baisch, Donna Clopton, Jim Petty, Dan Chatterton and Al Griggs.

building in 1967 from Walter Cranston, and became its sole occupant in 1969. The original Idaho Sporting Goods retail store included sales of a variety of outdoor sporting equipment including hunting, fishing, camping, skiing, and scuba equipment as well as shoes and clothing. The store also sold bowling equipment, school and team equipment, and had a trophy department.

Hugh Brady joined Idaho Sporting Goods on July 5, 1954 as an outside salesman. He called on schools and teams in Idaho, Nevada, and Oregon. His beginning wage was $600 a month and he paid his own traveling expenses. In 1957, Brady and Jack Kimmel purchased Walter Cranston's stock in Idaho Sporting Goods Company and they became equal partners in the business. Jack Kimmel's wages were set at $550 a month and Hugh Brady's, as a partner, were set at $450 a month.

Hugh Brady became the owner of Idaho Sporting Goods in May 1969 when he purchased Jack Kimmel's share of the business. Hugh's oldest son Patrick Brady began working for the company in shipping and receiving. After graduating from college in 1974, Patrick joined Idaho Sporting Goods as an outside salesman. Mike Brady joined the company in 1980 as an outside salesman. John Brady worked for the company for 10 years and then decided

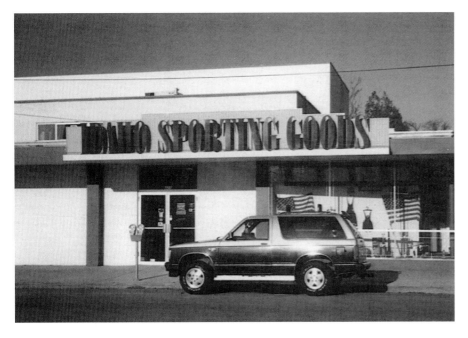

Front of the store in 1994, located on 10th Street, after remodeling.

Inside retail area in 1994. (left to right): Tim Brady, Pat Brady, Nick Brady, Cherie Brady, Hugh Brady and Kelly Brady.

to pursue other interests. Tim, Nick, Kelly, and Joanne Brady also joined the company. Hugh's father Ralph Brady worked as credit manager for the company for 20 years, from 1967-1987. JP Brady, Hugh's grandson, worked part time during this period as well, and JP is now a full time road salesman. Idaho Sporting Goods has had four generations of Bradys employed at one time.

In 1989, Idaho Sporting Goods opened a store in Pocatello, Idaho, and in 1992 another store was opened in Idaho Falls. Mike Brady manages both of these retail stores and calls on schools and teams in their areas.

The basic philosophy of Idaho Sporting Goods has been honesty with their customers. Customers are given quality merchandise and good service, and are satisfied. Idaho Sporting Goods believes in a team effort with all employees participating in quality service including the office crew, shipping

and receiving, the salesmen, the retail people, print shop workers, embroiderers, and the trophy employees. All work toward this common goal of excellence. Idaho Sporting Goods looks toward the future with optimism because of a successful past, a legacy of quality service, outstanding employees, and loyal customers.

Store on State Street after remodeling in 1994.

THE IDAHO STATESMAN

The Civil War was in its fourth bloody year when the first issue of *The Idaho Tri-Weekly Statesman* was pulled from the press on July 26, 1864.

Confederate sympathizers in Idaho clearly outnumbered those who favored the Union when *The Statesman* began publication. But James S. Reynolds, its fiery editor, left no doubt where the new paper stood.

In that first issue he wrote, "Politically, it may as well be understood, once for all, that we are opposed to this rebellion in every phase of its causes, or its results, and to everybody who is not opposed to it."

Founder James S. Reynolds was a printer intercepted on his way West by a group of business leaders who believed it was time for a city of more than 1,000 to have its own newspaper. Starting a Republican paper in a territory dominated by Democrats was courageous, and Reynolds was to have plenty of opportunities to defend his position and show his nerve.

The paper's first publisher helped to establish a tradition of

Publisher Margaret Cobb Ailshie and some of her employees break ground for the fifth Idaho Statesman *building at 6th and Bannock streets on June 15, 1950. Next to her is James Brown, general manager and later publisher.*

editorial independence that is maintained today by the staff of *The Idaho Statesman*. The newspaper championed women's suffrage, mine safety, respect of our natural resources and support for higher education.

Frontier journalism was noted for strong language and speedy retaliation, which was often physical. Reynolds took a humorous approach to reader antagonism during a visit to Silver City in 1865. He told his readers he had left town to avoid a half-dozen fights he planned to settle that week, but warned "those who may be expected to come for us" that he had made adequate preparations for them on his return by securing the services of "an eminent surgeon, two coroners and six intelligent jury men..."

Demand for news of the Civil War was so great in 1864 and '65 that printers worked all night cranking out 1,000 copies of each issue. Horsemen rushed these

The second Idaho Staesman *home, located at Capitol Boulevard and Idaho Street, where the Key Financial Center now stands.*

papers to Boise Basin and Owyhee mining camps at dawn, according to A.J. "Jud" Boyakin, a longtime *Statesman* writer and sometime editor.

Boyakin quit the paper several times to start rival journals with a Democratic slant, in opposition to *The Statesman*'s radical Republican stance. After each folded, his old employer cheerfully rehired him; excellent newspapermen were hard to find, whatever their political persuasion.

Part of the game in those days was lambasting rival editors. *The Statesman* waged a running battle with the *Idaho World* in Idaho City. The tradition of scurrilous insult between Reynolds and James O'Meara of the *World* was carried on with a vengeance by their successors.

The Statesman's first home was

remembered by a number of oldtime newspapermen as "a small structure of cottonwood logs containing two rooms, the rear one with a back entrance like the open end of a sawmill."

Accounts of its location vary, but it was probably somewhere on the north side of Main Street between Sixth and Seventh, where Boise City Hall now stands. In the beginning it had a dirt floor, no door and no glass in the windows.

The second *Statesman* building was a modest frame structure that stood on the northwest corner of Capitol and Idaho, where Key Financial Center stands today.

The third home of the paper on the northwest corner of Sixth and Main was purchased at auction. The happiest feature of this location, according to numerous items in *The Statesman* thereafter, was its next door location to John Broadbeck's brewery.

Judge Milton Kelly bought the paper in January 1872, turning it into a daily in 1888. Kelly, too, bore his share of verbal abuse and dished it out with enthusiasm. For this he was assaulted, clubbed and stabbed on Boise's Main Street. Libel suits were unheard of in those palmy days, and more direct satisfaction was sometimes secured.

The year following the conversion to a daily, Kelly sold the newspaper to the man whose family would operate it for more than 70 years. *The Statesman* Publishing Co. was formed in 1889, and a number of distinguished publishers became well-known Idaho figures. Best remembered are Calvin Cobb, his daughter Margaret Cobb Ailshie, and James Brown. A New Yorker who practiced law in Oregon before moving to the Idaho Territory, Calvin Cobb was an

autocratic guardian of *The Idaho Statesman*'s destiny for four decades. Cobb was at the helm when the classic Georgian building at Sixth and Main streets, which is still standing, was erected in 1910. He died in 1928, leaving the paper to his daughter, Margaret Cobb Ailshie.

As *The Idaho Statesman*'s first woman publisher (and one of the first in the nation), Ailshie insisted on a lively editorial policy, deploring "a dull newspaper." In 1952, she moved the newspaper from its third home at Sixth and Main in Old Boise to a two-story marble building at Sixth and Bannock. James Brown, her general manager, succeeded her as publisher after her death in 1959.

Margaret Cobb Ailshie commissioned famed modern architect Pietro Belluschi of Portland to design the fifth Statesman building at Sixth and Bannock, now Capitol Park Plaza. *The Idaho Statesman* moved to its current home on Curtis Road, formerly part of the Western Idaho Fairgrounds, in 1972.

"Mr. Brown," as employees knew him, was the last individual owner *of The Idaho Statesman*. When he retired in 1963, he sold the paper to Federated Publications, Inc., a six-paper chain.

In June 1971, Federated merged with Gannett Co., Inc., the nations largest newspaper group. The first Gannett publisher was Robert B.

Curtis Road and I-184 in West Boise has been the home of the Idaho Statesman since 1972. The building will undergo expansion in 2001-2003.

Miller, Jr., who presided over the move to the current location. Miller was succeeded in turn by Eugene Dorsey, Gary Sherlock, Gordon Black, Pamela Meals, and in 1999 by Margaret Buchanan.

The newspaper currently employs more than 425 men and women. It is the largest media source in Idaho, with newspaper distribution covering nearly half the counties in Idaho, as well as adjacent communities in Oregon and Nevada. Each day a distribution and carrier force of nearly 1,000 people deliver daily and Sunday newspapers to hundreds of thousands of readers.

In 1998 *The Idaho Statesman* launched a series of four local Internet products. In October 1999, news content was added. Three additional stand-alone information and advertising web sites have followed. By fall 2000, more than 1,000,000 *Idaho Statesman* Internet pages were viewed each month. New and existing site development will continue with reader demand expected to double annually for the foreseeable future. The primary Internet address is www.IdahoStatesman.com.

Information for this article was generously provided by Arthur Hart, director emeritus of the Idaho Historical Society.

IDAHO TIMBER CORPORATION

Idaho Timber Corporation was formed in May 1979 by native Idahoan Larry D. Williams. He began his lumber career in a local sawmill in his hometown of Midvale, Idaho, later moving to Chandler Corporation in Boise, Idaho, and continuing a progressive climb to executive vice president. It was after his resignation from Chandler that this young, progressive lumberman completed the organizational steps needed to form Idaho Timber Corporation. One could say, with reasonable concern, the late-'70s would not have been the most opportune time to go into the lumber business. Recession was being predicted, interest rates were inching toward 21 percent and inflation was nudging 13 percent. Even so, Mr. Williams took the plunge to start a small lumber brokerage firm with five employees.

Emerging from the adversity of the late 1970s, and early 1980s, Idaho Timber has successfully combined sales and resource management with quality manufacturing to become a nationally recognized leader in the forest products industry.

Since its inception, Idaho Timber has experienced continual growth, beginning with its first manufacturing facility, located in Whitefish, Montana, which was acquired within the first two months of business. By the end of the first year another manufacturing plant was started in the company's home city of Boise. Even faced with skyrocketing interest rates and a generally poor economy, Idaho Timber realized it had to continue its growth. Now employing approximately 60 people, meeting payroll and expenses with the current bank line of credit was becoming increasingly diffi-

cult. However, due to the excellent credit standing of the company, and with everything owned as collateral, the bank increased the operating line of credit, allowing the necessary growth. Williams remembers, "...the day we reached our first $2,000,000 month in billed sales we were so excited we closed the office and took the employees out for a luncheon celebration." That was about halfway into the second year in business, and gave the com-

Idaho Timber Corporation of Boise manufacturing plant and sales office, Boise, Idaho.

pany great hopes that it could end that year with nearly double the sales of the first year. The hopes and wishes came true, with great effort on everyone's part, and from that point on it has continued its growth. Steadily adding facilities as opportunities and people presented themselves, the company's yearly sales volume increased at a healthy pace. "Those bad times in the lumber industry made some key people available," remarks Williams. "It allowed us to get the kind of people that our new venture demanded—experienced, hardworking and dedicated people." In the company's sixth year there were seven members of the senior management team, with an average age of only 39 years, yet therein was a total of 112 years of experience in the lumber industry. Sales in that year reached nearly $100,000,000.

By the time Idaho Timber celebrated its 10th anniversary, the company had 10 active facilities, from Oregon to Florida. Annual sales reached $125,000,000.

Executive staff members, left to right: Jack Beverage, vice president, sawmill operations; Bryant Rudd, chief financial officer and vice president; George Karr, vice president; Ted Ellis, president; Larry Williams, chairman and CEO; Mike Johnson, vice president.

With experienced leadership and dedicated people, and the advantage of a more healthy economy, the company continued to prosper.

Managers of the company are provided the opportunity to affect their own futures through an ownership interest in their respective operations. All employees share a stake in its profitable operation through annual profit-sharing distributions.

Sales for the year ended March 2000 exceeded $370,000,000, and the company now employs over 850 people. In its 21st year in business, the company operates sawmills and manufacturing facilities strategically located throughout the U.S. According to Mr. Williams, chairman & chief executive officer, the secret of the company's success is, again, the people—dedicated, knowledgeable, hardworking, team players who set examples with "charged-up, go get 'em attitudes." Plants have been built around the people, and people around the plants. This is a high volume, low margin business, and Idaho Timber has been successful at maintaining a very conservative approach, continually monitoring its operations.

The company's most diverse operation is Idaho Land & Livestock, a wholly-owned cattle and land company located in Tuttle, Idaho. This company runs 1,100 head of mother cows, on 55,000 acres of private and Forest Service lands.

The parent company and corporate headquarters is located in Boise, Idaho. This office handles all legal, finance, accounting, credit, rail and truck traffic functions for all divisions across the country. In the year 2000, the Idaho Timber Corporation group consists of: Idaho Timber Corpo-

Idaho Timber Corporation corporate headquarters, Boise, Idaho.

ration of Montana, 1979; Idaho Timber Corporation of Boise, 1980; Idaho Timber Corporation of Texas, 1981; Idaho Timber Corporation of Idaho, 1983; Idaho Timber of Florida, 1984; Idaho Timber Corporation of Oregon, 1986; Timber Corporation of Kansas, 1987; Idaho Land & Livestock, 1989; Idaho Cedar Sales, 1992; Idaho Timber Corporation of Missoula, 1992; Idaho Timber Corporation of Carthage, 1993; Rio Grande Forest Products, 1996; Sagebrush Sales Company, 1998; Idaho Timber Company of Colorado, 1998; and Idaho Timber Corporation of North Carolina, 1998.

The various acquisitions over the past 21 years have positioned Idaho Timber's manufacturing, distribution and sales locations strategically across the United States. The company's facilities cover a combined total of over one million square feet of manufacturing and storage buildings, situated on 230 acres. The company ships in excess of 2,000 truck & trailer loads of lumber, per month, out

of its facilities, in addition to logs from its timber lands—a steady volume of high quality Ponderosa pine, Douglas fir, Hem-fir, spruce, Southern yellow pine and cedar. This product line consists of a mix of strips, boards, studs, dimension, pattern stock, fencing, post and rail, radius edge decking, export clears, roof and floor trusses, panel products, railroad ties and landscape timbers.

Mr. Williams is quoted as having said, numerous times over the past 21 years, "We aren't going to get any bigger." Obviously, that wasn't the case. Handling the complexities of timberland management, sawmills and manufacturing plants, regional distribution and sales takes a corporation with people at the center. Idaho timber has those people, and for its suppliers and customers, this is the Idaho Timber advantage.

"Sustaining forest resources for the future in harmony with responsible land management is the vision of Idaho Timber," says Williams. "Our proven ability to supply the highest quality products and service in balance with our vision is what sets us apart."

Sawmill operation headrig, circa 1986.

IDAHO TROUT PROCESSORS COMPANY

Earl Melville Hardy was born in Midway, Utah, on September 5, 1918 to Myrtle Watkins and Earl M. Hardy. Earl's father was a respected businessman and community leader, and held the Standard Fuel Company oil and coal distributorship in the immediate region. Upon his father's death when Earl was 14, Standard Oil Company obtained the distributorship. In the midst of the Depression, Earl successfully bid for the rights to cut timber and begin producing lumber from an abandoned mill. He supported his family and several other families during that time from the mill operations. After several seasons, he sold the mill to pursue his schooling. Years later, Earl walked the site of the mill, found whiskey bottles in the sawdust from the time of his operation, and said, "No wonder some of those boards weren't cut very straight."

In 1937, he enrolled in Business College in Salt Lake City, Utah.

Earl Melville Hardy, founder of Idaho Trout Processors Company. Courtesy, family photograph.

Clear Lakes Trout Farm with Idaho Trout Processors Company plant in left background, Buhl, Idaho, ca. 1980. Courtesy, corporate archives.

From 1938-1941 he was an auditor with the Public Service Commission in Salt Lake City, and it was in this capacity that he first traveled to Idaho. In Salt Lake City, he met and later married LaVane Matheson. Together they had three children.

Always patriotic, Earl was one of the first men to volunteer for active military duty at the onset of World War II. He assumed that he would be assigned for duty overseas, but because of his business background, he was transferred to Pocatello, Idaho, where he was responsible for military requisitions. After the war Earl and his family moved to Boise, where he continued his accounting practice, and also his fascination with Idaho and its abundance of water. As a boy growing up in Utah, Earl had fished every excellent fishing hole along the Provo River and he continued to be an avid fisherman in his early years in Idaho. Depression and war experiences had convinced him of the importance of food production to the country's survival, so with his love of water, fish, and an interest in sustainable agriculture, he was determined to begin trout production. In 1948, he and another accountant, Alfred

Iverson, began Rainbow Trout Farms in Buhl, Idaho, with high hopes and a loan.

Earl was president and Al vice-president of Rainbow Trout Farms. In September 1948, Earl filed on water rights for 10.6 cubic feet per second of water and obtained a land lease for one year to see if he and Al could survive the year. The first trout eggs were hatched in a tent during one of the coldest winters on record. Wildlife was starving and ducks came into the tent in droves to eat the small fish, so the first winter was a bitter lesson in survival. After the first year, Earl and Al continued to lease the land, and eventually entered into a contract to buy it. There was originally one other employee, Carl Cagle, who walked over the nearby hill from his family's farm to work with the fish. The first capital expense recorded in corporate records was $17.87 paid to Boise Payette Lumber Company for lumber to build hatching troughs. Originally, trout eggs were purchased from a local company. The first fish were raised in dirt

Sorting fish at Rainbow Trout Farms, October, 1955. Courtesy, corporate archives.

ponds that had been excavated. Production was labor intensive and all of the work was done by hand: sorting the trout, cleaning ponds and screens, and feeding and processing the fish. Within a relatively short period of time the small hatchery began to spawn its own trout from a prize strain of rainbow trout from eastern Idaho. September 1949 sales were 50 pounds for the month. Primary markets were California and Colorado. Earl told the story of how he, hoping to increase sales, advertised trout in *Gourmet* magazine. He sold no trout from that ad, as far as he could tell, until 21 years later when a woman called from Denver, saying she had seen an ad in *Gourmet* magazine and wanted to place an order. Earl used to tell people, "Behold the power of advertising," as the ad had finally paid for itself, albeit, 21 years later.

While the trout were growing in the ponds to production size, the first processing plant was built at the farm north of Buhl and a hatchery building to hatch the eggs soon followed. With acquisition of a site at Filer, Idaho, it was possible to provide another produc-

ing farm. These two original farms are small by today's standards, as the trend in the trout industry has been towards an increasing scale of production. Production and sales are in the millions of pounds, compared to the thousands of fish raised in the early years. Earl Hardy and Al Iverson are considered pioneers of the Idaho rainbow trout industry and the 1948 Rainbow Trout Farm is the genesis of Idaho Trout Processors Company and its five state-of-the-art production facilities.

Idaho Trout Processors Company was incorporated on March 2, 1959. Corporate offices have been located in Boise since 1959, but the producing farms and two processing facilities are located in the Thousand Springs area along the Snake River in Buhl, Filer, Hagerman and Wendell, Idaho. The Snake River Plain aquifer generates pristine spring water at a relatively constant 58°F temperature, which is ideal for the growth of rainbow trout. The earlier processing plant at Rainbow became inadequate to handle the increase in farm production, and in 1964, another processing plant was built at Filer. When the Filer plant was first built, 1,500-3,000 pounds of trout per day were processed. Currently, 15,000-30,000 pounds are processed at the Filer facility each day.

Some of the worst years in the business cycle occurred when foreign competitors "dumped" their product into the States, undercutting Idaho producers who could not compete with inexpensive foreign labor and government subsidized product. The Company survived and the demand for rainbow trout increased throughout the years. In 1961, Earl became a vice-president and director of Blue Lakes Trout Farm in Twin Falls,

Idaho. In 1967, Earl developed Clear Lakes Trout Farm and in 1976, he acquired Rim View Trout Company to increase productive capacity. The dirt ponds of earlier years were replaced with concrete raceways and state-of-the-art feeding systems. Earl innovated systems that became the industry standard for years and some remain the standard to this day.

After the Filer plant was built, another large, modern plant at Clear Lakes Trout Farm, Buhl was built to handle the increased demand. The processing plants are automated and efficient, with much of the earlier labor-intensive work replaced by machine. Idaho Trout Processors Company markets its fresh and frozen rainbow trout across the nation and in Canada.

Idaho Trout Processors Company and the related Rainbow Trout Farms, Clear Lakes Trout Farm, White Springs Trout Farm, Fisheries Development Corporation, and Rim View Trout Farm recently celebrated their 50th

Company origin: Sheepherder's tent, Rainbow Trout Farms, Buhl, Idaho, December, 1948. Courtesy, corporate archives.

anniversaries. Earl always respected the potential in people, one reason that Idaho Trout Processors Company has been able to attract and retain excellent employees and managers. Idaho Trout incorporates a team approach to management and is fortunate to work with dedicated employees who demonstrate both strong work ethics and family values.

It was over 15 years before Earl paid himself a salary from the trout operations, preferring to keep the capital working in the companies. His accounting practice and construction company helped to finance his dream. In 1952, Earl formed Cain and Hardy, a general construction company in Boise. Earl was president and R.D. Cain was the general contractor. In 1957, Earl formed a real estate development company bearing his name. The Company built the second Bogus Basin Ski Lodge, All-Saints Episcopal Church, and residential and commercial devel-

The Egyptian Theatre, Boise, Idaho, 1927, Frederick Hummel, Architect. Earl Hardy purchased and restored the theatre when it was scheduled for demolition. Courtesy, Idaho State Historical Society

Earl Hardy, Box Canyon Springs, 1983. Photo by Terrence Moore.

opments. Earl was a partner in the Idaho Office Building Company in downtown Boise from 1964 until the early-1970s.

Earl witnessed the development of the West. Traveling on State Highway 30 between Boise and Buhl in 1948, the night was black, rarely broken by headlights. Fifty years later, Interstate 84 is a river of light at night. Manley's Café in Boise and Jack's Coffee Cup in Hammett finally closed, and along with them a chapter in the history of American rural life. Earl's life and profession reflected the changes that were taking place across the American landscape as he watched the upland desert transform from native vegetation and sagebrush to the introduction of pivot-point irrigation and high-lift pumping. Changes in the landscape reflected the economic shift from small family farm to agribusiness. Earl recognized that the landscape was always chang-

ing, with different livelihoods and histories unfolding. His desire was to find some way to preserve and honor those Native Americans, pioneers, and ordinary visionaries whose histories and dreams were embedded in their homes, public spaces and landscapes.

Earl loved the landscape of the West. He may have represented the last generation of men who combined a sense of manifest destiny with an American romance for an Arcadian ideal they found in the West. Earl was a true steward of the environment and Idaho's natural resources. He believed that it was possible to contribute productively and to husband

John Watkins' home, Midway, Utah, ca. 1868. John Watkins, Architect. Courtesy, Watkins family archive.

resources well at the same time. In fact, he knew it was a necessity. For Earl, geography proved to be destiny. The land, and his love for it, gave him his trout farming profession and planted the seeds for the Foundation that bears his name.

The Hardy Foundation: In 1997, Earl formed a non-profit charitable foundation, The Hardy Foundation, to continue the preservation work begun earlier in his life. The Foundation's purpose is to preserve historic and/or architecturally significant structures; to preserve historically important and geographically diverse land areas; to educate the public on the benefits of preservation; and to make these sites and structures available for public research and enjoyment.

The Foundation currently owns several buildings listed on the National Register of Historic Places, including a home designed in 1868 by Earl's great grandfather, John Watkins, an architect for Queen Victoria in London who emigrated to the western United States. The Egyptian Theatre, also listed on the National Register, is located in Boise at the corner of Capitol Boulevard and Main Street. Built in 1927, the Theatre was scheduled for demolition under the Urban Renewal program. Earl purchased the Theatre in the early 1970s and completed the first renovation in 1980. It is one of the finest examples of Egyptian Revival architecture in the country, is Boise's only downtown movie theater and continues to function as a Boise landmark due to its beauty, visibility and popularity. A second renovation that will restore the Theatre to its original 1927 glory is in progress. Several other historic homes have been preserved by the Foundation to insure that the legacy of past generations is maintained and strengthened.

In keeping with the Foundation's philosophy, in 1998 Earl sold a 350-acre property to the State of Idaho to guarantee its future preservation. The State and The Nature Conservancy created a public-private partnership to preserve Box Canyon, a mile-long canyon featuring 200-foot basalt walls and the 11th largest natural spring in North America. The Canyon is significant because of its spring system, biological diversity, geology, archaeology, and history. The intent is to limit development and retain the Canyon's natural state, while still allowing public access. The Earl M. Hardy Box Canyon State Preserve will be available for future generations of Idahoans to enjoy.

Articles about Earl and his projects have been written in the *World Who's Who of Commerce and Industry*; *Who's Who in the West*; *Smithsonian*; *National Geographic*; *US News & World Report*; *Architectural Digest*; and *Sunset* magazines, as well as other publications. However, Earl was always more interested in making a contribution than creating any publicity for himself.

He was a builder and a visionary, dedicated to his family, to the companies he created, and proud to contribute to the country in whose vision he believed. Earl began his endeavors in an era when a person's word was his bond, and he never deviated from a style of management founded on integrity. Earl was always more demanding of himself than he was of others, and to those who knew him, his life was lived in service to others in pursuit of high ideals.

Earl Melville Hardy passed on February 13, 1999. The many people whose lives he touched and enlivened remember him with respect and love.

IDAHO WINE MERCHANT

Ed and Sheila Robertson knew they were in the wine business when their first shipment arrived in Boise before the builder had completed their pre-planned warehouse in Garden City. The wine had to go somewhere, so they licensed their home at 1819 West Jefferson Street as a wine warehouse. That was in November 1977, the beginning of an extremely cold winter. The wine filled every room of their modest home and overflowed into the garage and sun porch, where electric heaters kept the wine from freezing. Sheila was eight months pregnant with their second child Christian, who was born the day after Christmas.

The business was a response to a growing interest in the United States—and Boise—for imaginative food, fine wine and specialty beer. During the Vietnam and Cold Wars, military personnel were stationed in Southeast Asia and

Europe where many learned the culinary and wine traditions of those regions. During the same period, Peace Corps volunteers fanned out all over the globe, likewise learning to appreciate exotic foods and beverages. When these travelers returned to the United States, they brought their new tastes with them. Ed and Sheila were among those returnees. Ed had served five years as an Air Force supply officer at duty stations in Asia and Europe.

In Boise, Ed's brother Stephen, opened Annabel's in 1974 on Vista Avenue. The restaurant specialized in seafood and fine wines. In 1975, he opened Mussels Fish Market on Overland Road and sold both fish and wine. Both businesses were instant successes. The Hewlett-Packard Company had arrived in Boise in 1975 and brought a small tide of educated and traveled people who sought out interesting food and wine, finding it at Annabel's and Mussels.

Encouraged by Ed's mother Louise, to return to Boise to help

Sheila and Ed Robertson.

Stephen with his growing businesses, Ed and Sheila arrived in Boise with eighteen-month-old daughter Brandy, in November 1975. Ed's father and grandfather had each operated small businesses in Nampa, so entrepreneurship seemed quite natural to the young family.

In 1976 Ed opened a wholesale seafood business, Boise Fish & Oyster Company. At the urging of Brooks Tish, a Nampa State Farm Insurance agent and his brother Stephen, Ed established Idaho Wine Merchant in 1977. Within a year, he opened branch warehouses in Ketchum and Moscow and serviced restaurants, grocery stores and wine shops throughout the state. The company added specialty beers to the product line in 1978. In 1979 he computerized the wine business, improving efficiency. The two businesses grew rapidly, aided by the general prosperity in Boise and Sun Valley in the late 1970s. The Robertsons sold the seafood business in 1979.

Left to right; Eric Johnson, Brian Austin and Ollie.

Idaho Wine Merchant moved from Garden City to its present location at 3105 Neff Street in 1982.

In the early years, as both the wine business and the Robertson children were growing, the two youngsters were often at the warehouse, initially in a playpen, but eventually helping with whatever needed to be done. Their responsibilities gradually increased until they accompanied their parents on business trips to Belgium, England, France and Spain. In 1999, Christian, age 22, returned to the business as a sales representative. Sheila taught wine classes for restaurant and store employees and conducted wine appreciation courses at the YWCA and in private homes for the interested public. She sold wine and stocked shelves in area grocery stores.

When the upward-trend of their sales chart began to reverse during the 1980s recession, the Robertsons turned some of their energies to community services. Both completed the Chamber of Commerce Leadership Boise program. Sheila volunteered at the Idaho Conservation League, YWCA, and KBSU Radio, and served on the board of Idaho Department of Parks and Recreation. Ed focused on wildlife, salmon recovery, and public land issues. The Idaho Wildlife Federation recognized him as Conservationist of the Year in 1989 and he served as its president in 1991–1993. The two spearheaded fundraisers for Mountain States Tumor Institute hospice with "Winterfest" (1983–1986) and for "a Wild a Fair" (1986–1987),

which benefited wildlife conservation. They contributed to the Sun Valley Arts and Boise Beaux Arts wine auctions. When the recession years ended, Ed gave up his "40 hours-per-week volunteer work" and concentrated more than full time on re-growing the business. He sold the Ketchum branch in 1988 and in 1990 moved the north Idaho branch from Moscow

The Antinori family winery has been producing world class wines for over 600 years.

to Coeur d'Alene. The current portfolio offers nearly 900 different products from the wine and beer producing regions of the world.

The Robertsons continue to nurture their customers' and employees' interest in wine and beer. Each autumn since 1996 they have traveled to Europe and invited customers and employees to travel with them for nine days of immersion in a particular region's food, wine and culture. Their goal is to acquaint customers with the basics of European travel and

then to encourage them to organize their own trips.

It has been possible for the Robertsons to blend community ideals with their work culture at Idaho Wine Merchant. In the first years of the business they began to reduce waste and increase the use of recycled products. They built their current office building with many used or recycled materials. Energy-efficient lighting is used in the warehouse and office. A garden on the property grows vegetables, grapes and raspberries, but most of the property is landscaped for birds and butterflies. Employee dogs are welcome in the warehouse; and schedules accommodate high school and college students. Dress is appropriately casual and employees who bicycle to work have access to a shower.

Fine wine doesn't necessarily mean expensive wine. The term is a descriptor setting crafted products apart from wines that are marketed as commodities and which bear the heavy burden of advertising and marketing costs. Idaho Wine Merchant buys from many family-owned producers in California, the Pacific Northwest, Australia and Europe. Some of the European families have been making and improving their products since the 13th century. To taste these wines is to appreciate them!

The industry is much more competitive than it was in the early years with distributor and importer consolidations and an oversupply of commodity beers and wines. Idaho Wine Merchant has maintained its initial focus and still caters to those who enjoy creative food at home or in a restaurant and want to complete their experience with a fine wine or classic beer.

INTERMOUNTAIN GAS COMPANY

Low-cost energy is a key ingredient to successful economic development. When it comes to energy, Intermountain Gas provides its customers with comfortable, efficient, and affordable natural gas. The availability and low cost of natural gas is a major contributor to the enhanced quality of life and prosperity that the Company's customers and communities enjoy.

Boisean Nat Campbell and his wife Myrtis were the driving force behind Idaho's first natural gas energy operation. The possibility of offering Idahoans an alternative energy source sparked their interest in 1950, when natural gas was being introduced to the Northwest. The Campbells worked diligently for the next six years to secure the franchise and bring natural gas to southern Idaho. In December 1955, Intermountain Gas Company, an Idaho corporation, received the necessary certification from the Idaho Public Utilities Commission to distribute and sell natural gas at retail. Intermountain's first customer was connected a year later.

Homes throughout southern Idaho rely on natural gas for heating, water heating and other gas appliance operation.

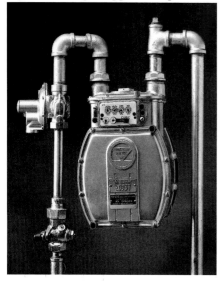

In 1985, Intermountain's ownership changed from that of a publicly-traded company to privately-held by an investor group. The new owner/directors, that included Idaho business professionals, combined their variety of complementary backgrounds and experiences with that of the management and employees to form a new basis for natural gas services. Strategies were formulated to encourage and reward entrepreneurial initiative, and to assure that the company would be properly positioned to take advantage of structural changes that were occurring in the natural gas industry. Efforts were undertaken to enhance Intermountain's responsiveness to markets and customers, and to solidify Intermountain's inherent ability to deliver competitive energy services and maintain the highest standards of safety and reliability. Concurrently, Intermountain's management focused on customer price stability through increased productivity of human, physical and financial resources.

Today Intermountain Gas, the local distribution company, provides natural gas energy to 75 cities in 29 counties over an area that covers 50,000 square miles. In an area that stretches from Weiser and Payette on Idaho's western border, through Sun Valley in the central mountains, to St. Anthony on the eastern border, this utility maintains over 7,700 miles of transmission, dis-

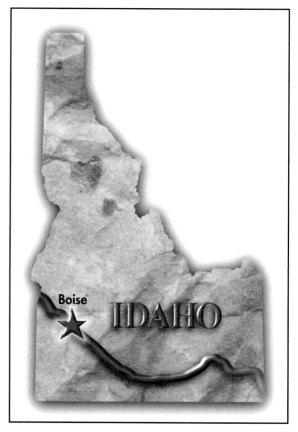

Intermountain Gas Company distributes natural gas energy to 75 cities in 29 counties along the Snake River corridor that traverses southern Idaho.

tribution, and service lines. Intermountain delivers natural gas to more than 200,000 customers throughout southern Idaho. In addition, the company operates a six million therm liquefied natural gas storage facility in its Western region. Residential and commercial customers account for 45 percent of annual sales, while industrial customers utilize 55 percent. Intermountain Gas plays a significant role as a major energy provider to industrial users such as potato processors, the dairy industry, chemical fertilizer manufacturers, and electronic manufacturing, to name a few.

Intermountain Gas Company's strengths originate in its workforce

Commitment to efficient use of natural gas today secures future, long-term benefits for Idaho. Partnering with the City of Boise resulted in the conversion of the Boise Urban Stages transit fleet to compressed natural gas (CNG). Reduced pollution from the natural gas buses and Intermountain Gas' fleet of CNG vehicles improves the air quality and also lowers operating expenses. This can translate into lower prices for its customers.

The future promises exciting opportunities for Intermountain Gas Company and the natural gas industry. Cogeneration, fuel cells, and creative pricing designs are just a few of many future developments which will continue to contribute to the efficiency, quality, and reliability of natural gas energy for all of the Company's customers.

Intermountain Gas introduced a program for the City of Boise to convert its Boise Urban Stages transit fleet to compressed natural gas (CNG), resulting in less pollution from bus operations and cleaner air for Boise.

of 330 employees. Known for their loyalty and commitment to the quality customer service, their teamwork is the basis for the company's efficient operation. The company's lean management structure and operating style enables employees to efficiently evaluate situations, solve problems, and quickly implement solutions to take advantage of opportunities. Every customer, irrespective of size, is important to the Company's success.

Intermountain Gas also excels in community involvement. Employees are encouraged to go beyond minimal involvement and pursue leadership positions in local economic development efforts, as well as in civic and service groups. This diversity of involvement contributes to the very success of the areas in which they live.

As technologies advance, Intermountain continues to look for

Intermountain Gas Company headquarters is the main hub for operations serving over 200,000 customers throughout southern Idaho.

better and more efficient ways to serve its customers and manage its operations. Advanced communication equipment allows a customer to make a local call from anywhere in the service area to a centralized customer service group with every customer record at its fingertips. Extended office hours, level pay arrangements, and, in remote locations, automated meter reading devices, help maintain the highest level of quality and service for the customer. Intermountain Gas uses a state-of-the-art SCADA (Supervisory Control And Data Acquisition) system to monitor and control gas flows and pressures, as well as read and control measurement points across its entire distribution system.

JORDAN-WILCOMB CONSTRUCTION, INC.

J.O. Jordan, founder of Jordan-Wilcomb Construction, Inc., arrived in Boise in 1901, just 11 years after Idaho had attained statehood. Forty-year old Jordan was a carpenter from Tennessee. The city was beginning to flourish and develop. Boise was named the capitol of the new Idaho territory in 1864. Between 1905 and 1912, after statehood was established in 1890, the state capitol building was constructed in Boise. The city was bustling and housing was needed. Jordan seized the opportunity and applied for his first building permit sometime prior to 1910. As a contractor, he began building houses in Boise.

In 1922, J.O. Jordan and his son J. Cecil Jordan formed a partnership as residential building contractors. The business became known as Jordan and Son. They were a small, family business and worked with as little overhead as possible. J. Cecil Jordan remarked, "In those early years the company's office was carried in the hind pocket of our trousers." Residential construction was their primary focus for a number of years.

Later they took advantage of the commercial opportunities in Boise. In 1927, Jordan and Son obtained their first commercial contract, to

The Ada County Courthouse, a Boise landmark, under construction in 1938.

The Boise State Administration Building (1940), a project of Jordan-Wilcomb Construction Company.

build the Egyptian Theatre located at the corner of Capitol Boulevard and Main Street. From that first commercial project they began to build Boise and a legacy. Their philosophy has been to confine their construction business to their hometown. The company has grown with Boise and 98 percent of their building contracts have been local.

J. Cecil Jordan was an astute businessman. Much of the firm's success can be attributed to the solid groundwork and management practices he established early in its development of the business. J. Cecil became active in the Boise Chamber of Commerce in 1930, when Jordan and Son became a member. He served on the board of directors in 1940 and on the executive board of directors from 1952-1954.

In the early years of Jordan and Son, J. Cecil tried to avoid contracting work outside the Boise area. When asked in a 1980 interview why he made this decision he replied, "Well, you have to go out and live somewhere else during construction and that's no fun at all. And another thing, if something happens to the darn thing, you have

to travel back and fix it. That's no fun, either. You spend more money than you make traveling back and forth just trying to make someone happy. We decided that if someone wanted to compete with us, they would have to do it in our own backyard...and that has worked pretty well."

When asked what innovations he had seen in construction J. Cecil responded: "Crane work. Back when we built the Egyptian Theatre we didn't have cranes. Imagine putting heavy steel trusses up and other heavy things without a crane. It was quite a job. It's a different program altogether, now."

By 1948, a third generation became actively involved in the business, and the family timeline was being established. With that came yet another name change. The company reorganized and a new partnership was formed. This time the partners were J. Cecil Jordan, his son J. Richard Jordan and his son-in-law Richard Wilcomb. The company became Jordan-Wilcomb Company.

The Boise State University Multi-Use Classroom Building completed in 1997.

The new partners continued to maintain a low-key approach. They shied away from advertising and publicity, but in time became a visible part of Boise, as their buildings continued to spring up out of the ground.

By 1980 the company had obtained contracts for and completed construction on dozens of schools; federal, state and county buildings; commercial buildings; public utilities; hospitals; churches; hotels; motels; theatres; and medical facilities. Each of these was essential to the growth and development of the community.

As so often happens in successful family businesses, the young people are encouraged to get a higher education before joining the company. Both Richard Wilcomb (J. Cecil's son-in-law) and J. Richard Jordan (J. Cecil's son) came into the business after college and serving time in the military during World War II.

Tim Wilcomb (Richard Wilcomb's son) grew up on the construction site. After obtaining a master's degree in international business, he had planned to pursue another career. He ultimately chose the family business and became a partner in 1979, carrying the business into the fourth generation. After graduating from Boise State University and working for Boise Cascade Corporation for several years, Bill Mooney Jr. (J. Richard Jordan's son-in-law) became part of the fourth generation and a principal in the company in 1986.

The family/business timeline continued. In 1982 Jordan-Wilcomb Construction, Inc. became the construction branch of Jordan-Wilcomb Company. Tim Wilcomb and Bill Mooney Jr. became the majority owners of Jordan-Wilcomb Construction, Inc. in 1995.

The principals in the company continue to be actively involved in each project. They have a hands-on approach and each job is managed and supervised by one of the principals. They have established credibility and integrity, which has helped them to build their business through referrals.

In spite of the company's success it still maintains a low-key approach and has resided in the original office space at 406 South Sixth Street since 1938. The principals will not take on a greater workload than they themselves can handle, honoring a commitment to owner satisfaction on all of their construction projects. The company's business philosophy has served it well for nearly a century. More recent projects are The Idaho Elks Rehabilitation Hospital, Idaho Shakespeare Festival Outdoor Theater, renovation of the YMCA downtown facility and renovation of the Intermountain Gas Company headquarters.

The Jordan-Wilcomb legacy moves into the 21st century as it continues to build Boise.

Rendering of the Idaho Elks Rehabilitation Hospital, completed in Fall 2000.

J-U-B ENGINEERS, INC.

J-U-B ENGINEERS emerged in 1954 as the culmination of a series of events beginning in 1951 when Sumner M. Johnson apprenticed to Raymond J. Briggs and Associates of Boise. The following year he received his Professional Engineer registration and became a full associate. While working on assignment in Las Vegas he met Robert W. "Bob" Underkofler. Shortly thereafter Bob left his work in Las Vegas and came to Boise looking for new opportunities. It happened that Sumner needed help on subdivision surveying and engineering work, and when Bob approached him he responded, "I can use you for a couple of weeks." Those two weeks ran into an association of 25 years. The two formed a partnership, with offices in Boise and Nampa, which later expanded to include William W. Briggs from Briggs and Associates.

Originally the primary services were engineering and surveying, predominantly for land development and municipal engineering services in the Boise valley, as city engineer for the neighboring city of Nampa. As the area grew during the 1960s, J-U-B grew as well. By actively seeking more work in the public sector and continuing its broad base of land development projects, the company continuously added more staff. During this time the firm expanded its services to include structural engineering, which has continued to be a major component of the services that J-U-B provides.

As the company continued to grow, the partners saw the need to bring key staff members into ownership of the company. Therefore, in 1969 they proceeded to incorporate the firm as J-U-B

Above
William W. Briggs, senior vice president, was an associate of Briggs and Assocites prior to becoming a principal of J-U-B in 1962.

Below
The recently completed J-U-B building in 1980.

Engineers, Inc., a business specializing in engineering, surveying and planning.

In 1971 J-U-B merged with Riedesel and Straubhar of Twin Falls, bringing the number of offices to three. During the explosive growth of the mid-1970s, fueled by the grant programs associated with the Clean Water Act and by funding for airports, J-U-B continued to expand its public works engineering until the department equaled that of land development. J-U-B added offices in Coeur d'Alene, Idaho; Kennewick, Washington; and Pocatello, Idaho. By the late '70s J-U-B was the largest Idaho-based consulting firm in the state. In 1979 the Boise office alone had grown so much that the firm built its own office at 250 South Beechwood Avenue. That structure still serves as corporate headquarters.

Arlin Broske, who joined the firm in 1957 as business manager and assistant corporate secretary-treasurer, was the first woman stockholder. She continued with the firm for 40 years, keeping the principals organized and doing the billing.

During the early-'80s the Idaho economy suffered a serious and

Sumner M. Johnson

prolonged downturn. As a result, J-U-B found itself shrunk from 165 employees to 45, and prospects for the company were grim. At this juncture Bill Briggs retired from J-U-B and started his own firm. Sumner Johnson, who had previously retired, returned to lead J-U-B's reorganization. The existing stockholders took as much money as they could out of their own pockets to leverage into loans and began rebuilding the firm. Reorganized and refinanced, the company was set on the road to growth. J-U-B Engineers, Inc. has become one of the leading consulting engineering firms in the Pacific Northwest, with five offices in Idaho, two in Washington and two in Utah, and employing over 250 people.

J-U-B has engineered a significant number of the residential subdivisions in Boise from the mid-'50s to the present. The company has also done much of the master planning and many of the sewer models for the City of Boise as well as the structural work for the Capitol Mall and

buildings on Boise State University campus.

The company has always placed a very high value on education and encourages its employees to continue their development. Members of the firm also participate at all levels of education as volunteers and as elected officials on school boards, in addition to the company's monetary support. Sumner Johnson served a term as president of the Idaho Society of Professional Engineers and on the Nampa School Board for some time, and Robert Underkofler was executive secretary to the Idaho Board of Registration of Professional Engineers and served as president of the Consulting Engineers of Idaho.

Throughout its history, J-U-B has been a community-based engineering firm. Its employees are part of the communities in which they work and reflect the values of those communities. During his tenure of leadership with the company, Sumner Johnson consistently emphasized to J-U-B's employees the importance of meeting the ethical standards of the profession. This tradition of con-

Robert W. Underkofler

sistent dedication to the principles of integrity and community involvement continues to be of prime importance in the organization and has played a major role in the general success and respect enjoyed by the company as a whole.

Dormitory on the campus of Boise State University.

METALCRAFT, INC.

Metalcraft, Inc. is a precision sheet metal fabrication and machining company, historically serving the electronics, semiconductor, and medical industries, that was founded in 1986 by Richard G. Cortez. Mr. Cortez, the son of Mexican-born migrant workers, began his sheet metal career as a Fab 1 sheet metal trainee with the Hewlett-Packard Company in Palo Alto, CA in 1962. He turned that opportunity into a 24-year career with HP, retiring as section manager of the sheet metal and finish shop at HP's Boise site. Upon retirement, Mr. Cortez realized that he possessed the skills and ambition needed to open Metalcraft. He liquidated his personal assets and invested every dollar, including his HP retirement fund, into this pursuit.

As with many start-ups, Metalcraft's early years were filled with much adversity, and sacrifice. Opening with one NC punch, one NC brake, one computer and five employees, the company suffered an inexperienced workforce, a lack of customers and a financial situation that was touch-and-go. There were times when Richard went for months without receiving a paycheck from Metalcraft, yet the company persevered. With time, the employees had gained valuable production experience, and the customer base had consistently increased. Metalcraft found itself rapidly approaching its production capacity. Although sales were increasing and the company growing, the bottom line was still dismal. Metalcraft was faced with the need for additional equipment, but lacked the financial stability to secure a line of credit. The company was at a crossroads: it could continue to operate with its limited capital,

Ken Contez, president and Richard G. Contez, CEO.

workforce and equipment, or make the commitment to expand. Richard dedicated his company, as well as himself, to growth and its accompanying challenges. In 1988, Richard formed a partnership with an associate from HP, and transformed the company into a corporation. This partnership allowed the company to secure the capital investments necessary to accommodate the growth that the organization was enjoying. The partnership was dissolved in 1992 upon his partner's retirement, leaving Richard as the sole stockholder.

Metalcraft's commitment to growth led to a diversified customer base, an increasing pool of talented employees and a technically advanced equipment inventory—all operating within the original 8,000 square-foot, leased facility. In 1993, with the assistance of an SBA loan, Metalcraft began moving into its very own 21,000 square-foot facility. Not only did Richard

reorganize the physical plant at this time, but he also restructured the management team. Ken Cortez was hired as general manager to join Richard's management team, which had been comprised of Richard and his business manager. As intended, substantial growth followed, and has continued since. Although many growth-related problems of production and personnel have arisen over the years, Richard has used his acquired ability of problem solving to overcome these various obstacles.

The results of Richard's efforts speak for themselves. Metalcraft is to be an ISO 9002 registered company with a customer base of over 300 and annual sales approaching $10 million. The company is administered by a management team that includes the president, sales manager, business manager and operations manager. Production employees are cross-trained for increased productivity, which improves employee retention, and includes in-house Spanish and English courses taught to help accommodate Metalcraft's bilingual environment. Richard's ability to identify talent, and the development of the management team and production staff have enabled the company to evolve into what it is today—a stable, respected competitor in the precision sheet metal and machine trades.

Richard's dedication to improving the stability of Metalcraft allowed him to become a very involved and well-respected member of the community. The focus of Richard's community work has been education, as he feels that it is imperative to equip young people with the necessary tools to become self-sufficient. As president and charter member of the Hispanic Business Association, Richard and Metalcraft organize and sponsor the Jalapeno Open Golf Tournament. The proceeds from this event fund scholarships, which afford Hispanic youths the opportunity to attend college or vocational school. Proceeds from the 1999 tournament totaled over $10,000.

Richard has been recognized on numerous occasions for his outstanding service to business, as well as to the local community. In October 1993, he was honored in "Portrait of a Distinguished Citizen" by the *Idaho Statesman*. In May 1994, as president of Metalcraft, he was awarded the U.S. Small Business Minority Small Business Advocate of the Year—Region Ten, for significant contributions on behalf of small

business. Also in 1994, Senator Dirk Kempthorne recognized Richard "as an asset to the community" in a tribute presented to the U.S. Congress, and the City of Boise named him grand marshall of the annual Holiday Parade. In 1995 he was appointed to the Idaho Commission on Hispanic Affairs by then Governor Phil Batt, and, also in 1995, Metalcraft was the Blue Chip Enterprise Initiative State Award recipient. In 1997 Richard was named the Boise Area Chamber of Commerce "Small Business Person of the Year." He was quoted in the November 1994 issue of *Money* magazine, and June 1995 issue of *Nation's Business* magazine.

By Summer 2000, Richard had assigned the daily administrative duties of the company to the management team that includes the president, vice president of operations and sales, vice president of administration and finance, operations manager, production manager and quality manager. In

addition to performing countless civic and business duties Richard has served on the Boise State University College of Engineering Advisory Board; the Governor's State Science and Technology Advisory Council; the Governor's International Trade Advisory Council, Governor's Workforce Development Council; and as a board member of the Boise Metro Chamber of Commerce.

The Metalcraft of the future will be ISO 9002 certified, continue to diversify its customer base; expand the plant by 10,000 square feet; continue capital investments in new equipment, processes, and technology; and will see the employee base reach 100 total. Richard Cortez is a perfect example, for non-Hispanics as well as Hispanics, on how to take advantage of an opportunity, and by exercising this liberty has empowered numerous others to do the same.

Metalcraft plant, 2000.

NAGEL BEVERAGE COMPANY

During the early growth years of Boise, in the late 1800s, a gentleman from Baker City, Oregon saw an opportunity to make his mark in the business world.

On September 20, 1895, John Nagel purchased the soda water business of Ada County. The business mainstay was soda water delivery to 10 Southwest Idaho county saloons. All deliveries were done by horse-drawn wagons. The physical location of the business was in the Davis Levy building on the northwest corner of Fifth and Idaho streets in Boise, Idaho.

With the ever-growing public demand for soda water it became evident to founder John Nagel that he needed to expand his business, and in 1905 Nagel Beverage Company relocated to 13th and Main Streets. This new facility gave John the opportunity to begin bottling flavored soda waters.

Copy of 1895 deed for purchase of Ada County Soda Water Business.

Nagel Beverage Company 13th & Main Street in Boise, Idaho.

Being a savvy businessman, John Nagel obtained Nagel Beverage Company the franchise rights for Pepsi-Cola, in 1935. This would give John both growth and stability opportunity for his family-owned business. Nagel Beverage became a franchisee for Squirt that same year. With the brand rights for bottling two top sellers, Pepsi-Cola and Squirt, John Nagel was now able to begin seeking business opportunities outside of the Boise Valley. John saw and seized such an opportunity for expansion to the south of Boise in the fast growing community of Twin Falls, Idaho. He was able to open Twin Falls Pepsi that same year by procuring a partnership with community leaders from the Twin Falls area. The opening of this plant allowed John Nagel to expand product delivery routes to include South Central Idaho counties. Nagel Beverage also had obtained distribution rights for other brands, including Mission Orange Soda, Acme Beer and Schlitz Beer.

Well over 40 years after establishing his soda water business, and expanding it into a franchise bottler for top selling soft drinks Pepsi-Cola and Squirt, John Nagel Sr. passed away. The torch of leadership for this family-owned business was passed onto John's son John F. Nagel.

With the United States of America coming out of the war victorious, it was time once again for John F. to concentrate his efforts on building the family business. Having the same business acumen as his father, John F. applied the profits from Nagel Beverage Company back into the business. A new state-of-the-art bottling line was installed at the 13th and Main plant in the 1950s, helping to increase overall sales for Nagel Beverage.

After dedicating his adult life to ensuring that the soda water busi-

After studies of the current plant and endless hours of deliberation, a decision by the Nagel family was made to build outside the current city limits, where they could drill a well for their water needs to bottle product. They purchased land on Irving Street. In 1972, the new Pepsi-Cola plant opened for business.

With Pepsi-Cola making great strides in becoming the leader in cola products, especially in the Boise Valley and outlying areas, the plant needed to be larger. So in 1982, a new addition was built onto the existing plant at 5465 Irving Street.

In 1988, Jack Nagel unexpectedly passed away. His mother Mildred E., sister Anne Nagel Mathews and a daughter Victoria survive Jack.

Having survived both her husband and son, Mildred E. Nagel

Nagel Beverage Company, circa 1940.

ness his father had built would be there for future generations, John F. Nagel passed away in 1969. He left a wife Mildred E., a son Jack and a daughter Anne. With large shoes to fill Jack Nagel, at the age of 26, assumed the role of running Nagel Beverage Company after his father's death. A daunting task for such a young man to undertake, Jack, having inherited his grandfather and father's good business sense, had the foresight to look outside the business and project where the company needed to be in the future. While production of Pepsi-Cola products increased (three-fold since his father had installed the latest in bottling equipment), Jack could see that in order to meet the public's growing demands and produce all the new products introduced by Pepsi-Cola Corporate, Nagel Beverage would have to, once again, expand their bottling facility.

Twin Falls Pepsi Building, 1934, sister company of Nagel Beverage Company of Boise, Idaho.

stepped into the role of Nagel Beverage Company president with her daughter Anne Nagel Mathews assuming the role of company vice-president.

1995 was a milestone year for Nagel Beverage Company, celebrating their 100-year anniversary in the Boise community. Under the leadership of Mildred and her daughter Anne, Nagel Beverage Company remains in the forefront as a leader and good corporate citizen in the community they so dearly love.

Reflecting upon Nagel's past accomplishments and the Company's best position for future growth potential, Mildred, along with her daughter Anne, created a 20-year business plan, projecting where they felt business opportunities would become available to both Nagel Beverage and

Our young men go off to defend the country and women enter the workforce at Nagel Beverage Company to help fill the void.

Nagel Beverage Company president John F. Nagel—Nagel's second generation.

its sister company Twin Falls Pepsi.

In 1996 Nagel Beverage Company re-acquired the franchise rights for 7-Up, increasing Nagel Beverage Company's market share.

Once again, Nagel Beverage was looking towards expanding to meet the growing consumer demand for product. In 1996 the production line was revamped and new equipment purchased and installed to assure the company's ability to fulfill all the consumer needs of their Southwest Idaho and South Central Idaho delivery regions. Nagel Beverage Company's delivery region is west to the Oregon border, east to Glenns Ferry, Idaho, north to New Meadows, Idaho and south to the Nevada border. Its

New bottling line was installed at Nagel Beverage in 1950.

Nagel Beverage Company's new facility on Irving Street, 1972.

sister company Twin Falls Pepsi, delivers west to Bliss, Idaho, east to Raft River, Idaho, north to Galena Summit and south to the Nevada border.

Mildred E Nagel, president of Nagel Beverage Company, feels a great sense of community involvement has always been foremost in the minds of Nagel Beverage Company. Thus, in memory of her late husband John F. Nagel and son Jack, she established a charitable foundation. The John F. Nagel foundation is very committed to youth charities and southwest Idaho charities. Pepsi sponsorship of community sporting events (baseball, tennis, hockey and football), Youth Sports (Capital Youth Soccer and PAL sponsorship) and Little League Baseball are integral parts of Nagel Beverage Company's commitment to giving back to the community that has given them so much.

Nagel Beverage Company is also a key contributor to youth education. Nagel Beverage Company has established a High School Scholarship Program with annual contributions to southwest Idaho High Schools. Nagel Beverage is also committed to higher education, and is a main benefactor to Southwest Idaho colleges and universities, providing numerous scholarships and methods of financial support, where needed.

Nagel Beverage is an employee-oriented, family-owned business that takes great pride in the fact that they are still locally-owned and managed after 105 years.

Plant expansion located at 5465 Irving Street in Boise, 1982.

R & M STEEL COMPANY

It all started in State College, Pennsylvania. Robert C. (Rob) Roberts founded the R & M Steel Company when he was 22 years old, in 1968.

Rob took a welding class because he wanted to build a hitch to pull a mobile home. He bought his first portable welding machine, then welding leads, and finally, the battery. It took time to earn and save up the money for each item.

The City of State College had a new ordinance requiring fire escapes on all of the buildings that had apartments for the college students. Rob had a load of steel dropped off to each site, measured and manufactured it right there, installed it and went on to the next one. There was just "a zillion of them" to do.

R & M Steel Constructors was the company's original name. When incorporated in November 1973, the company became R & M Steel Company, Inc., with Rob Roberts as president. Throughout the world the company is now simply known as R & M Steel.

R & M Steel offers complete manufacturing service from custom design, through delivery of pre-engineered metal building

Original shop at 7700 W. State Street, Boise, ID, 1971.

systems for virtually any application. All buildings meet applicable codes and incorporate state-of-the-art design and fabrication technology. The systems are designed for quality, simplicity, fast and economical installation, and low maintenance cost. Competitive pricing has facilitated both national and worldwide distribution.

A team of trained professionals is available to assist designers, builders and first-time users. Custom designs are available for retail, industrial, manufacturing, warehousing, service centers, truck terminals and distribution centers, mini storage, office space, multiple lease, school facilities, and agricultural facilities. R & M Steel specializes in custom design and manufacture of aviation building systems such as FBO facilities, maintenance hangars, individual hangars, corporate hangars, T-hangars, flight training facilities, and shade ports.

R & M Steel's scope of work allows the local community to share in the economic benefits of the project. Local suppliers, contractors and other professionals do

the work of site preparation, concrete work for foundations and slabs, metal building system installation, interior finishing, landscaping, and supplying and installing exterior finishes if the exterior is other than steel.

Rob graduated from Western School of Heavy Equipment in the Spring of 1968, and his wife Mavis completed a teaching contract in Pennsylvania at Bald Eagle Elementary School in June 1969.

Rob left the fire escape building business and moved the family, including their five children, to Boise, Idaho, arriving in August of 1969. As he developed the portable welding business, Rob continued to think about other work to do. He came up with the idea of erecting structural steel.

The first job that R & M Steel Constructors did in Boise was the Catholic Student Center at Boise State University, erecting the steel joists and metal deck. It was across the street from the BSU

Rob Roberts at Western School of Heavy Equipment, Weiser, Idaho. 1968.

1998 Kenworth truck.

campus. Rob hired a crane; he and Mavis set the steel.

Some other memorable jobs during R & M Steel Constructors' first years were erecting the towers and antennas at Deer Point up at Bogus Basin in 1970 through 1974. Unfortunately, the clients would always wait until November, when it was snowy and icy to decide to begin this type of project, rather than early in the year. Rob and his son George worked together erecting the first towers and antennas, which varied in size and height. Some were 100 feet and some were 200 feet tall. Eventually it became too difficult getting anybody that would work a couple of hundred feet off the ground. They would get to the top and "freeze-up," or be afraid to go up at all. It was just too scary for them. Rob did do some tower erecting by himself, but it was too

much for one person. He finished the last tower project and simply stopped doing any more.

Early steel erecting projects also included Grand Central, several B.S.U. Student Union Building additions, Great Western, and Lowell-Scott Junior High School.

R & M Steel's work evolved into manufacturing structural and miscellaneous steel, Division Five, for a variety of projects in Boise, including, Albertson's grocery store, the first major expansion to Boise Air Terminal, the tunnel

connecting the State Capital to the Len B. Jordan building, and Meridian High School.

In the early 1970s Mavis was managing the wrought iron division.

Rob started working on developing metal building manufacturing. By 1971, R & M Steel was designing and manufacturing pre-engineered metal building systems. Rob did all of the drawings and structural engineering, and continued to refine and develop the process. A licensed engineer reviewed the work and signed and sealed the drawings.

In 1971, five acres were purchased at 7700 West State Street in Boise, where the company relocated. The concrete barn was remodeled for use as a shop. The great drafting table and related equipment were purchased that year. There were four or five employees working in the shop at that time. The majority of the land was in pasture grass with a few head of cattle.

Rob and George manufactured and erected the second shop building in the Fall of 1973. The first semi tractor and trailer, an International, was purchased that year as well. Typically, wheat would be hauled to Portland, steel hauled back to Boise to be used

Second shop, completed 1973.

in the manufacturing process, and the completed steel building system was delivered to the client.

Jobs were acquired by word-of-mouth recommendations at that time and through the '70s and early-'80s this was effective for about a 300-mile radius.

The third shop building was manufactured and erected by Rob and several other employees over a 4th of July weekend in 1975. At the beginning of the weekend there was nothing there, and by the end of the weekend the 80 by 100-foot building was completed. The remodeled barn became exclusively office space.

Rob Roberts designed and manufactured a sub arc, which is an automatic beam welding machine that puts in two welds simultaneously. That was a milestone in manufacturing. He also manufactured several sub arc machines for other companies.

Aviation has had a significant influence on the company. In 1981 Rob learned to fly. He holds a commercial pilot's certificate with multi-engine, instrument, and flight instructor ratings. The corporation purchased a Cessna 182. A resurgence of interest in general aviation has provided great opportunities for Rob and the com-

Sub arc and welding shop.

pany and he continues to fly for business and pleasure. The company specializes in meeting the aviation building systems needs of the aviation community.

In the 1980s the metal building market collapsed as metal building companies were going out of business on a daily basis. Rob began developing a dealer network. R & M Steel experienced steady growth in that time period and during each successive year.

R & M Steel was one of the first companies to do computer drafting work as it related to metal buildings.

By 1980, Rob was doing computer-aided design and engineering, which allowed him to do more precise and accurate work. In 1985 R & M Steel purchased the Rap Cad program, proceeded to modify it and began producing computer-drawn metal building plans. This was a great step forward; it really made a big difference.

George was instrumental in developing the computer estimating, computer design, and computer drafting programs. The computer-

estimating programs are still in use in the year 2000. In 1985 he began doing the computer drafting, and has continued working in the engineering department with increasing responsibilities.

A doublewide was purchased in 1991 and used as the main office. R&M Steel employed 13 people at that time.

Rob's son Robert K. joined the company in 1990. He started in the shop and later was shop superintendent for a number of years. In the Summer of 1999, Robert decided to pursue other interests and left the company. Dave Randall was promoted to shop superintendent.

In 1994, Rob remarried. His new wife Nancy Rose Carter began bringing lunch every day. Rob had warned her that this steel business gets into your blood, the excitement grows, and you begin to feel like you just have to be a part of it. He was right, again. Nancy Rose joined the company in 1995.

Rob and Nancy with Piri Puruto III in Rarotonga, 1995.

Cedco Blue Diamond, Las Vegas, NV. (Building project example.)

Nephews Sean and Link Porterfield designed and installed two websites for the company in 1998. The pre-engineered metal building systems division is serviced by www.rmsteel.com. The aviation building systems division is serviced by www.aviation buildingsystem.com. A request for quote or an employment application can be completed and submitted from either website.

Rob uses old-fashioned, conservative business principles to make sure the company is strong, profitable and enduring, so that he and the employees will all have the opportunity to have a highly-successful lifetime career and a comfortable retirement. Growth is carefully controlled. Each employee is trained to be a master of their profession and encouraged to reach their highest level. Rob believes the work should be fun, something they enjoy, that gives a great feeling of satisfaction. Income is kept high and benefits are excellent. In the 30 years of operation, there has never been a layoff. That, is an incredible record!

The company mission is met on a daily basis: To provide the highest quality metal building system on the market. The working ethic for all employees comes from Rob's Boy Scout background, "friendly, courteous, kind, obedient, cheerful, thrifty, brave, clean and reverent." The company's success is attributed to the high quality of product, simplicity of the design and installation of the building system, and the high quality of workers within the organization. The company motto is "Steel Building Excellence—Since 1969."

It is exciting to travel nearly anywhere in the world and see R&M Steel metal building systems in service: all around Boise, throughout the mainland United States, and in Alaska, Hawaii, Canada, Mexico, American Samoa, Germany, Japan, North Africa, Guam, Micronesia, Latvia, Madagascar, Tonga, Aruba, the Caribbean, the Philippines, Puerto Rico, and Israel.

The list of metal building projects in Boise alone is immense. A few of the most widely-known are: T-hangars at Gowen Field; M-K aviation; M-K rail locomotive repair shop; Masco buildings 1, 2, and 3; Idaho 1st National Bank hangar; Boise Cascade hangar; Western Aircraft office; B.U.U.F. Church; Idaho Department of Transportation maintenance buildings; Handy Concrete Mix and Truck Lines; and Clemons Sales.

Entering the year 2000, R&M Steel is a $10 million company with 33 employees. The need for expansion had been pressing for many years.

The latest expansion began in 1998. Rob and Nancy purchased 80 acres of industrial/farm ground in Caldwell, Idaho. Currently, the new 90,000 square foot facility is under construction and expected to be completed in September 2000.

R&M Steel Company is expanding its commitment to their customers by offering the new facility that features state-of-the-art equipment for the design and manufacture of complete pre-engineered metal building systems, including a variety of roof and wall panels and standing seam roof systems.

Designed for maximum efficiency, the plant will significantly increase R&M Steel's production capabilities, and reduce lead times for delivery of metal buildings anywhere in the world.

R&M Steel Company received many alluring relocation incentives to expand out-of-state, but Rob has refused to leave the great state of Idaho. Boise is home.

R & M Steel Company's new 90,000 square foot plant under construction, August 2000.

SAINT ALPHONSUS REGIONAL MEDICAL CENTER

On a cold and wintry December day in 1894, four devoted nuns of the Sisters of the Holy Cross proudly opened the doors of Boise's first hospital. It was to be called Saint Alphonsus, and it represented a concerted effort by the Sisters and the people of Boise to build better healthcare for all people of the community. In the century that followed, that cooperative and dedicated spirit united time and time again, constructing a major medical center that serves a tri-state area with leading-edge technology, compassionate care and a constant eye to the future.

When the Sisters first came to the people of Boise with their idea, they needed $3,000 to purchase land. The citizens of Boise and neighboring towns raised the funds for a site at Fifth and State streets. The Sisters fulfilled their goal, opening a hospital named after Saint Alphonsus Ligouri, a 16th-century Italian missionary, and Alphonse Glorieaux, Boise's first Catholic Bishop known for his dedication to serving the spiritual, educational and healthcare needs of Idahoans. Boise had its first hospital, a modern facility that combined up-to-date medicine with a gracious staff who never turned away anyone in need.

During the hospital's first year, the four Sisters treated 56 patients. Those unable to pay received the same attention as those who were able. A barter system, as well as paying in cash, remained an acceptable means of payment at Saint Alphonsus into the mid-1940s.

Year after year, the hospital continued to provide Boise with the latest medical innovations. In 1906, Saint Alphonsus brought Idaho its first X-ray machine and its first School of Nursing. In 1902

Saint Alphonsus Hospital was the first hospital in Boise, established in 1894 at Fifth and State streets by the Sisters of the Holy Cross.

and 1912, additions were made which increased the building's capacity to 139 beds. In 1919, the American College of Surgeons recognized Saint Alphonsus' medical staff for putting Idaho in the "forefront of states active in medical progress."

During the 1920s and 1930s, services burgeoned with the number of patients treated climbing to over 3,100 in 1936. The only deep-therapy X-ray apparatus between Portland and Salt Lake City was obtained for Saint Alphonsus, and during World War II, it became a blood-drawing center

The Saint Alphonsus Idaho Neurological Institute leads the state in medical care for the brain, neck and spine, and the Radiology Department is home to some of the most sophisticated equipment and techniques available in the United States.

for the American Legion. By the end of the war, occupancy rates soared for hospitals everywhere. The Boise community and Saint Alphonsus, as well as sister Boise hospital St. Luke's, launched a joint effort to fund expansions in 1947. The outcome was a new 60-bed wing at Saint Alphonsus built in 1951, where two years later Idaho's first short-term psychiatric ward opened its doors.

A two-year study completed in 1963 revealed a major hospital space shortage in Boise. After considering the physical condition of the Fifth and State streets building and the growing population of Boise, which had swelled

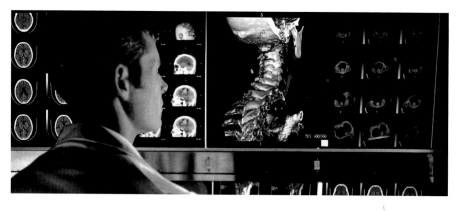

Saint Alphonsus operates Idaho's longest-standing emergency air medical transport, Life Flight.

to 35,000, a decision was made to relocate Saint Alphonsus. A site on Curtis Road near the planned freeway connector and Fairview Avenue, Boise's major east-west thoroughfare, was selected. Once again, the community came forward to support the expansion. More than 60 civic leaders and 1,000 dedicated Boiseans contributed over $1.3 million to the project.

In April 1972, after nearly a decade of planning, research, and fundraising, patients were moved to a new 229-bed hospital. The $14.4 million facility, like the original $3,000 Saint Alphonsus hospital, represented the latest in healthcare. The years that followed brought a new outpatient surgery department and a $1 million expansion to the emergency-trauma department. A new neurology/neurosurgery department was completed on the sixth floor of the hospital and the critical care unit doubled in size. By 2000, Saint Alphonsus Regional Medical Center had become a 281-bed hospital serving an area that is home to over half a million people.

The hospital has never stopped growing and changing in response to the region's needs. Today, Saint Alphonsus is Idaho's only Level II Trauma Center, making it the

state's flagship medical center for emergency-trauma care. In addition, it operates Boise's longest-standing emergency air medical transport, Life Flight. It has been named to the nation's Top 100 Hospitals list by independent health research firms for both orthopedic and cardiac care, and has been named as one of the 100 Most Wired hospitals for its innovative use of computer technology.

Saint Alphonsus Centers of Excellence also offer advanced and compassionate care for cancer, maternity, behavioral health, pediatrics, and women's and

seniors' health, among others. Its Idaho Neurological Institute leads the state in medical care for the brain, neck and spine, and the Radiology Department is home to some of the most sophisticated equipment and techniques available in the United States. Saint Alphonsus has expanded into the region through affiliated physician practices, off-campus rehabilitation units and mobile health facilities, and has reached out to the community with wellness education. It is the center of an integrated network of health delivery, and has never stopped helping those in need.

The four pioneering Sisters who opened Boise's first hospital would be astounded by the facility's progress. They would also be delighted that their philosophy has endured. Caring for the spiritual, emotional and physical needs of the community has, and always will be, the primary task of Saint Alphonsus Regional Medical Center.

Today, Saint Alphonsus is Idaho's only Level II Trauma Center, making it the state's flagship medical center for emergency-trauma care.

SCP GLOBAL TECHNOLOGIES

SCP Global Technologies has been providing products and services for the semiconductor industry since 1975. With a focus on innovative technology, SCP's equipment has become the tool of choice for many of the world's leading integrated circuit chip manufacturers. This success has propelled SCP to become the world's second largest supplier of semiconductor cleaning equipment and one of the Treasure Valley's fastest growing high-tech manufacturing companies. With the increasing demands for high throughput and ultra-clean process equipment, the fully automated wet station has become the core of SCP's product line.

SCP Global Technologies began operations in California's Silicon Valley, under the name Santa Clara Plastics, as a small custom machine shop and manufacturing company. The company later moved to Garden City, Idaho in 1978 to avoid the escalating costs in Silicon Valley. Approximately 15 Santa Clara Plastics employees made the move from California to Idaho to help establish the company in the Treasure Valley.

In 1981, Preco, Inc. acquired Santa Clara Plastics, which remains a division by Preco to this day. Preco is the leading manufacturer of reverse motion alarms for industrial equipment.

In 1996, Santa Clara Plastics changed its name to SCP Global Technologies to reflect the company's new focus on worldwide expansion and the development of industry-leading technology. SCP's vision is to be the leading worldwide supplier of cost-effective surface preparation technology, systems and services to the semiconductor and related industries.

In 1998, the company established SCP Global Technologies

SCP surface preparation system.

Europe to provide world class process, service and support for Europe. And in 1999, SCP Global Technologies Asia Pte. Ltd. was founded to sell, distribute and service SCP surface preparation systems throughout Asia. SCP is well on its way to accomplishing this goal, climbing from number eight in market share in 1996 to number two in 1999.

To continue to gain market share and add new technologies, SCP has aggressively added highly-trained engineers and technologists from within the industry. In 1998, the company established a New Product Development department that is dedicated to the development of state-of-the-art process technology and products to meet the increasing demand for higher throughput and lower cost equipment. SCP also has one of the industries' best

customer demonstration labs, to support customers with process and product development.

SCP's state-of-the-art man-ufacturing facility is based in Boise. Production and packaging is conducted in a Class100/Class1000 cleanroom to maintain the cleanliness standards required in today's semiconductor fabs. Products are moved from SCP's cleanroom to the customer's fab without ever being exposed to harmful contaminants. Moving forward, SCP will continue to add capacity to support technology and growth, and reduce equipment lead-time on delivery.

SCP offers one of the most comprehensive customer support structures in the industry, offering 24-hour service, 7 days a week through its Global Customer Support Network. This network includes field service and parts distribution centers throughout the United States, Europe and Asia. Its worldwide support centers provide knowledge-driven service and quick parts delivery around the globe, ensuring unmatched service and delivery to maximize customers' uptime.

SCP Global Technologies has come a long way from its inception in 1973 as a small custom machine and manufacturing company employing 13 people. Today, SCP employs well over 900 people located throughout the United States, Europe and Asia and its campus encompasses seven buildings in the Westpark Industrial Park of Boise.

PRECO, INC.

In 1947, Edwin R. Peterson was thinking about how he was going to make a living. The Staten Island, New York native had recently completed his duties as a captain and pilot in World War II. During the war Peterson was trained at Boise's Gowen Field; after the war he returned to Idaho's capital city.

A self-proclaimed "inventor and tinkerer," Peterson founded Preco, Inc., in a 10x20 foot tin shed on South Sixth Street in Boise. Its primary business was the rebuilding of water pumps, generators, and batteries. As the business grew, there was soon the need for larger quarters, and the company moved to a location on Fairview Avenue.

In 1967, Mr. Peterson infused major growth into the company by inventing the first reverse-motion alarm. A new industry was thus formed. Preco is a leading manufacturer of the devices that make the "beep-beep-beep of the back-up alarm sounds on construction sites and on large vehicles all over the world. The growth caused by the demand for back-up alarms necessitated the need for more management, and in 1975 Peterson hired Jack Y. Robertson as chief executive officer. Under Robertson the company grew, and with growth came profits, expansion, and diversification.

Preco acquired Santa Clara Plastics in 1981, which has since moved from its original location in Santa Clara, California to Boise,

Preco, Boise, Idaho.

Idaho and evolved into SCP Global Technologies, the industry leader in semiconductor wafer cleaning systems. In 1987 Preco opened a manufacturing operation in Morton, Illinois which has become a leading electronic custom manufacturing concern in the industrial electronics industry.

Additionally, in 1996 Preco acquired Ampro Computers, Inc. Ampro is based in San Jose, California and is an innovator in the embedded computer industry. By 1996, the company had reached an overall employee base of more than 600 employees. Preco was now a serious force to be reckoned within the areas of industrial electronics, semiconductor cleaning equipment, and embedded computers.

In that same year of 1996, Edwin R. Peterson sold the company to his son Mark, who had spent the previous 13 years working his way through the ranks of Preco and SCP Global Technologies. This allowed the elder Mr. Peterson (well beyond the age of retirement for most people) to focus on what he loved best: tinkering, flying in one of his several aircraft, and inventing new "gadgets." Mark took over as CEO and Jack Robertson assumed the role of chairman of the board.

Mark Peterson sought to grow and strengthen Preco, Treasure Valley's oldest and most stable electronics manufacturing company. He emphasized new product and process development to fuel growth. The Preco companies recruited executive and technical talent from the "best in class" high technology companies in the country. Personnel from Boeing, Hewlett-Packard, Sun Microsystems, Micron Technology, Apple Computer, Motorola, and others were brought together with

Preco executives to exchange ideas, vision, and knowledge.

The Millennium found the original Boise-based Preco electronics operation with new product lines augmenting the old core products. These included sophisticated radar object detection systems and computers that reside on industrial vehicles, to allow voice, data and video communication on and off board. The Morton-based Preco organization opened a new, state-of-the-art facility for electronic custom manufacturing services and has become a leader in industrial electronic manufacturing.

SCP Global Technologies had become the second largest provider of semiconductor cleaning solutions in the world as a result of being the leading innovator in semiconductor cleaning and drying equipment. SCP sales continue to grow with the most prevalent silicon manufacturing companies all over the world. In the meantime, Ampro Computers had invented what became an embedded computer standard, the "PC104" configuration, which quickly popularized itself in a number of industries, including medical, aviation, and transportation, to name a few.

The little firm that Edwin R. Peterson founded in the tin shed on South Sixth Street is now based on Maple Grove Road near the Franklin intersection. Preco's facilities now comprise over a 250,000 square feet of manufacturing space in three states, with sales and service offices throughout the United States, Canada, Mexico, Ireland, Israel, and Singapore. The Preco Group employs over 1,300 employees in six different countries, and it is the largest, privately-held electronics manufacturing company in Idaho.

ST. LUKE'S REGIONAL MEDICAL CENTER

The red brick walls of St. Luke's are symbolic of the enduring strength of Idaho's largest medical center. St. Luke's was founded in 1902 by the Rt. Rev. James B. Funsten, an Episcopal Bishop and missionary, who saw Boise's need for "sufficient proper facilities for the care of the sick." St. Luke's began as a six-bed frontier hospital located in downtown Boise. By 1907, the hospital had tripled in size and continued to grow with the community. In 1928, a four-story building was constructed at the medical center's present site at First and Bannock Streets, increasing the hospital's patient capacity to 135. Today, St. Luke's is a 323-bed, state-of-the-art health care facility specializing in cardiac, cancer, women's and children's services. But even in the present-day world of technology, St. Luke's continues to maintain the spirit of philanthropy inherent in its beginnings.

The St. Luke's mission is "to improve the health of people in [its] region." To this end, St. Luke's has maintained an open door policy, which means that no person will be denied care regardless of ability to pay. St. Lukes' status as a non-profit organization means that all profits are returned to the medical center for building improvements and medical equipment. A history of careful long-range planning and budgeting, as well as the generosity of local donors, has allowed the St. Luke's story to continue as one of expansion. As the population of southwestern Idaho increases, medical center services and facilities are constantly added and upgraded to meet the health care needs of a swelling populace.

By 1990, it was apparent that the rapidly-expanding area west

Rev. Funsten and the St. Luke's School of Nursing graduating class of 1915.

of Boise was in need of its own hospital. St. Luke's commitment to meeting the region's growing health care needs meant the construction of St. Luke's Meridian Medical Center, a 525,000 square foot facility where families living in western Ada and eastern Canyon Counties could find convenient, quality care close to their homes. In early 2002, St. Luke's Meridian Medical Center will open as a full-service community hospital, plans for which include a 24-hour emergency department, maternity care, and other inpatient and surgical services.

In 1995, St. Luke's was approached by the citizens of the Wood River Valley regarding building and maintaining a hospital for the people in the Sun Valley/ Blaine County area. After nearly five years of planning, fund-raising and construction, St. Luke's Wood River Medical Center is slated to open in December 2000, bringing improved and enhanced medical facilities to a community committed to providing its people with the finest health care resources available.

In 1970, St. Luke's became the only Level III (most sophisticated level of care) Neonatal Intensive Care Unit (NICU) in Idaho; they also have the state's only Level III Pediatric Intensive Care Unit. In 1999, St. Luke's formally dedicated its Children's Hospital, a hospital within St. Luke's Boise site devoted to the care of thousands of children each year. Today, St. Luke's Children's Hospital's NICU provides care to over 900 critically-ill infants each year; some babies treated there are born as much as 16 weeks early or weigh little more than one pound. Since the early 1990s, the average number of infants in St. Luke's NICU has risen 50 percent, from nearly 20 babies to nearly 35 babies per day. Due to the unit's increasingly frequent operation at its maximum capacity, construction to enlarge this very special service began in Summer 2000. But the NICU wasn't the only service needing additional space— construction to enlarge the Emergency Department was also begun.

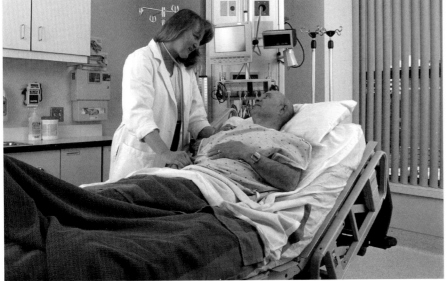

Experience, technology and compassion are the St. Luke's hallmarks. Photo by John Rogers

highest level of cardiac care in Idaho has been available at St. Luke's since 1968. That year, the first open-heart surgery in the state was performed, and there was no looking back. Over the following three decades, great strides were made in the diagnosis and treatment of cardiovascular conditions, and St. Luke's has been, and continues to be, committed to providing the best to its cardiac patients. From their specialized care units to their partnerships to provide care and coordinate the transfer of cardiac patients from rural areas, St. Luke's Heart Institute is synonymous with Idaho heart care services.

Brick by brick, St. Luke's has built a reputation over the past 100 years that reflects both pride in its past and an eye toward the future. Now southwest Idaho's sixth-largest employer, St. Luke's continues to grow with its community to provide the finest medical services to everyone in the region, through every stage of their lives.

Plans for the new St. Luke's Emergency Department (ED) include twice the space of the early 1980s expansion and feature a more efficient design and larger treatment rooms; areas dedicated solely to pediatric patients and another for cardiac care are included. The 1983 ED was designed with a projected capacity of approximately 25,000 patients, but even though minor operating changes enabled the department to see more patients, over 36,000 patients were treated at St. Luke's ED during 1999.

Another service that has seen tremendous growth over the past 30 years is St. Luke's Mountain States Tumor Institute (MSTI), a wholly-owned subsidiary that first opened its doors in 1969, providing the latest diagnostic and treatment services for cancer patients in a 100,000-square-mile area. A 1976 expansion allowed MSTI to add educational and research programs to better meet the region's needs for sophisticated cancer care. During the late 1990s, MSTI facilities expanded once again, increasing the patient care areas and adding a spacious

waiting area and medical resource library. Through the facility expansion in Boise, a full-service facility in Nampa and clinics in Caldwell and other cities, MSTI now provides over 75,000 treatments for children and adults on an annual basis.

Expansion is characteristic of St. Luke's, and never more so than when new family members arrive. St. Luke's has been delivering babies for nearly a century, and they are Idaho's most popular "port of entry"—over 5,000 babies greet the world each year at St. Luke's. In the 1980s, St. Luke's established a service to provide air as well as ground transport for high-risk moms and babies, and during the 1990s, a 32-bed Mother/Baby Care Unit and an Antepartum Unit for pregnant women at risk for, or experiencing, pre-term labor were added.

St. Lukes' family-centered approach also extends to their Heart Institute, where patients find not only a high-tech, but also a high-touch atmosphere. The

St. Luke's Regional Medical Center, in the heart of downtown Boise. Photo by John Rogers

SYMMS FRUIT RANCH, INC.

Richard A. Symms had eight acres of fruit trees-peaches, plums, apricots, cherries, pears, and several varieties of apples. He had horses and a wagon to take them to market in Jordan Valley. The 50-mile trip to sell his fruit, plus milk and eggs, was a "three-day ordeal," says his grandson, R.A. (Dick) Symms. It was the mid 1910s. Symms had planted his first fruit trees on Sunny Slope in the spring of 1914, realizing the dream of becoming a fruit farmer that had brought him and his family from Kansas. Previously, he had been a dairyman.

Today, Symms' descendants, into the fourth generation, operate the largest fruit production in the state of Idaho. They have 2,800 acres of fruit trees and another 1,000 acres in vegetables, cattle, feed, and seed.

The dream didn't begin as expected. Symms read about the fertile Willamette Valley in western Oregon and wanted to move there. He drew a parcel in an Oregon land lottery and, in 1913, the family headed west. Symms, his wife, Eva, and their three children, Darwin, Leta, and Doyle traveled by train. The closest rail point to the parcel of land was Caldwell, Idaho. So, they bought a team of horses and a wagon and set out to find his 40 acres, which was actually located near Jordan Valley, not the Willamette Valley. The road ended about 100 miles short, at the Snake River. The area was part of a federal reclamation project, which had built canals and reservoirs between 1904 and 1912, and made the land available for homesteading. With no bridge available to cross the Snake, the family settled in Sunny Slope and started to work on realizing Symms' dream.

Fourth generations family fruit growers. Jamie Mertz, Left, Dar Symms, Center, Dan Symms, Right. A commitment and tradition of quality since 1914.

It was different from the land lotteries. Those were put together by private developers and weren't always legitimate. The family has thought about going to see if they can find those 40 acres, but no one has done it yet. It would be interesting to know if Richard A. Symms' name was ever on the land register. Richard Symms began in 1913 by renting a farm. The next year, he bought an 80-acre homestead relinquishment from a family that decided not to stay. Symms put eight acres into fruit trees. The rest was mostly sagebrush; it was not farmed right away. Because of the adjacent sagebrush land, the biggest problem was jackrabbits. They would eat the trees in the winter, killing many of them. The original acreage, now known as the "Home Eighty"

is at the heart of the ranch. Four of the original trees-three apple and one pear-are still living and producing.

During the '20s, Symms Fruit Ranch (SFR) started shipping produce by rail, at first to the Midwest and later to the eastern states. In 1928 and 1931, respectively, Darwin and Doyle joined their father in the business. With 30 acres in fruit, they created their now world-famous SSS label. The three S's did double duty, standing either for the three Symms' or for Symms Sunny Slope. Richard died in 1934 and his sons struggled through the

'30s. By the early '40s, they had more than 60 acres, In 1961, the year that Darwin's eldest son, R.A. (Dick), joined the company, there were 380 acres of fruit trees. Steve, Darwin's other son joined in 1963 and Jim and Kathy Mertz, Doyle's daughter and son-in-law, came on board in 1971. Growth continued through the 1960s and '70s, with the family adding wine grapes and the Ste. Chapelle Winery to their mix in 1977. The winery was sold 20 years later.

Steve, meanwhile, left the business in 1972, turning to politics. He served four terms in the U.S. House of Representatives followed by two terms in the U.S. Senate. His son, Daniel, however, turned to the ranch. In 1983, he became the first member of the fourth generation to participate. By then, Symms Fruit Ranch had grown to more than 3,000 acres. Two more members of the fourth generation, James W. Mertz and Dick's son, Darwin II, became part of the business in the early '90s.

Just as Richard sold his first fruit fresh to consumers, so the majority of SFR's produce still goes to the fresh market. Most is shipped by truck to chain stores around the nation, and about one third goes into the International market. The company started exporting in the 1980s and now has major customers in Taiwan, Hong Kong, Singapore, Indonesia, Malaysia, Thailand, Vietnam, Brazil, Columbia, Venezuela, Costa Rica, Mexico, Canada and parts of Europe and the Middle East. Most of the produce for these destination goes in containers by ship, though cherries, which are more perishable, often go by air.

Packaging is a major part of the SFR operation, with the modern, computerized packing and storage

facilities covering more than 250,000 square feet. There is cold storage for 800,000 bushels of fruit. Produce is sized, sorted and graded, mostly into corrugated cardboard cartons, which have replaced the wooden crates, once common. The equipment packs about 15 semi truckloads of produce daily, and SFR employs between 200 and 800 people, depending on the season.

While fruit—now apples, peaches, cherries, nectarines, plums, prunes, pears and grapes— accounts for roughly 80 percent of sales, the company also grows potatoes, sugar beets, asparagus, onions, grain, corn, hay and alfalfa for seed. The potatoes and beets go to processors; onions and asparagus to the fresh market; and the alfalfa to companies, which clean its seeds and sell them to farmers who grow forage. The company uses the grain and hay on its own feed lots, where for nine

Symms Fruit Ranch headquarters and surrounding orchards. Lake Lowell in background, is part of reclamation project for irrigation in the Boise Valley.

months of the year it feeds 1,000 head of cattle for market.

"We are proud of our heritage in the fruit business," say R.A. (Dick) Symms. "And with three members of the fourth generation involved, we expect to celebrate 100 years as a family owned and operated farm in 2014."

WASHINGTON GROUP INTERNATIONAL

On July 7, 2000 Morrison Knudsen Corporation acquired Raytheon Engineers & Constructors, creating an engineering and construction firm that ranks among the largest in the industry.

The combined company is renamed Washington Group International, Inc., an organization that carries forward the traditions of skill, responsibility, and integrity that marked Morrison Knudsen from the time it was founded in Boise, Idaho in 1912.

The company was founded by 27-year-old Harry W. Morrison and 50-year-old Morris Hans Knudsen. Their first project was construction of a pumping plant on the Snake River near Boise, performed for $14,000. Knudsen served as president of the company until 1939, four years before his death at age 81.

From meager beginnings consisting of $600 in cash, a few horses, some old pan-type scrapers and a dozen wheelbarrows, MK grew into an international company with annual revenues of over $2 billion. In recent years, the company has employed between 20,000 to 25,000 people.

In the early 1930s, MK became a major force in heavy construction with its involvement in what has been called one of history's greatest dam-building efforts—Hoover Dam on the Colorado River.

Harry Morrison's guiding hand, and his pioneering of the now common joint-venture concept of pooling talent and resources for exceptionally large projects, brought together the famed group of western builders known as Six Companies, Inc. The group completed the prodigious Hoover Dam project two years ahead of schedule, in 1935.

Following construction of Hoover Dam, MK participated in construction of the San Francisco Bay Bridge.

With the start of World War II, MK joined other contractors in another great joint-venture known as Contractors, Pacific Naval Air Bases. Over 1,200 construction workers on these projects were taken prisoner by the Japanese in December 1941, after a courageous stand with U.S. Marines. Along with those seized, 98 were killed.

Post-war years included two outstanding accomplishments in frigid lands—the Distant Early Warning (DEW) Line, a chain of bases and radar installations across northern Canada; and the "White Alice" communications system in Alaska. An MK-led joint-venture performed a massive program of military construction in Vietnam during U.S. military operations there.

During the post-war years the company greatly expanded its operations "overseas," after making inroads as an international builder in Central and South America during the early 1940s. Landmark international projects include:

• The world's deepest bridge piers for Ponte Salazar Suspension Bridge across the Tagus River estuary at Lisbon, Portugal.

Side-boom tractors lower a section of pipe into a trench in 1976 during Morrison Knudsen's construction of a 153-mile long segment of the Trans Alaska Pipeline. MK also constructed storage facilities at the port city of Valdez.

• Portage Mountain Project in Canada, a huge underground powerhouse, 890 feet in length and hewn in solid rock with a labyrinth of appurtenant chambers, tunnels and shafts for a 2,270,000-kilowatt hydroelectric development.

• Construction of support facilities in the Kingdom of Saudi Arabia for a self-contained, self-supporting city known as King Khalid Military City.

• A 1,200-mile long extra-high-voltage power transmission line in Zaire.

• The $2 billion Cerrejon Coal Project in Colombia, consisting of a port, railroad and mine facilities, ranking as one of the largest ever performed by a single contractor.

On the home front, MK operations have reached to all corners of the nation. The company was an early participant as the nation looked to space as the next great frontier. MK constructed several principal facilities at Cape Canaveral in Florida, the most spectacular being the mammoth Vehicle Assembly Building at John

Lucky Peak Dam takes shape 15 miles north of Boise, in 1952. The dam is one of six major dams built by Morrison Knudsen in Idaho, including three dams for Idaho Power Company in Hells Canyon.

F. Kennedy Space Center. This structure, at the time of its completion, was the world's largest building, from the standpoint of volume enclosed (125,500,000 cubic feet).

Among other landmark projects completed in the U.S. in recent years are:

• A 153-mile long section of the Trans-Alaska Pipeline, plus extensive rock excavation to prepare the site of the line's marine terminal at Valdez.

• Nearly four miles of 35-foot-diameter stormwater tunnels beneath Chicago, utilizing a tunnel-boring machine—at the time the largest such machine ever manufactured.

• Eleven-mile long section of the Tennessee-Tombigbee Waterway

in Mississippi, where a fleet of more than 180 units of heavy equipment excavated over 95-million cubic yards of earth.

• Construction management of the giant Saturn automobile assembly plant for General Motors in Tennessee. The complex encloses more than 4,000,000 square feet and encloses state-of-the-art equipment.

Throughout its history, MK has been busy in its hometown of Boise. MK played a role in construction of The U.S. Bank Plaza, the Wells Fargo Center, and the Hoff Building on the city's downtown skyline, and two major facilities at the State Corrections Department complex east of Boise. MK developed the ParkCenter business park and constructed Lucky Peak Dam just north of the city. Traffic facilities such as the Interstate Highway in and near the city, the Cole-Overland Interchange and rebuilt Flying Y Intersection are part of the company's hometown legacy. In the late

1950s, MK built Ann Morrison Memorial Park in honor of Harry Morrison's first wife, who died in 1957. Mr. Morrison was active in management of the company until 1968. He died in 1971 at the age of 86.

Today, Washington Group provides engineering, construction and program-management services in the energy, environmental, government, heavy-construction, industrial, mining, nuclear-services, operations and maintenance, process, transportation, and water-resources markets. In 1996, Dennis R. Washington, a Montana businessman, acquired a major stake in MK and became the company's chairman.

The company is still headquartered in Boise and is organized into five operating groups: Power; Infrastructure & Mining; Government; Industrial/Process, and Petroleum & Chemicals. Washington Group is a public company and its shares are traded on the New York Stock Exchange.

WESTERN RECYCLING

"Do not dwell on setbacks and put emphasis on the successes," is the foremost learning experience expressed by David Dean, President of Western Recycling. The history of Western Recycling—illuminated by prosperity and heartbreak—has provided the personnel of this company with repeated opportunities to practice this philosophy.

Western Recycling was founded by John Bunderson and Basil Harrison in February 1976. David and Luane Dean purchased Western Recycling in 1979. Along with Peggy Dean and an original work force of six employees in the capital of Boise, the company has grown almost three dozen employees in four offices.

Western Recycling purchases, processes and ships recyclable materials including cardboard, newspapers, computer paper, ledger paper, aluminum cans, glass and batteries. The company markets its recycled products to industries in the Pacific Northwest, primarily Washington, Oregon and California. Western Recycling also markets to aluminum smelters throughout the United States and exports some materials to Pacific Rim countries.

People who recycle cans, paper and glass sell their collected materials to Western Recycling at any of the company's facilities.

Baling plastic.

Load of cardboard headed to the mill in Springfield, OR.

Western Recycling also purchases recyclable materials from private business organizations and provides recycle pick-up services for businesses and government agencies.

Still headquarted in Boise, the company has remained in the same family since 1979, and it's roots have grown deeper. Since the early days of this company many of the employees have stayed and become managers and owners of Western Recycling. Riding to a national wave of increased awareness of limited resources and sensitivity for the environment, Western Recycling has provided an outlet for more than 900,000 tons of recyclable materials.

As owner and president, Dean along with general manager Rick Gillihan, has guided Western Recycling to increased sales and corporate expansion. In 1979 Western Recycling purchased one of the area's first recycling operations, Operation Squirrel. In 1984 Western Recycling opened a new facility in Nampa. And seven years later, in 1991, Western Recycling acquired American Recycling in Boise and Fruitland. Dean's suc-

cessful business philosophy is simple: take care of employees and provide the best possible service to customers.

Dean moved to Idaho with his family when he was 10 years old. After graduating from Boise State University with a bachelor's degree in accounting/business administration, his first professional job was as a certified public accountant for Touche Ross & Co. His career was focused in accounting for several years, until he purchased Western Recycling. When asked why he purchased the recycling operation, Dean replied that he and his wife Luane enjoy the challenge of running a business and feel good about the positive impact the company has on the environment.

According to Dean, growth of the Idaho/Northwest recycling business is a product of greater awareness about the value of recycling, rising problems with landfills, and increased school education programs. The increased demand for recycled materials has been driven by the

Dave and his wife, Luane.

overall health of the national economy and the number of mills converting to the use of recyclable paper and metals. The strength of the export market has also presented new opportunities and bolstered the industry.

The success and growth of Western Recycling has been matched by challenges and tragedy. In July 1979, just three months after the Deans purchased the company, the original Boise facility was completely destroyed by fire. Fortunately, no Western Recycling employees were in the building that Sunday morning.

The blaze was first reported at 4:30 a.m., with a second alarm sounding a few minutes later. Firefighters responded with 25 crew members, three pumper trucks, one ladder truck and a tanker. When the fire was finally extinguished more than four hours later, Western Recycling was burned to the ground, with the building and all its contents completely destroyed. One truck

inside the building was destroyed and two trucks outside were burned. Other lost equipment included the baling machines and two fork lifts.

Western Recycling tediously recovered from the devastating fire. The company moved into a temporary location—across the street from a major competitor—while searching for a new location. The manager of a northwest paper mill, Walt Reitz who believed in Dave and Luane's ability to make the business a success leased Western Recycling a baler offering the expensive equipment at a price substantially lower than market value. Over the course of several long months, Western Recycling operated as much as possible, gradually rebuilding and restoring the entire business.

In the years following the fire, Western Recycling survived continued hardship as an economy in recession dramatically affected the recycling industry during the late 1970s and early 1980s. As the demand for finished goods dropped, so did the need for the recyclable materials that go into making those

goods. In turn, recyclers were forced to drastically drop the prices paid to customers bringing recyclable materials, and forced to reduce the prices collected from the sale of those materials.

In an industry inherently sensitive to economic conditions, several Idaho recycling companies and programs were closed during the recession. In 1978 the North End Recycling Project, a program that collected recyclable materials from residences and business, was discontinued after seven months when organizers conceded that the project was not economically feasible. Two other local recycling businesses closed in 1982. Western Recycling weathered the difficult years, patiently waiting for the economy to turn itself around.

The employees of Western Recycling are focused on a future of continued growth, always poised to take advantage of new opportunities. In 1986, Dean and several Western Recycling employees co-founded Western Records Destruction, Inc. The company is contracted by business organizations to destroy confidential documents. The idea came from the recycling business, as several of Western Recycling's customers expressed concern about including sensitive documents in their paper recycling program. Dean and his colleagues identified a solution and started a sideline company.

Western Recycling plans to continue expanding recycling services in southwestern Idaho and other geographic areas, as market opportunities arise. With a history of steady growth and average annual sales in the millions of dollars, Dean attributes Western Recycling's success to its employees and a collective corporate focus on quality and customer service.

HARMON TRAVEL SERVICE, INC.

It would be hard to find a more classic example of achieving the American dream than the success story of Earl and Eleanor Harmon in creating one of Idaho's finest full-service travel agencies.

It began in the 1950s when the Harmons were running a "mom-and-pop" grocery store and gas station in the tiny town of Hammett, on U.S. Highway 30 about 80 miles southeast of Boise. Before Interstate 84 was built, the Harmon store was a flag stop for Greyhound buses between Portland and Salt Lake City. Hammett, with about 200 people, rarely supplied a passenger for the buses, but they occasionally stopped to pick up or deliver freight. A Greyhound district sales manager first told Earl and Eleanor about something called "escorted bus tours" and helped organize their first one.

Eleanor, who was raised on a farm near Wendell, Idaho, had never been east of Salt Lake City. Earl had never been to California. Their first tour left in February 1958, bound for Utah, Arizona, and California. Their passengers had paid the grand sum of $79 for the eight-day trip.

For the Harmons, there was much to be learned on that first

Earl and Eleanor Harmon have turned the family business over to sons David, (left) and Bob.

grand adventure, from overcoming Eleanor's fear of the microphone, to maintaining a schedule, and to dealing with the unexpected things that happen on any trip. These inexperienced "country kids," as Eleanor puts it, turned out to have a real talent for keeping people happy and for planning tours that attracted travelers. While Earl continued to work hard to support a family that grew to seven children, Eleanor set up her tour office on their kitchen table.

In 1962 the Harmons moved to Boise, where Earl took a job as station manager for Trailways Bus Company. Eleanor continued to organize and operate group tours from her kitchen. Earl credits her with being the real force behind the development of Harmon Tours, and eventually, today's Harmon Travel. A New England fall foliage tour became one of the young company's most successful tours. Repeated annually, the Fall tours ranged from 17 to 38 days— one of the longest bus tours

offered anywhere at the time. (Today's tour starts with an air leg from Boise to Buffalo and Niagara Falls.)

Eleanor's imagination and creativity led to her development of travel experiences never before offered by any other agency. A riverboat tour from Portland to Lewiston on the Columbia River is one she pioneered; she is constantly exploring new possibilities of tours for Idahoans.

Harmon Travel now employs 25 people in its large and attractive Boise headquarters. Sons Bob and David, who have worked in the family business since they were teenagers, are now in charge, leaving Eleanor and Earl free to travel. Eleanor still seeks new travel adventures around the world and leads selective tours to places she finds exciting. She says of the business she and Earl created over 40 years ago, "Not bad for a couple of country kids."

An early tour group pauses for a roadside photo, with Earl and Eleanor kneeling at far right.

WESTERN STEEL MANUFACTURING COMPANY

The corner of 26th and Main streets was an undeveloped site in 1946. Curbs or gutters did not exist on the dirt road that channeled into downtown Boise's major thoroughfare. But it was a good location for the newly formed Western Steel Manufacturing Company founded by Roy Norquist, a veteran of steel fabrication. Norquist had started out building fuel tanks and grain bins with his uncles in Kansas City, Missouri. That family enterprise evolved into Butler Manufacturing Company—among America's foremost steel fabricators.

Western Steel Manufacturing Company began operations in a 50-foot by 150-foot plant. The firm originally produced small and medium-size structural and plate steel products; however, by the time it celebrated its 30th anniversary, Western Steel ranked among the major steel fabricators in the Pacific Northwest. Its capabilities ranged from the framework of multi-story buildings to hydroelectric-power dam components. The scope of operations grew, too. The firm lists among its credits structural steel systems for an atomic energy facility in South Carolina, a power plant in Wyoming, and a dredge for a South American mine.

By 1973 the original facility, hemmed in by Boise's sprawling commercial center, proved inadequate. Expanded quarters were essential to the organization's progress. Western Steel moved to a 10-acre site adjacent to the Boise Municipal Airport and the Boise Industrial Foundation. The new plant and office facility contained 33,600 square feet. Another 400,000 square feet of outside area was given over to the storage of fabricated jobs and material.

At the new site, the company continues to maintain its traditional standards of professional integrity, financial responsibility, and quality workmanship combined with continually upgraded equipment. A rigid quality control program includes the use of American Welding Society qualified welders, documentation of mill test reports, and specifications on all material purchased for product fabrication. All fabricated steel is produced to AISC certifications.

The Western Steel name and reputation are built into many of Boise's landmarks and showplaces. In addition to these structures and many throughout the state of Idaho, the firm has performed fabricating services throughout the Intermountain West and Pacific Northwest for clients ranging from individuals to government agencies.

The company's commitment to quality and service are reflected in its community involvement, especially its support of Boise State University. Western Steel Manufacturing Company participates in the school's placement program and offers on-site training opportunities for vocational-technical majors.

An interior photo of one of the cranebay areas where the fabrication of steel products takes place.

In 1965, Roy Norquist entered semi-retirement. His son, Galen, who had joined the business in 1950, was named president and chief executive officer at that time. A third generation, Steve Norquist, joined the firm in 1981.

In 1993, 10,000 square feet were added for additional plant and office facilities. In 1997, a new remote controlled tower crane was installed for exterior material handling, and periodically new fabricating equipment has been acquired.

In 1994, Galen Norquist semi-retired and Steve Norquist was named President and CEO.

Primary projects are institutional, industrial and commercial buildings and structures.

Professional industry membership include AISC, PNSFA, AWS, and AGC.

The Norquist's have both served as presidents and board of directors members of the Pacific Northwest Steel Fabricators Association.

ZAMZOWS, INC.

Gus Zamzow with his crew in 1950: Bernie Zamzow, Carmlita Zamzow, Gus Zamzow, and Stan Zamzow.

Zamzows is a company with a remarkable history. Founded in 1933 by August and Carmalita Zamzow, Zamzows is still owned by the same family. Zamzows' Fairview store has been located on the same corner since 1933. And co-founder Carmalita Zamzow is 103 years young, and has lived in three different centuries!

Yet if it weren't for the railroad, "Gus" and Carmalita might not have ever met. Five-year-old Carmalita House arrived in Boise by train from Knox County, Missouri in 1902. Her family settled near Meridian, where Carmalita attended school.

August L. "Gus" Zamzow (pronounced Zam-zoe) was from Minnesota. In 1913 he and brother Carl were headed for California, when the train stopped in Meridian. Gus got off to get a sandwich and the train left without him! Gus found work in Meridian as a farm hand and frequented Beam's Bakery, where a young Carmalita House was working. In 1915 they were married.

Gus continued his farm work and his family grew with the addition of five children, Bernard, Dorothy, Stanley, Margaret, and Evelyn. They settled down on a dairy farm located near the corner of Cole and Franklin in Boise.

In 1933, Gus and Carmalita

Old Fairview store in the early 1960s after the second remodeling. Note widening of Fairview Avenue and the now paved "Highway 30."

bought the Snodgrass Mill in rural Boise, changing the name to Zamzows Coal & Feed. The business was founded on the idea of selling the best products, with good customer service, and honesty in all matters. Gus handled the business, while Carmalita did the mixing and created displays.

Zamzows used The University of Idaho formulas. Carmalita mixed the feed on the floor of the Old Fairview store using rakes and scoop shovels. In addition to feed, the store sold gasoline, coal, baby chicks, tools and seed.

Sons Bernard and Stanley began working at the store and bought the business from their parents in the late-'40s. In 1953 the company bought a feed processing mill in Meridian. It was expanded in size and modern milling equipment was added.

In the early-'60s, a third location was added in Kuna. In 1973, Bernard's sons Jim and Rick purchased Zamzows from their father. The Fairview store, which had been rebuilt in the early '70s, was expanded. The Meridian Mill was remodeled into a retail store, and a fourth store was built in Emmett.

Zamzows pioneered many new products in the Treasure Valley. Zamzows was the first store to offer premium pet food, and became a distributor for Iams. In 1986 a second Boise store was added on State Street. In 1989, an office/distribution center was added in Boise to serve what was now a growing five store chain.

By the '90s, Rick Zamzow was now president of the Company, while brother Jim was chairman of Zamzows, Inc. and president of Dynamite Marketing, a direct-marketer of vitamin & mineral supplements. This was a decade of massive

expansion for Zamzows. In 1990 a Nampa store was added. In 1993 a third Boise store on Federal Way was added. In 1995 a new Meridian store was built under the Meridian Water Tower. In 1999 a new 30,000 square foot office/distribution center in Nampa replaced the Boise facility, and a new store in Eagle was added. Year 2000 plans call for a new store on State Street, expanding the Nampa Distribution Center, and adding a second Nampa retail store at that location.

Zamzows still formulates many of their own products. Zamzows Feeds are still manufactured at the Meridian Mill. Zamzows Organic-Based Lawn Foods are specially designed for Treasure Valley soils. Zamzows Save-A-Tree has improved the health of thousands of trees. And Zamzows Premium Pet Foods are used by thousands of pets.

What does the future hold for Zamzows? Rick's daughter Anne is an assistant manager at Zamzows, while Jim's son Joshua works at Dynamite and has a son named August, who is Carmalita's great-great grandson. Thus, the circle of life continues for August Zamzow. His wife, family, and great-great grandson August Jr. carry on in his name. The company he started is now seven stores strong with over $12 million in annual sales. But Zamzows' mission remains the same: "To sell the highest quality, environmentally-sound products at a service level beyond our customers' expectations."

A Timeline of Boise's History

c. **1800** Peiem and his family provide leadership to 1,500-2,000 of his traveling Western Shoshoni based in the Boise area.

1811 Donald Mackenzie leads a detachment of the overland Astorians through the Boise Valley, followed soon after by Wilson Price Hunt's band of Astorians.

1824-1832 Hudson's Bay Company fur brigades work in the Boise area.

1836 The Whitman-Spalding party of missionaries, including the first white women to come through the valley, travel through the area, marking the beginning of emigrant travel to the Oregon Country.

1837 Captain B.L.E. Bonneville, with the assistance of Washington Irving, publicizes the Boise Valley.

1843 John C. Fremont's party surveys the Oregon Trail. Kit Carson was its scout.

1846 Boise becomes United States territory, and Oregon Trail traffic through the area increases.

1862 Major floods affect Boise and the channels of the Boise River; Richard (Beaver Dick) Leigh establishes a ferry across the Boise River just upstream from the city's eventual location.

1863 Idaho Territory is created; U. S. Army Fort Boise is established and the city is plotted adjacent to the fort by settlers who have come to the valley to grow crops with which to supply miners in the Boise Basin.

1864 Boise becomes the territorial capital.

1867 The first, nationally-chartered bank in Idaho opens in Boise.

1872 Boise's own United States assay office (now a Registered National Historic Landmark) opens; samples of gold and silver ore no longer have to be sent long distances for valuation.

1881 Historical Society of Idaho Pioneers formed in Boise.

1886 The Territorial Capitol is completed.

1887 The Oregon Short Line Railroad provides the first rail service to Boise, via a spur line from Nampa.

1889 The Idaho Constitutional Convention meets in Boise.

1890 Idaho becomes a state, with Boise as its capital; the first residential and commercial geothermal hot-water company in the country is established in Boise.

1891 Electric streetcar service begins.

1892 Boise's Natatorium opens for swimming and other social activities.

1894 St. Alphonsus Hospital opens.

1897 The Idaho Intermountain Fair opens in Boise.

1900 St. Luke's Hospital opens.

1907 Trial of William D. (Big Bill) Haywood for conspiracy in the assassination of former governor Frank Steunenberg brings national press and other celebrities to Boise. Idaho Historical Society formed as a state agency. The Boise & Interurban electric railway begins service to valley towns.

1909 Diversion Dam is completed, bringing badly needed irrigation water to the valley. Idaho Children's Home Finding and Aid Society opens.

1911 Wright and Curtiss planes fly at the fairgrounds.

1912 The central portion of a new state capitol is completed.

1916 Arrowrock Dam, at the time the highest dam in the world, is completed.

1919 The first Music Week in the country begins in Boise.

1920 Idaho's state capitol is completed.

1925 Main-line rail service to Boise begins, and a new depot is opened.

1926 First commercial air mail service in the United States, with Boise as its base, established by Walter A. Varney at what is now the campus of Boise State University.

1927 Charles A. Lindbergh visits Boise with his *Spirit of St. Louis*.

1931 United Airlines formed out of Varney Airlines and others.

1934 Boise Junior College is founded, to become Boise State University in 1974; the Six Companies, organized by Boise-based Morrison-Knudsen Corporation, contract to build Boulder Dam.

1939 Joe Albertson opens his first grocery store in Boise.

1940-41 Boise Municipal Airport and the Army Air Corps' Gowen Field are constructed.

1955 Lucky Peak Dam, a flood-control structure, is dedicated.

1962 Boise becomes a Standard Metropolitan Statistical Area of the U.S. Department of Commerce.

1965 Boise Junior College given four-year status.

1968 Mountain States Tumor Institute established.

1969 Annual legislative sessions begin in Boise.

1970 Boise (now National) Interagency Fire Center established.

1971 Birds of Prey Reserve established.

1973 Boise State College achieves University status.

1978 Voters pass initiative limiting property taxes to one percent of market value.

1982 Pavilion opens at Boise State University, providing a venue for major sports and popular concert events.

1984 Morrison Center for the Performing Arts opens on the Boise State University campus, with top-quality concert and recital facilities. Former Senator Frank Church dies.

1985 National Governors Conference held in Boise. Jimmy Jausoro awarded a National Heritage Fellowship by the National Endowment for the Arts for his work to preserve Basque culture.

1986 Boise Towne Square Mall opens on the west side of the city, concluding a years-long argument over a downtown mall.

1990 Boise celebrates the centennial of Idaho statehood.

1992 Boise Mayor Dirk Kempthorne elected to the United States Senate.

1996 Foothills fire creates threat of major floods in downtown Boise and leads to construction of catchment ponds in Fort Boise Reserve.

1997 Amtrak passenger service to Boise discontinued. The Western Idaho Fair celebrates its centennial in Boise.

1998 Albertson's, Inc. becomes the second largest grocery chain in the United States. Dirk Kempthorne elected governor of Idaho.

1999 Boise's New Year's Eve celebration of the arrival of the year 2000 featured on national television.

2000 Boise Metropolitan Statistical area population grows to 408,817.

Boise City and Urban Area Population, 1863-2000

	CITY LIMITS	METROPOLITAN STATISTICAL AREA	ADA COUNTY
1863 (September 23)	725		
1864 (September 10)	1,658		
1870 (June 1)	995		2,675
1880 (June 1)	1,899		4,674
1890 (June 1)	2,311	3,391	8,368
1890 (September 19)	4,026		
1900 (June 1)	5,957	7,207	11,599
1910 (April 15)	17,358	21,365	29,088
1920 (January 1)	21,393	23,887	35,213
1930 (April 1)	21,544	27,236	37,925
1940 (April 1)	26,130	38,595	50,401
1950 (April 1)	34,393	56,487	70,649
1960 (April 1)	34,481		93,460
1970 (April 1)	74,990	97,752	112,230
1980 (April 1)	102,160	154,735	173,036
1990 (April 1)	125,738	295,900	205,800
2000 (April 1) (est)	170,327	408,817	283,357

All these are United States census reports, aside from 1863 and 1864, which were official territorial census compilations, and September 19,1890, which was based upon a Board of Trade name register that showed rapid growth (and perhaps some census oversight) that summer.

Bibliography

Alegria, Henry. *Seventy-five Years of Memoirs.* Caldwell, Idaho: Caxton Printers, 1981.

Anderson, Eloise H. *Frontier Bankers: A History of the Idaho First National Bank.* Boise: Idaho First National Bank, 1981.

Athearn, Robert G. *Union Pacific Country.* Chicago: Rand McNally Company, 1971.

Atkinson Associates. *Boise City, 1985: General Plan Study.* San Mateo, California: Atkinson Associates, 1962.

Beal, M.D. *Intermountain Railroads: Standard and Narrow Gauge.* Caldwell, Idaho: Caxton Printers, 1962.

Bird, Annie Laurie. *Boise, the Peace Valley.* Caldwell, Idaho: Caxton Printers, 1934.

Boise, City of Trees: A Centennial History. Idaho Historical Series Number 12. Boise, Idaho: Idaho State Historical Society, 1963.

Bradley, Cyprian, and Edward J. Kelly. *History of the Diocese of Boise, 1863-1952.* Boise: [Roman Catholic Diocese of Boise], 1953.

Bristol, Sherlock. *Pioneer Preacher.* Chicago: Fleming H. Revell, 1887.

Caldwell, Harry H. *Economic and Ecological History Support Study for a Case Study of Federal Expenditures on a Water and Related Land Resource Project: Boise Project, Idaho and Oregon.* Moscow: Idaho Water Resources Research Institute, 1974.

Carlton, Neil H. "A History of the Development of the Boise Irrigation Project." Unpublished M.A. thesis, Brigham Young University, 1969.

Chaffee, Eugene B. *Boise College: An Idea Grows.* Boise: Syms-York Company, 1970.

_____. "Early History of the Boise Region, 1811-1864." Unpublished M.A. thesis, University of California, Berkeley, 1931.

Crowder, David L. "Moses Alexander: Idaho's Jewish Governor, 1914-1918." Unpublished Ph.D. dissertation, University of Utah, 1972.

d'Easum, C.G. *Fragments of Villainy.* Boise: Statesman Printing Company, 1959.

Donaldson, Thomas. *Idaho of Yesterday.* Caldwell, Idaho: Caxton Printers, 1941.

Dougall, William G. "The Boise, Idaho, Public Transportation Dilemma: A Case Study of Problems Affecting Transit Systems in Cities of Under 100,000 Population." Unpublished M.B.A. thesis, University of Washington, 1972.

Edlefsen, John B. "A Sociological Study of the Basques of Southwest Idaho." Unpublished Ph.D. dissertation, University of Wisconsin, 1948.

Eggers, Robert F. "A History of Theater in Boise, Idaho, from 1863 to 1963." Unpublished M.A. thesis, University of Oregon, 1963.

Firman, Robert G. *A History of the Boise Public School System.* Boise, Idaho: Boise Chapter of the Retired Teachers Association, 1975.

Foote, Mary Hallock. *The Chosen Valley.* Boston: Houghton Mifflin Company, 1892.

Gentle, Marguerite S. "A Historical Study of the Independent School District of Boise City during the Period from 1881 to 1890." Unpublished M.A. thesis, The College of Idaho, 1963.

Gerassi, John. *The Boys of Boise: Furor, Vice and Folly in an American City.* New York: The Macmillan Company, 1966.

Gray, Mary Pearl. "A Population and Family Study of Basques Living in Shoshone and Boise, Idaho." Unpublished Ph.D. dissertation, University of Oregon, 1955.

Grover, David H. *Debaters and Dynamiters: The Story of the Haywood Trial.* Corvallis: Oregon State University Press, 1964.

Gulick, Grover C. [Bill]. *They Came to a Valley.* Garden City, N.Y.: Doubleday & Company, 1966.

Hart, Arthur A. *Fighting Fire on the Frontier.* Boise, Idaho: Boise Fire Department Association, 1976.

Hart, Arthur A. *Historic Boise: An Introduction to the Architecture of Boise, Idaho, 1863-1938.* Boise: Boise City Historic Preservation Commission, 1979.

Hedges, James B. *Henry Villard and the Railways of the Northwest.* New Haven, Connecticut: Yale University Press, 1930.

Hicks, John D. *Republican Ascendancy, 1921-1933.* New York: Harper and Brothers, 1960.

Hidy, Ralph W., Frank Ernest Hill, and Allan Nevins. *Timber and Men: The Weyerhaeuser Story.* New York: The Macmillan Company, 1963.

Illingworth, Gertrude P. "A Historical Study of the Establishment of Boise City and Fort Boise." Unpublished M.A. thesis, University of Southern California, 1937.

Irving, Washington. *Astoria, or Anecdotes of an Enterprise beyond the Rocky Mountains.* Philadelphia: Carey, Lea, and Blanchard, 1836.

_____. *The Rocky Mountains; or, Scenes, Incidents, and Adventures of the Far West; Digested from the Journal of Captain B.L.E. Bonneville.* Philadelphia: Lea and Blanchard, 1837.

Jensen, Dwight W. *Visiting Boise: A Personal Guide.* Caldwell, Idaho: Caxton Printers, 1981.

Johnson, Claudius O. *Borah of Idaho.* New York: Longmans, Green, and Company, 1936. Reissued, with a new introduction, Seattle: University of Washington Press, 1967.

Johnson, Vicki S., and Patricia S. Mickelson. *Nine Walking Tours of Boise.* Boise: Boise Walking Tours, 1979.

Jones, Timothy W. *Archaeological Test Excavations in the Boise Redevelopment Project Area, Boise, Idaho. With Chinese Artifact Analysis by George Ling and Boise History by Michael Ostrogorsky.* Moscow: University of Idaho Anthropological Research Manuscript Series No. 59, 1980.

Jordan, Grace E. *The Unintentional Senator.* Boise: Syms-York Company, 1972.

McCullough, F.M. "The Basques of the Northwest." Unpublished M.A. thesis, University of Portland, 1945.

McKenna, Marian C. *Borah.* Ann Arbor: University of Michigan Press, 1961.

Malone, Michael P. *C. Ben Ross and the New Deal in Idaho.* Seattle: University of Washington Press, 1970.

Morris, Frank Daniel. *Pick Out the Biggest: Mike Moran and the Men of the Boise.* Boston: Houghton Mifflin Company, 1971.

Morrison, Ann. *... Those Were the Days.* Boise: eM-Kayan Press, 1951.

Muench, Christopher and Paul Buell. *The Ah-Fong Apothecary of Boise Idaho: A Brief History and Analysis.* [Prepared for the Idaho State Historical Society under an Association for the Humanities in Idaho grant, 1982.]

Murphy, Paul Lloyd. "Irrigation in the Boise Valley, 1863-1903: A Study in Pre-federal Irrigation." Unpublished M.A. thesis, University of California, 1948.

Robb, Thomas H. "Routes to Southwestern Idaho, 1855-1884." Unpublished M.A. thesis, University of Idaho, 1971.

Ross, Alexander. *Fur Hunters of the Far West.* London: Smith, Elder & Company, 1855.

Scheffer, Martin. *Boise Citizens Survey, 1975.* Boise, Idaho: Boise Center for Urban Research, 1975.

Sears, Jesse Brundage. *... The Boise Survey: A Concrete Study of the Administration of a City School System.* Yonkers-on-Hudson: World Book Company, 1920.

Silen, Sol. *La Historia de los Vascongados en el oeste de los Estados Unidos* [Boise, 1918].

Smith, Robert S. *Doctors and Patients.* Boise: Syms-York Company, 1976.

Sorensen, Mervin G. "History of Boise City, Idaho." Unpublished M.A. thesis, Colorado State College of Education, 1949.

Stallcup, Marvin E. "Music in Boise, Idaho, 1863 to 1890." Unpublished Master of Music thesis, University of Montana, 1968.

Talbot, Ethelbert. *My People of the Plains.* New York: Harper & Brothers, 1906.

Tuttle, Daniel S. *Reminiscences of a Missionary Bishop.* New York: Thomas Whittaker, 1906.

Unruh, John D. *The Plains Across: The Overland Emigrants and the Trans-Mississippi West, 1840-60.* Urbana: University of Illinois Press, 1979.

ARTICLES

Alexander, Thomas G. "Mason Brayman and the Boise Ring." Idaho Yesterdays (Fall, 1970), 14/3:21-27.

Barrett, G.W. "Reclamation's New Deal for Heavy Construction: M-K in the Great Depression." *Idaho Yesterdays* (Fall, 1978), 22/3:21-27.

Bieter, Pat. "Reluctant Shepherds: The Basques in Idaho," *Idaho Yesterdays* (Summer, 1957), 1/2:10-15.

Chaffee, Eugene B. "Boise, the Founding of a City." *Idaho Yesterdays* (Summer, 1963), 7/2:2-7.

Davis, L.J. "Tearing Down Boise." *Harpers* (November, 1974), 249:32+.

Dougall, William G. "Clang, Clang, Clang, Went the Trolley." *Idaho Heritage* (September-October, 1976), 14-17.

Edlefsen, John B. "Enclavement among Southern Idaho Basques." *Social Forces* (December, 1950), 30:155-158.

Etulain, Richard W. "Basque Beginnings in the Pacific Northwest." *Idaho Yesterdays* (Spring, 1974), 18/1:26-32.

Hibbard, Don J. "Domestic Architecture in Boise, 1904-1912: a Study in Styles." *Idaho Yesterdays* (Fall, 1978) 22/3:2-18.

Hussey, John A. "Building Most Valuable: The Story of the Idaho Assay Office." *Idaho Yesterdays* (Spring, 1961), 5/1:2-13.

Jessey, Thomas E. "St. Michael Fackler and Saint Michael's Cathedral." *Idaho Yesterdays* (Fall, 1961), 5/3:2-6.

Lay, Bairne. "Cities of America." *Saturday Evening Post* (January 18, 1947), 219:22-23+.

McFadden, Thomas G. "Banking in the Boise Region: The Origins of the First National Bank of Idaho." *Idaho Yesterdays* (Spring, 1967), 11/1:2-17.

McIntosh, Clarence F. "The Chico and Red Bluff Route: State Lines from Southern Idaho to the Sacramento Valley." *Idaho Yesterdays* (Fall, 1962). 6/2:12-19.

Olson, James S. "The Boise Bank Panic of 1932." *Idaho Yesterdays* (Winter, 1974-1975), 18/4:25-28.

Ostrogorsky, Michael. "Fort Boise and the 'New Confederacy.'" *Idaho Yesterdays* (Winter, 1979 and Spring, 1979), 22/4:25-31, 23/1:18-24.

Paul, Rodman W. "When Culture Came to Boise: Mary Hallock Foote in Idaho." *Idaho Yesterdays* (Summer, 1976), 20/2:2-12.

Rhodenbaugh, Beth. "Boise, the City of Trees." *Scenic Idaho* (1950), 5:5-21.

Wells, Merle W. "Heat from the Earth's Surface: Early Development of Western Geothermal Resources." *Journal of the West* (January, 1971), 10:53-71.

Acknowledgements

Boise's history extends over so brief a time period that my own memory covers exactly half that length. For events after 1930 (when I moved to Boise), this account features personal recollection supplemented by library reference for additional detail. Personal friends who came to Boise as many as 40 years earlier provided information from their experiences, going back to about 1890. So chapters dealing with Idaho's statehood era depend primarily upon oral history. For Boise's early days and Idaho's territorial period, standard documentary research offers two chapters of conventional community history. Additional archaeological and ethnological interpretation and Indian history resources were contributed by Sven Liljeblad, Earl Swanson, B. Robert Butler, and Brigham D. Madsen. Local periodical and newspaper coverage-especially from 118 years of *Idaho Statesman* files-contain information invaluable for this study.

Idaho State Historical Society and State Historic Preservation Office staff who contributed in a great variety of essential ways to this volume include Jennifer Eastman Attebery, Judith Austin, Lisa Berriochoa, Gary Bettis, Madeline Buckendorf, Doris Camp, Carol Cooper, William G. Dougall, Karin Ford, Thomas J. Green, Arthur A. Hart, Elizabeth Jacox, Larry Jones, Suzanne Lichtenstein, Jeanne Marsh, Sandy Rikoon, Robert Romig, William P. Statham, Ann and Ken Swanson, Donald Watts, and Marj Williams. In addition to many other important contributions, Arthur Hart organized and prepared textual explanation for illustrations he selected from various Idaho State Historical Society collections.

Boise State University staff who have provided valuable assistance include Eugene B. Chaffee, G.W. Barrett, Pat Bieter, John Caylor, John Keiser, John Mitchell, Robert C. Sims, and Warren Vinz. Other Idaho contributors-past and present-include Eloise Anderson, Ira Anderson, Leonard J. Arrington, George R. Baker, Willis Burnham, George Bowditch, Frank Chalfant, John Corlett, George H. Curtis, Dick d'Easum, Ernest Day, Alice and Leslie Dieter, Bobbie Doss, Richard G. Eardley, Vernon Emery, Harold Finch, H.H. Hayman, Bill Hopper, Ray and Pat Jolly, Harry S. Kessler, Mary Lesser, Glenn Lungren, Harlan Mann, Edith Mathews, John Matthew, Gib Michalk, J.M. Neil, Ernest Oberbillig, Peter Perry, J.V. Root, C.J. Sinsel, Milton Small, Susan Stacy, Paul Tate, J.M. Taylor, Ron Twilegar, Reece Theobald, Faith Turner, Alice Walters, Donald Wells, and Lyman Wilbur. Special recognition also goes to exceptionally helpful Idaho State Library, Boise Public Library, Boise State University Library, and Idaho State Law Library reference staffs.

Merle Wells

Index

Chronicles of Leadership Index

ADA County Highway District, 172-175
Agri Beef Co., 176-177
Albertson's, 178-179
American Ecology Corporation, 180-181
Bogus Basin Ski Resort, 182-183
Boise Samaritan Village Healthcare and Rehabilitation Center, 184-185
Boise State University, 186-187
Cosho, Humphrey, Greener & Welsh, P.A., 193
Davies & Rourke Advertising, 188-189
DeBest Plumbing, 190-192
Delta Dental Plan of Idaho, 201
Employers Resource Management Company, 194-195
Fearless Farris Stinker Stations, 196-197
Givens Pursley, Llp, 198-200
Hansen-Rice, Inc., 202-203
Harmon Travel Service, Inc., 248
Hawley, Troxell, Ennis & Hawley, 204-205
Holland Realty, Inc., 206-207
Idaho Sporting Goods Company, 208-209
Idaho Statesman, The, 210-211
Idaho Timber Corporation, 212-213
Idaho Trout Processors Company, 214-217
Idaho Wine Merchant, 218-219
Intermountain Gas Company, 220-221
Jordan-Wilcomb Construction, Inc., 222-223
J-U-B Engineers, Inc., 224-225
Metalcraft, Inc., 226-227
Nagel Beverage Company, 228-231
Preco, Inc., 239
R & M Steel Company, 232-235
Saint Alphonsus Regional Medical Center, 236-237
St. Luke's Regional Medical Center, 240-241
SCP Global Technologies, 238
Symms Fruit Ranch Inc., 242-243
Washington Group International, 244-245
Western Recycling, 246-247
Western Steel Manufacturing Company, 249
Zamzows Inc., 250

General Index
Numbers in italics indicate illustrations

A

Ada County, 10, 22-23, 67, 124-125, 152, 153, 160, 162, 163
Ada County Courthouse, *23*
Ada County Highway District, 167, 172-175
Ada Theatre, 121, 123
Adams, Charles Francis, 48
Adams, Samuel, 20
AFL-CIO, 146
Agee, William (Bill), 124, 157, *157*

Agnew, James D., 19
Agri Beef Co., 176-177
Air travel, 159, 161
Alaska Building, 152
Albertson, J.A. (Joe), 111, 122, 165; Albertson's Market, 111, 128, 158
Albertson's, 178-179
Aldrich, Nelson, 84
Alexander, Moses, 62, *64*, 84, 86
Alexander Building, 152
Alexander's Store, 147
Alkali Flat, 47-48
Alvord, Benjamin, 18
American Ecology Corporation, 180-181
American Indian (ethnic group), 162
American Institute of Architects, 153
Amtrak, 159
Anderson, C.C., *115*
Anderson Ranch Dam, 110, 113
Andrus, Cecil D., 122-124, *155*, 167
Ann Morrison Park, 117
Anne Frank Human Rights Memorial, 169
Aram, John, 110
Archibald, Nate, 164
Arid Club, 147
Arrowrock Dam, *84*, 84-85
Art in the Park (annual event), 168
Ashe, Arthur, 164
Ashley, William H., 14-15
Asian (ethnic group), 162
Astor's Pacific Fur Company, 13-14
Atlantic & Pacific Supermarket, 124

B

Baldridge, H.C., *90, 91*
Balkan (ethnic group), 162
Ballard, D.W., *27*, 27-29, 37, *38*
Ballet Idaho, 168
Bank of America Center, 155, 158
Bannock Indians, 41-42
Barber Lumber Company, 75
Baseball, 64
Basketball, 65
Basque, 74, 146, 162
Basque Center, 162, 163
Basque Museum and Cultural Center, 162, *162*, 169
Beatty, James H., 63
Bennett, T.W., 41, *41*
Bennett, William R., *153*
Bishops' House, *63*
Black (ethnic group), 162
Blair, Bonnie, 164
Blount, Mel, 164
Bogus Basin, 117, 123
Bogus Basin Ski Resort, 182-183
Boise Actors' Guild, 168
Boise Art Museum, 154, 168
Boise Barracks, 42. *See also* Fort Boise
Boise Basin, 17-18
Boise Cascade, 121, 145, 153, 157, 158
Boise Centre, 155
Boise City, *47, 53,* 161
Boise City Hall, *139*
Boise City Historic Preservation Commission, 168
Boise Contemporary Theater, 168
Boise Factory Outlets, 158
Boise Gallery of Art. *See* Boise Art Museum
Boise Hawks (baseball team), 164

Boise High School, *72, 90;* football team of, *89*
Boise Junior College, 64, 103, 117, 120
Boise Little Theater, 168
Boise National Forest, 84
Boise-Payette Lumber Company, 81, 97, 110
Boise Philharmonic Orchestra, 117, 168
Boise Police Department, 163
Boise Public Library, 61, 117, 169
Boise Redevelopment Agency, 151, *152,* 153
Boise Ridge, 10
Boise Ring, 40-41, 49, 50
Boise River, *9,* 13, *102,* 122, *129, 157,* 160, 169, *169*
Boise River Resource Management and Master Plan, 165
Boise Samaritan Village Healthcare and Rehabilitation Center, 184-185
Boise State College, 120
Boise State University, 120, 145, 147, *163,* 164, 166, 168, 186-187
Boise Tower, 156
Boise Urban Stages (mass transit system), 160
Boise Valley, 11
Boise Valley's New York Canal, 78
Bon Marché, 153, 158
Bonneville, Benjamin L.E., 15
Book Fest, 169
Book Shop, The, *155*
"Boomtown U.S.A." (newspaper feature), 155
Borah, William E., 62, *64,* 75-76, 84, 86, 94-95, 100, 102, 123
Borah High School, 116
Boxing, 164
Boz Theater, *99*
Brayman, Mason, *41,* 41-42
Bristol, Sherlock, 19
Broadway-Chinden connector, 160
Bronco Stadium, *163*
Bruneau Treaty, 30
Bryant, H.H., 92
Budge, Hamer, 123
Buffalo Horn, 41
Bunn, William Malcolm, 49-50

C

Caldron Linn, *12*
Campbell, William S., 69
Canyon County, 152, 153
Capital Christian Center, 162
Capital City Development Corporation, 154
Capitol Mall, 120
Capitol Terrace, *160*
Carley, Joan, 152
Carnegie, Andrew, 61
Cartee, Lafayette, *27, 34;* home of, *45*
Carvino, James, 163
Centennial parade, *155*
Center for Horticulture Technology, 166
Central Christian Church, *77*
Central Pacific Railroad, 34-35, 37, 43
Central School, *46*
Central Station, *66*
Chaffee, Eugene B., 103, *103*
Chamber of Commerce, 102, 114, 119-120, 145
Chapman, W.W., 38
Ch'i-ch'ao, Liang, 72

Chiles, Joseph R., 19
China Reform Association, 72
Chinese, 71-72, *163*
Church, Frank, 123, 159
Church, John, 163
Churches: Central Christian Church, *77*; First Baptist Church, *39*; First Methodist Church, *40*, 77; First Presbyterian Church, *39*; Presbyterian Church, *61*; St. Paul's black Baptist Church, 162; Swedish Evangelical Lutheran Church, *117*
City Hall, *114*, 154
Civilian Conservation Corps, *96*, 101
Clemente, Roberto, 164
Coffin, Frank R., 60; home of, *62*
Coles, Brent, 153, 159, 163
Columbia Band, *104*
Columbia Theatre, 61, *99*, *105*
Columbia Village, 158
Columbian Club, 61
Comanche Indians, 12
Connick, Charles (work of), *136*
Conradi, Joseph (work of), *90*
Cosho, Humphrey, Greener & Welsh, P.A., 193
Costco, 158
Coxey, Jacob S., 63-64
Crater Lake, 11
Craters of the Moon National Monument, *10*
Crawford, James, 21
Crawford, Slocum and Company, 19
Creighton, John, 19
Crook, George, 30
Crookham, George, 113
Cummins, John, 30
Curtis, E.J., *51*
Curtis, J.F., 50

D
Daly, Joe, *71*
Darrow, Clarence, 76, *76*, 78
Davidson, Christopher, 165
Davies & Rourke Advertising, 188-189
Davis, Julia, *19*
Davis, Thomas Jefferson, *19*
Davis, Tom, 19, 25, 65
Dayton Hudson Development Firm, 121
DeBest Plumbing, 190-192
Delta Dental Plan of Idaho, 201
Department of Commerce and Development, 114
Depression, Great, 97
Dewey, W.H., 70
Diamond Sports, Inc., 164
Dillards, 155
Dillon, Sidney, 43, 47
Discovery Center of Idaho, 169
Disney, Walt, 166
Diversion Dam, 79, *113*
Dodge, Grenville M., 34, 37
Dorion, Marie, 14
Driscoll, J. Lynn, 100
Drugs, 163, 164
DuRell, B.M., 19, 29-30

E
Eagles Hall, 152
Eardley, Dick, 147, 149, 151, *152*, 153
Eastman Building, *148*, *152*
Eazkaidunak, 146
Eberle, William D., 123-124

Egyptian Theatre, 93, *98*, *141*, 152
Eighth Street bridge, 160
Eighth Street historic district, 168
8th Street Marketplace, 158
Electric Bond and Share, 121
Elks Building, 152
Elks Lodge building, *92*
Elks Rehabilitation Center, 127
Employers Resource Management Company, 194-195
Enough is Enough, 164
Environment, 164-168
Environmental Protection Agency, 167
Erving, Julius, 164
Esther Simplot Performing Arts Academy, 168
Ethnic groups: American Indian, 162; Asian, 162; Balkan, 162; Basque, 74, 146, 162; Black, 162; Chinese, 71-72, *163;* Germans, 86; Hispanic, 161, 162; Japanese, 74, 106; Pacific islands, 162; South America, 162; Soviet Union, 162
Evans, John, *153*
Extended Systems, 158

F
Fearless Farris Stinker Stations, 196-197
Federal Trade Commission, 158
Federal Writers' Project, 101
Fenn, Stephen S., 41
Fery, John B., 145, 159
First Baptist Church, *25, 39*
First Idaho Regiment, *54*
First Methodist Church, *40, 77*
First National Bank of Idaho, 29, 100, 146
First Presbyterian Church, *39*
First Security Bank, 100
First Thursday (art event), 168
Fisher, Vardis, 101, *102*
Flicks, The, 169
FMC corporation, 151
Football, 65, 164
Foote, A.D., 52, 56, 58, 64; home of, *52*
Foote, Mary Hallock, 52, *52*, 56; home of, *52*
Forbes Magazine, 156
Fort Boise, *14*, 14-15, 18-19, 30-31, 42, 85
Fort Hall, 15
Fortune 500, 157
Friends of the Garden, 165
Fritchman, Harry, *72*

G
Garden City, 112
Germans, 86
Getzler, Sue Robinson, 105
Gilson, Horace C., 25, 27-28
Givens Pursley, Llp, 198-200
Glorieux, A.J., 61
Golf, *65, 88*
Gould, Jay, 42-43
Governor's Guards, 55
Gowen Field, 103, 106
Graham, Matt, 53
Green, John, *43*
Greenbelt, 153, 164, 165
Greenbelt Appreciation Day, 165
Grimes, George, 17
Grove, The, *152*, 153, 155, 158

Grove Hotel, *143*, 155, 158
Gwinn, Tony, 164

H
H. Seller's Valley Store, *50*
Hailey, John, 48, *49*
Hailey Ring, 49
Haley, George P., *49*
Hansberger, Robert V., *121*
Hansen-Rice, Inc., 202-203
Harad, George, 159
Hardy, Earl, 152
Harmon Travel Service, Inc., 248
Hart, Arthur, 153
Hart's Exchange, 28, *28*
Hausrath, Ann, 166
Hawley, James H., 63, *63*, 75-76
Hawley, Troxell, Ennis & Hawley, 204-205
Hayes, Rutherford, 41
Hayne, Julia Deane, 22
Haywood, William D., 75-76, 86
Hells Canyon Dam, 113-114
Hewlett Packard, 127, 156
Highway 21, *164*
Hispanic (ethnic group), 161, 162
Historic Sites Review Board, 169
Hockey, 155, 164
Hodges, Kathy, 169
"Hogan the Stiff," *71*
Holladay, Ben, 21, 26
Holland Realty, Inc., 206-207
Hosford, Neil, 155
Hotel Boise, 97, *101*, *120*
Howard, Oliver Otis, 41, *42*
Howell, Ken, 152
Howlett, Solomon R., 28-29
Hudnut, J.O., 37
Hudson's Bay Company, 14-15
Hulls Gulch, 166
Hummel, C.F. (work of), *77*
Hummel La Marche & Hunsaker, 153
Hunt, Wilson Price, 13
Huntington, C.P., 43

I
Ice-skating, 65
Idaho and Oregon Land Improvement Company, 46-47
Idaho Black History Museum, 162, 169
Idaho Botanical Garden, *138*, 165, 166, *166*
Idaho Building, 152
Idaho City, 17, 20, *164*
Idaho Council of Churches, 145
Idaho First National Bank, 155
Idaho Historic Preservation Council, 168
Idaho Historical Museum, 117, *117*, *132, 140*, 168
Idaho Historical Society's Historic Preservation office, 168
Idaho Oldtime Fiddlers, *146*
Idaho Power Company, 113-114
Idaho Shakespeare Festival, 168, *169*
Idaho Sneakers (tennis team), 164
Idaho Soldiers Home, *64*
Idaho Sporting Goods Company, 208-209
Idaho Stallions (football team), 164
Idaho Stampede (basketball team), 164
Idaho State Federation of Labor, 90

Idaho State Historical Society, 117
Idaho State Library, 117
Idaho Statehood (centennial), *154*, 155
Idaho Statesman, 21, *155*, 166;
    building of, *21*
Idaho Statesman, The, 210-211
Idaho Theater for Youth, 168
Idaho Timber Corporation, 212-213
Idaho Trout Processors Company, 214-
    217
Idaho Wine Merchant, 218-219
Idanha Hotel, 69, 121, *142*, 152
Innertube float trips, *169*
Interagency Fire Center, 122
Intermountain Fair, *80*
Intermountain Gas Company, 220-221
Intermountain Railway Company, 81
International Association of Chiefs of
    Police, 163
International Trade Commission, 156
Interstate 84, 160, 161
Interstate Commerce Commision, 159
Irving, Washington, 13
Irwin, John, *169*

J

Jacobs, Cyrus, 19, *20*, 58; home of, *20*;
    store of, *16*
Jacobs, Mrs. Cyrus, *20*
Jacobs-Uberuaga house, 162
Jaialdi (Basque festival), 162, *163*
James C. Howland Urban Enrichment
    Award, 155
Japanese, 74, 106
J.C. Penney, 153
Johnson, Andrew, 28
Johnson, Kevin, 164
Johnson, Peter, 124
Johnson, Rafer, 164
Johnson, Walter, 78, *89*
Joiner, Truman, 121
Jordan, Len B., 123
Jordan-Wilcomb Construction, Inc.,
    222-223
J.R. Simplot Company, 157; Food
    Group, 157; Land & Livestock
    Group, 158
J-U-B Engineers, Inc., 224-225
Julia Davis Park, 19, 114, 154, 162,
    168
Junior Little Theater, 168

K

Kaiser, Herman, *105*
Katherine Albertson Park, 165
Keino, Kip, 164
Kelley, John, 105
Kelly, Milton, 30, *30*
Kelly's Hot Springs, 30, 58-59
Kempthorne, Dirk, 151, 153, 154, *157*,
    163
Kersey, Jackie Joyner, 164
Killeen, Vaughn, 163
Kimmel, Husband, 107
King, Ernest J., 107
King, James, 60; work of, *64*
Knock 'em Dead dinner theater, 168

L

Lamond, John, 6
Landry, Tom, 164
Lawrence, James, *32*
Lay, Bierne, 111-112

Leigh, "Beaver Dick," 19
Lejardi-Coleman, Nicole, *162*
Lemp, John, 47-48; home of, *44*
Les Bois Park, *164*
Lewiston, 20-22, 24, 27
"Liberty Car," 55, *56*
Light in the Window, A, (library history),
    169
Lindbergh, Charles, 90, *90*
Link's Business College basketball
    team, *89*
Little Theatre, 117, 145
Log Cabin Literary Center, 169
Logan, Thomas E. (home of), *133*
Lombard-Conrad, *141*
Loughrey, Bob, *152*
Louie, Gwong, *73*
Lower, Geoff, *169*
Lucky Peak Dam, 113, 165
Lugenbeel, Pinckney, *18*, 18-19
Lynch, Peter, 158
Lyon, Caleb, 22, *24*, 24-27, 30

M

MacArthur, Douglas, 107
McClellan, "Uncle John," 19, *19*
McCormick, Pat, 164
McDevitt, Charles, 124
McGee, James A., 50
McKay, Thomas, 15
Mackenzie, Donald, *13*, 13-15
McKinley, William (memorial parade
    for), *68*
McMillan, John, 69
McMillan, Thomas, 69
Mandarin Inn, *73*
Mann, Cynthia, *46*
Mason, John, 154
May, Charles, 20
"Mechanafe" (advertisement for), *95*
Medical Arts Condominium, 127
Medini, F. Roena. *See* Miller, Frankie
Memorial Bridge, 160
Memorial Stadium, 164
Meridian, 67, 158
Mervyns, 153
Metalcraft, Inc., 226-227
Metroplan, 151
Metropolitan Statistical Area, 152
Micron Technology, 156, *156*, 157, 159
Miles, Don, 153
Miller, Frankie, 105
Mills, Billy, 164
Miner, T.F., 6
Misseldt, Joe, *36*
Missouri Beef Packers, 128
Montgomery, Jim, 163
Moody, Silas, *51*
Moore, C.W., 19, 29; home of, *45*
Mormon, 49-50, 101-102, 145, 148
Morris, William B., 40
Morrison, Harry, 103, *110*, *115*, 147
Morrison, John T. (home of), *58*
Morrison, Velma, 147, 167
Morrison Center for the Performing
    Arts, *141*, 168
Morrison-Knudsen (M-K), 103, 110, 128,
    145, 157, *157*, 159, 160, 161; MK
    Rail, 157, 161, *161*; MK Transit,
    157
Motive Power Industries, 161
Moulton, Elvina, *61*
Mountain Men, 15, *15*, 132

Mountain States Regional Medical Pro-
    gram, 126
Mountain States Tumor Institute, 126
Municipal Gallery of Art, 117
Murphy, Dale, 164
Museum After Hours, 168
"Museum Comes to Life" (celebration),
    168

N

Nagel Beverage Company, 228-231
Naked Truth Saloon (advertisement
    for), *36*
Nampa, 158, 159
Natatorium, 59, *59*, *107*
National Conservation Area, 167
National Governors Conference, *153*
National Landmark U.S. Assay Office.
    See U.S. Assay Office
National League of Cities, 155
National Register of Historic Places,
    160, 162, *162*, 169
Native Americans, *163*
Nelson, Morley, 166, *167*
New Deal programs, 101-102
New York Times, 155
Newell, R.J., 113
Nez Perce Indians, 41
North end, *153*, 169
North West Company, 14
Northern Pacific Railroad, 38
Nye, William (home of), *44*

O

Ogden, Peter Skeen, 15
Oinkari Basque Dancers, 146, *147*
Old Boise district, 152
Oldfield, Barney, 90
Old Idaho Penitentiary, *138*, 162, 165,
    166, *166*
Olney, Richard, 63
One Capital Center, *142*
Open Heart Surgery Program, *127*
Opera Idaho, 168
Orchard, Harry, 76
Oregon Short Line, 46-48; depot of, *60*
Oregon Trail, 9, 13, 15, *154*, 160
Ore-Ida, 121, 128
Ore-Ida Women's Challenge, *164*
Ostner, Charles, 38; work of, *38*, *47*, *143*
Ouderkirk, Judy, 166
Overland House, *22*
Overland Stage Company, 21
Owyhee Hotel, 79

P

Pacific islands (ethnic group), 162
Palmer, Joel, 19
Palmer, Mary Ellen. *See* Jacobs, Mrs.
    Cyrus
Parenting Magazine, 155
Parrott, Samuel (store of), *70*
Paulsen, John C., 60; work of, *114*, *139*
Paulson, Larry, 163
Pavilion Family Theatre, 78
Payette, Francois, 13
Payette Lake, 10
Pele, 164
Peregrine Fund, 166
Permanent Building Fund Advisory
    Council, 120
Perrault, Joseph, *51*
Pierce, Don, 163

Pierce, Elias Davidson, 15
Pinkham, Joe, 63
Pinney, James A., 61, 78, 93, *98*
Pinney Theatre, *92, 98, 99*
Pioneer route, 159
Pioneer Tent Building, 152
Placerville Volunteers, 18
Planning and Development Committee, 121
Planning and Zoning Commission, 151
"Point of Origin" (sculpture), 154
Pollard, James, 30
Polo, *89*
Pope, James P., 100, *100*
Popma, A.M., 126
Potter, John S., 22
Presbyterian Church, *61*
Price, John, 151, 153
Price, Vaughan, *140*
Prickett, H.E., 30
Pride, D.P.B., 49, *51*
Public Land order 5777, 167
Puckett, Kirby, 164
Purvirve, William, 19

R

R & M Steel Company, 232-235
Rafting, *169*
Ralston, W.C., 38
Raytheon Engineers & Constructors, 157
Redevelopment Agency, 121
Redway, A.G., 20
Regional Urban Design Assistance Team, 153
Reid, John, 13-15
Retton, Mary Lou, 164
Reynolds, James S., 21, *27*
Rice, Dan, 22
Ridenbaugh, W.H., 40
Ridenbaugh Canal, *113*
Ridenbaugh Mill, *40*
Riggs, Ada, *23*
Riggs, Henry Chiles, 18-19, *21*, 21-22, 24
Ritchie, William R., 19
Ritz, Phillip, 25
River Festival, *165*
Riverside Park Theatre, 78
Robbins, Orlando " Rube," *42*, 55
Robie, Albert H., 21
Robinson, Andy, *71*
Robinson, David, 164
Robinson, Jeremiah, 83, 101
Rodriguez, ChiChi, 164
Roller-skating, 64
Roosevelt, Franklin D., 101
Roosevelt, Theodore, *76*
Ross, Alexander, 14
Ross, C. Ben, 102
Rudolph, Wilma, 164
Rummel, John, 153

S

Saint Alphonsus' Hospital, 61-62, 126-127
Saint Alphonsus Regional Medical Center, 236-237
Saint John's Roman Catholic Church, *39*, 78, *116*
Saint Luke's Hospital, 62, 126-127
St. Luke's Regional Medical Center, 240-241

Saint Margaret's Hall, 61, 102-103
Saint Michael's Episcopal Cathedral, *31*, 76, *77*, *136*
St. Paul's black Baptist church, 162
Saint Teresa's Academy, 61, 102
Salt Lake Hardware, 111
Sawtooth range, *112*
Schirage, William F. (work of), *72*
Scott J.L., 124
SCP Global Technologies, 238-239
Sears, 153, 155
Sears Roebuck, 111
Second Idaho Infantry, *85*
Selander, Glenn, 151
Sheewoki fair, 12
Shellworth, Harry, 101
Shoshoni Indians 11-12, 22, 42
Shoup, George L., 55
Simplot, J.R. (Jack), 111, *111*, 117, 156, 159
Slaughterhouse Gulch, *74*
Slight, T. (work of), *7*
Slocum, Jerry, 21
Smith C. DeWitt, 24-25
Smith, Jedediah, 14-15
Smith, Madison, 32
Smylie, Robert E., 123
"Snake Boy," 105
Snake Country, 13
Snake River, 10, *11*, 167
Snake River Birds of Prey National Conservation Area, 166
Snake River line, 34-36, 43
Snake War of 1866-1868, 30
Soccer, 65
Sonna, Peter, 105; work of, *51*
South America (ethnic group), 162
Southern Pacific Railroad, 43
Soviet Union (ethnic group), 162
Spanish-American War, 65
Spider Web Saloon, 32
Splawn Moses, 17
S-Sixteen Simplot Family Limited Partnership, 158
Stage Coach Theatre company, 168
Stall, Mark, 163
Standifer, Jefferson, 18
State Capitol, *114, 118, 125, 149*
State Historical Society, 123
Statehood Day, *155*
Statehouse, *82, 155*
Steel Heads, 164
Steidel, Louis, *104*
Steunenberg, Frank, 75, *75*
Stevens, Gary, 164
Streetcars, *57, 83*
"Streets for People," *155*
Swedish Evangelical Lutheran Church, *117*
Symms Fruit Ranch Inc., 242-243
Symms, Steve, 160

T

"Tammany Ring," 40
Tate, Mary, 153
Temple Beth Israel, *162*
Tennis, *88*
Texas Instrument's Memory Division, 157
Thayer, Clarence E., *78*
"The Delamar," *45*
"The Hall of Mirrors," *24*
"The Second Missouri Compromise,"

See Wister, Owen
Thomas, Harold, 114
Thunder Mountain, 69
Tourtellotte, John E. (work of), *117*
Towne Square Mall, 151, 153, 155, 169
Treaty of Fort Boise, 22
Triangle Dairy, 128
Troutner, Art, 114
Trus Joist, 114, 158
Turn Verein Building, 152
Turn Verein Society, 86
Tuttle, Daniel S., *25*
Tweed, William Marcy, 26
Twilegar, Ron, 153, 163

U

U.S. Assay Office, *38, 124*, 169
U.S. Commerce Department, 156
U.S. Conference of Mayors Drug Control Task Force, 164
U.S. Customs Office, 161
Union Block, 152
Union Pacific, 159, 161
Union Pacific Railroad, 34, 37-38, 42-43 87, 159, 161; depot of, *136, 137, 157,* 159, 161; locomotive 1289, *161;* locomotive 8444, *159*
United Water Corporation, 154
United Way, 126
"Uptown Boise," 153
Urban Properties, Inc., 121
US Bank Tower, *143*
USA Today, 157
U.S.S. Boise, 106

V

Veterans Administration Hospital, 127
Veterans Memorial Park, 122
Villard, Henry, 43, 46
Virginia City, 21

W

Wallace, William H., 20
Walmart, 158
Walsh, Stuart P., 120
Washington Group International, 244-245
Washington Group International, Inc., 157, *157*
Washington Mutual Capitol Plaza, 155, *160*
Washington Volunteers, 18
West Bannock. *See* Idaho City
West Coast Hotels, 155
Western Federation of Miners, 63
Western Idaho Fair, 164
Western Idaho Fairgrounds, 163
Western Recycling, 246-247
Western Steel Manufacturing Company, 249
Westpark, 151
Wetlands Coalition, 166
Weyerhauser Lumber Company, 81, 158
Whitney, Asa, 33-34
Willard, Charles F., *91*
Winmar Company of Seattle, 146-147
Wister, Owen, 29
Wood River. *See* Boise River
World Center for Birds of Prey, 166
World Sports Humanitarian Hall of Fame, 164
Wright, George, 18

Wyeth, Nathaniel J., 15

Z
Zamzows Inc., 250
Zimmer Gunsul Frasca, 153
Zubizarreta, Josu, *162*